THE CREATIVE CLASSROOM

THE CREATIVE
CLASSROOM

Teaching
without Textbooks

HENRY F. BEECHHOLD

CHARLES SCRIBNER'S SONS
New York

A-8.72(C)

Printed in the United States of America
SBN684–12369–X (trade cloth)
SBN 684–12983–3 (trade paper, SL)
Library of Congress Catalog Card Number 78–143946

ACKNOWLEDGMENTS

Acknowledgment is gratefully made to the following publishers who
have permitted the use of their materials in copyright:

Harper & Row, Publishers
from *The Schools* by Martin Mayer. Reprinted by permission of the
publisher.

Horizon Press Publishers
from Paul Goodman's *Compulsory Mis-education*. Copyright © 1964.
Reprinted by permission of the publisher, Horizon Press, New York.

Houghton Mifflin Co.
from "Ars Poetica" from *Collected Poems 1917–1952* by Archibald
MacLeish. Reprinted by permission of Houghton Mifflin Co.

Indiana University Press
from *The Educated Imagination* by Northrope Frye. Copyright © 1964
by Indiana University Press. Reprinted by permission of the publisher.

Little, Brown and Company
  from *The Complete Poems of Emily Dickinson* edited by Thomas H. Johnson. Copyright 1929, © 1957 by Mary Hampson. Reprinted by permission of the publisher.

W. W. Norton & Company, Inc.
  from *How They Murdered the Second "R"* by George Riemer. Reprinted by permission of the publisher.

Pitman Publishing Corp.
  from *How Children Fail, How Children Learn,* and *The Underachieving School* by John Holt. Reprinted by permission of the publisher.

Prentice-Hall, Inc.
  from *The Nongraded High School* by B. Frank Brown. Reprinted by permission of the publisher.

Random House, Inc.
  from *The Immense Journey* by Loren Eiseley. Copyright © 1957. Reprinted by permission of the publisher.

Charles Scribner's Sons
  from Viktor Lowenfeld's "Creativity: Education's Stepchild" from *A Source Book for Creative Thinking* edited by Sidney J. Parnes and Harold F. Harding. Reprinted by permission of the publisher.

Viking Press, Inc.
  from *Serious Games* by Clark C. Abt. Reprinted by permission of the publisher.

To Irene

and

to Adrienne and Matthew,
the next generation

ACKNOWLEDGMENTS

I owe many debts of gratitude, but none so much as to my wife, Irene, to whom this book is dedicated. She pushed the right button (and has at times had cause, I am sure, to regret it!). To John J. Livecchi, friend and fellow teacher, who tested and polished many of my ideas in the classroom. To my department chairman at Trenton State College, Professor Milton I. Levin, who eased certain burdens. And, finally, to the editorial staff at Charles Scribner's Sons, who had faith in the book when it was only an embryo, who put up with a lot of auctorial nagging, and from whom I have learned much.

But for all that warrants censure, see me.

H.F.B.

FOREWORD

Naïf I am to hope that the educational enterprise would have escaped the diseases that wrack other enterprises, and it is probably fatuous of me to proclaim my disillusionment. Yet enterprises are, after all, just people. And if we set aside the crippling view of life that in its most depraved form produces an Adolf Eichmann (that view of life which says, "I'm merely an insignificant part of a system over which I have no control and to which I am bound"), there is hope.

It is the job of administrations to administer. Administration, *an sich,* is empty and unproductive. At the same time, by some perversity of human behavior, the manipulative power of an organization is vested in those members of the organization whose productive power is virtually nil. It is (to come to the point) the teacher who produces, but it is the "front office" which makes the "life and death" decisions of the school. There's the rub. But it needn't be so. Sufficient and well-placed pressure can easily subvert the timid self-serving administration (*i.e.,* the typical administration). There is much to be said in favor of unionization of teachers, although union organization itself quickly lapses into the inevitable organizational state of entropy that characterizes all administrations. If the union could manage to get the educational decision-making power into the hands of the teachers, our schools might be better off for it. But let any of those teachers get the administrative itch and we are back where we started. Not that there aren't a few enlightened administrators around. I expect that those young ones who are fresh out of the classroom manage for a few years at least to keep out of the worst administrative ruts, but sooner or later they go glassy-eyed like the rest.

To set up a reaction is to start a dialogue (a pox on these fashionable words!) of sorts. And even if the first responses are negative, the vibrations and echoes are in the air and (my experience tells me) things begin to happen. An angry response is very likely a defensive response. If one is defensive, he probably feels in some degree uncertain about his beliefs. This is the chink in the armor through which new ideas can enter. Of course, if I were more concerned with sensibilities (as I might be were I younger and more accepting: "A man who reaches the age of forty without becoming a misanthrope never loved mankind"), I would come on less strong, less "heavy," as they say. But, our children are dying.

I will ask the reader, then, to look beyond the tone (if the tone suits him not) to the substance. If there be teachers and administrators to whom my strictures do not apply, then their knowledge that they do not will be sufficient. If there be teachers and administrators (there be!) to whom my strictures do apply, please remember, our children are dying.

There is much of value to be got from this book about the aims and the substance of education. (Why should I affect modesty on this point?) I have tried to be fairly comprehensive though not exhaustive, for an exhaustive treatment of the subject could not fit between one set of covers (and is, in any case, unnecessary). The teacher who cannot build effectively upon what I have offered here should be barred from the profession. The layman, likewise, should have no difficulty in grasping the fundamentals of good education.

Education is the biggest single "business" in this country, and is everybody's business. Unfortunately, few of those who for whatever motivations run for school boards, organize and run parent-teacher groups, and otherwise directly interest themselves in the schools know anything worthwhile about education. Having gone to school makes one no more usefully knowledgeable about schooling than driving a car makes one an automotive engineer. With the type of special involvem·nt the public has with education, the public should be able to do more than approve or disapprove budgets (or fuss irrationally about sex education). School-board members, for example, or PTA'ers or parents in general should be equipped to raise searching questions about what actually goes on in school. The classroom is the heart of the matter, and a school makes it or not depending on what happens in the classroom. The rest is window dressing. The five-minute patter on Parent's Night won't answer. Those little presentations are about as informative as a TV commercial (and far less entertaining). No one can take issue with the broadly stated goals of any school. That would be taking issue with truth, beauty, goodness, virtue, and The American Way of Life. The question remains: What goes on in the classroom?

If human growth, other than the purely physical, is an endless process of self-creation, then our "creativity component" is what we should be engendering in our school program. Hence, *The Creative Classroom,* which is a shorthand way of saying, *the classroom in which both teacher and student create education.* Reliance on a set of books designed to reach the widest possible audience (presumably offending none, pleasing all, suiting all—a patently impossible task) is contra-creative. Hence, the subtitle of the book, *Teaching without Textbooks.* (Not without *books,* but without *text*books.)

And if it seems ironic or contradictory that I offer what amounts to a textbook against textbooks, it is not, for this book is designed to free the teacher and the student. The usual textbook is designed to create dependency—after Book Grade 1 follows Book Grade 2, and so on, the whole curriculum being built (for all practical purposes) around the sequence of textbooks.

It is surely overweening of me to expect that this book will cause any great changes in our ways of education. But it takes some overweening to write such a book in the first place. And, our children are dying.

HENRY F. BEECHHOLD
West Trenton, New Jersey
1969–70

CONTENTS

THE CREATIVE CLASSROOM

1 TEACHING WITHOUT TEXTBOOKS

Comparing what two competing publishers have to say about the same research findings can have ludicrous results.

[Jeanne Chall, *Learning to Read*]

Since with two or three exceptions all texts are not only boring but based on the assumption that knowledge exists prior to, independent of, and altogether outside the learner, they are either worthless or harmful.

[Neil Postman and Charles Weingartner,
Teaching as a Subversive Activity]

From the very beginning we make books and reading a constant source of possible failure and public humiliation.

[John Holt, *The Underachieving School*]

Given their present motives, the schools are not competent to teach authentic literacy, reading as a means of liberation.

[Paul Goodman, *Compulsory Mis-education*]

That textbooks can be avoided has been demonstrated over and over again. At the Ifield Junior School in Crawley New Town, in southern England . . . there is not a textbook to be seen. Instead, the school as a whole has the look of an open-stack library on the new plan.

[Martin Mayer, *The Schools*]

THAT so "fundamental" a part of our educational methodology should be called into question must strike the reader as strange indeed. Yet the textbook as we know it is a relative newcomer to education. Habits, of course, are easily established, especially when vast sums of money are spent on their establishment. Thus, through a fatal combination of high-powered propaganda on the part of the publishing industry and the principle of least effort on the part of teachers and administrators, textbooks have become (more's the pity!) the backbone of American education. How relatively unimportant any particular teacher is, by contrast, is evident in the ease with which substitutes are plugged in and out, the real issue being, after all, keeping up in the texts.

The publishers' arguments in support of textbooks are irresistibly seductive:

> With all [that] teachers have to do, there is no reason for them to plan the organization of the course in detail. The author of the text-book can do that for them. There is no need for them to think up all the precise instructional language required for the teaching of mathematics, or science, or English. Nor should they have to rely entirely on their own resources for the planning of class discussions, practice materials, projects, activities, further reading. (American Textbook Publishers Institute, *Textbooks in Education,* quoted in *The Schools,* p. 379.

Thus, practically speaking, the teacher becomes the publisher's classroom agent. One might ask, in response to the "Institute" (a fancy name for a public relations operation), why in fact the author should plan any teacher's course in detail. How can the author anticipate all teachers, all students, all schools? Are they really all alike? Further, one might ask just what a teacher is supposed to do or know if he has not "to think up" the "precise instructional language" of mathematics and so on, for if he doesn't already know the language of his subjects, he has no business in the classroom, and if he is a teacher, "instructional language" is part of his professional equipment. The fact of the matter is that there is no "instructional language." There is the language of each discipline and there is the broad communication framework within which all teaching takes place. If a teacher is out of touch with, say, new developments in language study (linguistics), then he had better inform himself properly, not hope to keep a chapter ahead in the textbook. The belief, unconscionably perpetrated by textbook publishers, that a textbook series and a teacher's manual give the teacher "everything he has to know" about, let us say again, linguistics, is patently absurd. Were a parent to argue that he has just bought a book that the publisher claims will "provide him with all he needs to know in order to teach his child how to read or write or . . . ," will the teacher grant the parent's competence to teach on the basis of the publisher's promise? And in the matter of the teachers' "relying entirely on their own resources," the truth is that where a textbook series is used (and that means in virtually every school in the country), the teacher is rare indeed who fails to rely *entirely* on the textbook and accompanying teacher's guides. Dr. Ruth G. Strickland, professor of education at Indiana University, estimates that about half the nation's primary teachers slavishly follow the guides. According to Dr. Bruce Joyce, the former head of elementary education at the University of Chicago, "about 80 percent of the nation's elementary teachers use textbooks as their main teaching tool and source of knowledge." (Quoted by Hillel Black in *The American Schoolbook*, pp. 4–5.) What, then, one may properly ask, is the textbook-enslaved teacher but the publisher's agent? Black states it thus: "This reporter's observations suggest that more often than not the American schoolteacher serves as an adult presence who is no wiser or better than the textbooks her children use." My own observations suggest precisely the same thing.

The purpose of this book is to outline a program for teaching without textbooks. May I quickly say that I distinguish between books and textbooks, the latter being a species of "non-book." This is the same distinction made by Joseph Featherstone in his examination of the new infant schools (*i.e.*, K–3) in Great Britain: "Increasingly in the good infant schools, there are no textbooks and no class readers. There are just books, in profusion." (*The Primary School Revolution in Britain.*)

One might reasonably argue that it is the teacher and not the textbook that is the issue. A textbook is, after all, just a tool. But the fact is that where the textbook series is built into the curriculum (or, rather, the curriculum is built around the textbook series!), the teacher is in an important sense a function of the textbook. We are dealing here with a *system*, not merely this or that teacher. There is an inevitable interlocking of processes and activities in a school program; and where there is a considerable financial commitment to a text series, it is reasonable to assume that each teacher will be expected, even required, to use the textbooks assigned to his grade level in such a way that the teacher at the next higher grade level (using the next higher numbered book in each series) can properly "plug in." For all practical purposes, the textbook series does indeed determine the shape of the curriculum (which, incidentally, means that the textbook salesman with the most impressive sales presentation —and the most winning personality!—is the *de facto* curriculum consultant for the school system). If one argues that the school makes the decision, one can reply by saying that the decision is that of choosing from among a number of Tweedledums and Tweedledees. Furthermore, the decision is rarely made by the classroom teacher who will actually be using the books; though even when it is, the teacher no less than the administrators and "curriculum coordinators" (and parents, for that matter) have been pre-sold on the *idea* of using textbooks both by virtue of their own educational experience and the intense propaganda of the publishers spread through the professional journals and professional meetings, wherein the prestige of the organizations rubs off on the salesman's pitch.

Further still, the young and inexperienced teacher who enters the school system for the first time will be handed a textbook series and told, "This is what we use here." And since the typical textbook series is a complex of neatly organized, ready-made materials, and since the teacher is both insecure and anxious to make good, he will tie himself tightly to the materials as the safest way to do his job (and not rock the boat, of course) whether the textbooks have any educational merit or not. (I have concluded that they have very little, and whatever they have is not worth the price of having to use them.)

Further still, irrespective of the quality of the teacher, the student will be conditioned to the textbook as the source of educational values, for the textbook cannot help but take on the aura of great authority, given the biases already built in to student, teacher, and society at large regarding the primacy of the printed word. (Or if the student recognizes the book for a sham, he will generally go along with it as a strategy in playing the "education game.") Such conditioning can be avoided or negated only in a classroom where the teacher is free of the imposition of textbooks or, at least, free to examine them critically as one might examine an argument for its logic. The system, however, does not produce many teachers who are competent to judge the substantive quality of a textbook, nor would most teachers even think to do so except with regard to appearance, illustrations, degree to which the book makes using the book easy, and so on. Though it is true that teachers are continually dissatisfied with the way things are going in the classroom, they feel that somehow if they just had a "better book" things would be more to their heart's desire. This is the rationale behind the endless textbook swapping that goes on. "If only we had the XYZ Company series instead of this old-fashioned QRS Company series . . ." But before long, the wish having been granted, we are looking covetously at the JKL Company series. Promises, promises! It is eminently clear that textbook series are commercial ventures and that, like cigarettes and gasolines, the real differences among the several brands are minimal and insignificant. Whether, for example, a "language arts" text is "traditionally" or "linguistically" oriented is of small moment, for the practical result (*i.e.*, the books themselves) is the same: workbook exercises, formulas, and the rest of the educationally counter-productive nonsense that so effectively bores the student. In a new (that magical word) "linguistic" text/workbook series that even boasts of a "linguistics consultant" (how impressed we are with "consultants," how un-helpful they so often are), the program of the book typically asks the student to do a few more-or-less standard workbook exercises, which lead to a blue rectangle (new feature!) in which is printed the student's "discovery" (honestly, that's what it is labeled). It will be a dull student indeed who doesn't catch wise to this gimmick in about five minutes, and he will thenceforward spend his workbook time memorizing the contents of all the blue rectangles, for it will be obvious to him that these "discoveries" are what the teacher will be looking for on the weekly grammar test. Linguistics or no linguistics, "new" or old, educational baloney is educational baloney.

Jeanne Chall writes that "we could, perhaps, dismiss any questionable actions on the part of publishers as natural to the competitive publishing game. But isn't teaching children to read too serious a 'game' to be left to publishers?" (*Learning to Read,* p. 299.) I would expand her purview by saying that education is too serious a game to be left to publishers. If I seem to be laboring the point and belaboring the publishers, it is, I suppose, because I want to be heard above the publishers' diapason. The fact is that a plea to abandon textbooks in our school program must be considered a radical one, though one might (not without some guile) remind the reader of a Lincoln, who educated himself with the likes of Milton, Shakespeare, and the Bible, all "texts" in the best sense of the word, but surely not textbooks. That this is no very compelling argument is perfectly apparent, yet the fact that it is not by no means strengthens the counter-argument and may indeed weaken it if we conceive of a program of (a) student-generated curriculum materials (projects, problems, student-produced publications, etc.) and (b) classroom libraries of books of every kind. What specially written textbook story, for example, can touch *The Little Prince, The Wind in the Willows,. Charlotte's Web, Winnie the Pooh, Blueberries for Sal, Mouse House,* the Babar stories, etc.? Controlled vocabulary, (tiresome) repetition, simple-minded sentence structure—all the "theoretically sound" techniques of the basal readers are, it would seem, almost deliberately designed to bore the young reader. I put "theoretically sound" in quotation marks because, as Dr. Chall points out, the type, and quality, of "research" that goes into the readers is close to being laughable, and to faulty and irrelevant research are added the publishers' "interpretations" of the research. The net result of this academically shameful enterprise is classroom tedium. The linguistic sophistication of a three-year-old is on the average far advanced of the materials presented in early-grade readers. The authors of the basal readers confuse *decoding* with *comprehension* (as do the "reading specialists"). Decoding can be quickly taught (as I will detail in Chapter 4), whereas comprehension is an intellectual process that encompasses not only what we read but everything else we do that requires any kind of sequential and integrative thinking. At all events, let the reader not believe that the claims of salesmen, advertising brochures, or, for that matter, people like the "experts" connected with the writing and editing of school textbooks represent *veritas.* It's just that they have been shouting longer and have at their command the medium that impresses us members of the Gutenberg Galaxy most: print.

It is unfortunately true that our educational enterprise traditionally has not been served, except at its highest levels, by first-rate minds. Always, of course, there are exceptions, but when one draws a hypothesis he works from statistical norms. Hence, if there have been relatively few really stupid teachers and administrators, there likewise have been relatively few really bright ones. Not that brilliance alone can guarantee classroom success. I expect that at least some of our Nobel laureates would be dreadful high school or elementary school teachers. I suspect, however, that at the level where they are usually found, their mastery of their subject is sufficient to carry them. Where (self-) motivation is high, the quality of instruction is of small moment. On the other hand, where the educational process depends upon the creation and engendering of motivation, then the skill of the teacher as a teacher becomes paramount. But the teacher who is minimally informed and who depends upon established curriculum patterns and textbooks (naturally) is not likely to develop much skill in the art of teaching. The majority of teachers presently in the classroom are without question weak in substantive knowledge and at the same time impoverished in professional skills. With the emphasis in teacher education moving away from "methods" courses and toward "subject-matter" courses, part of the problem stands in favor of being solved. Unhappily, courses in teaching methodology take for granted the use of the textbook, a fact which colors the whole approach to teaching. On the issue of teacher intelligence, one can only hope that as the quality of teacher education improves and as the conditions of teaching improve (though they are not so bad these days!) we can expect a better quality of teacher. But if we continue to design educational programs in the same general mold we have been, then all we can hope for is the occasional non-conforming, "subversive," teacher, who bootlegs good education into the classroom despite the system and despite the parents (who are desperately in need of what might be called "educational literacy"). And may I add that what we must look for in our teachers beyond intelligence and academic credentials is their genuine desire to do something worthwhile in the classroom. The profession today is overloaded with time-servers.

One reads of all kinds of "crash programs," "workshops," "experimental programs," etc., and one naturally concludes that education in America is a hotbed of ferment and change. It isn't. Like the great majority of college students (as opposed to the one or two percent that is so well publicized), the great majority of schools, classrooms, and teachers are quiet, orderly, and devoid of intellectual excitement and accomplishment. It is a cliché that only the out-of-the-ordinary is newsworthy. One might assume on the basis of what we read in our daily newspapers that we are living in a kind of on-going St. Valentine's Day Massacre. Yet, though America is a notoriously murder-prone society, one can reasonably expect to die here of causes other than murder. Hence, our view of what is happening in education is a distortion of the deadly truth that not much is happening except in a negative way—where we can't see it and only occasionally get a hint of it.

Thus, it is best to design our program as though all curricula had disappeared from the face of the earth and taken with them all textbooks, school buildings, "traditions," and unreconstructable teachers and administrators. This, at any rate, is what I shall attempt here. I am not fond enough to suppose that my program will be swallowed whole, though I would hope that its principles might be. A program, after all, is only a possible manifestation of its underlying philosophy, just as each individual human being is only a possible manifestation of humanness. The fact is that the philosophy implicit here is anti-programmatic. That is, the teacher is encouraged to develop in concert with his students the specific activities that represent their educational needs and desires. This is not to suggest that the teacher abandon teaching and leadership, but rather that he abandon head-stuffing and tyranny.

In broad terms, we aim at the "self-creating" class. There is far more to the child at any age than we are aware of, especially those of us whose model of a child is built on conventional wisdom and the implicit textbook profile. In more ways than we can imagine, the child is father to the man. Hence, what we must provide is a responsive environment wherein the child is encouraged to explore and to produce as the dominant activities as opposed to the usual static environment wherein the child is told what he has to know and is required to sit and receive it.

> The notion of a curriculum, an essential body of knowledge, would be absurd even if children remembered everything we 'taught' them. We don't and can't agree on what knowledge is essential.
>
> .   .   .   .   .
>
> The idea of the curriculum would not be valid even if we could agree what ought to be in it. For knowledge itself changes. (John Holt, *How Children Fail*, pp. 175, 179.)

Education is a process of one's doing things, not a process of having things done to one (quite different, say, from getting a cavity filled). The operational metaphor of our usual educational environment is that of hospital (school) to patient (student)—in a context that bears a frightening similarity to a prison, on which point I shall have more to say in the next chapter—the teacher assuming the rôle of the doctor charged with curing the patient of his infirmity (presumed ignorance). The curriculum in my metaphor is, of course, the regimen, which when administered properly and followed faithfully will do the job. It's a sick system!

Thinking is the basis of genuine education. In the very young child, much thinking seems to be "pre-conscious," that is, he does not sit down and tell himself that he must do thus and such in order to learn language, for example, yet by the time he is three, he has acquired not only a sizable lexicon but an impressive facility in the manipulation of grammatical structures. Without formal schooling, the child would of course continue to learn and to find ways of fitting himself into the life around him. Lack of formal education was no deterrent to man's long pre-academic survival. Nor is it any deterrent to the societies which today have nothing resembling "schools." (John Holt, Paul Goodman, and other contemporary critics of American education raise the question of whether we are well advised to require all children to go to school.) Yet, the idea of schooling has merit after all. If that merit is to be realized, however, the aim of the school must be to bring thinking up to the conscious, manipulative level. If a person cannot consciously "use" his rational powers to rational ends, he can never be truly *educated*. He can be driven to memorize, but *memory* does not equal *education* (even the etymology of "education" is against it, for *educere* means "to draw out"). The point is easily demonstrated: who can "do" more with numbers, the child who has merely memorized the mechanics of arithmetical operations or the child who understands the logic of numbers? "It is easiest to teach mathematics to very young children, for they have inquiring minds and they are self-reliant, and want to understand things for themselves. It is much harder to teach adults, because so many adults have had their confidence shaken by bad teaching." (W. W. Sawyer, *Vision in Elementary Mathematics*, p. 5.) It is the inquiring mind we must nurture. Let me repeat, the *inquiring* mind. It is sad to relate that an inquiring mind is what few teachers have; and when an inquiring student meets with an in-curious teacher, a kind of death is the result. For soon the inquiring mind is transformed into a creature of the system, a player of the great American Game of Education. The rigged quiz games of the fifties were marvelously apt projections of our schooling. We soon learn that appearance, not substance, is what pays off.

A major cause of the long-term misdirection of education is the mistaken belief that the chief aim of classroom academic activity is to teach children to read, write, and figure. The truth is that the "three R's" are but particular surface manifestations of underlying logical and linguistic processes. If we turn directly to those proc-esses, we shall in the long run have far greater success with the sur-face "subjects" than we could ever hope to have through traditional approaches.

As for education's "life-adjustment" and "citizenship" goals—trivializations of fundamentally good ideas—one need only examine our crime, divorce, alcoholism, drug addiction, and mental illness statistics. (One of the highest per capita drug abuse—Demerol and other "hard" drugs—areas in the country is a certain "bedroom" county in the East where the problem among "comfortable" mid-dle/upper-middle-class housewives is close to epidemic proportions. Of course, the socio-economic status, as it is called, of these life-ad-justed matrons saves them from entanglement with the law, and the citizenship of the local physicians prompts them to keep their pa-tients well supplied.) If education takes place in an environment free of the fraud and coercion of the typical classroom, and if the child's energies are directed toward discovery and problem-solving, and if he is encouraged to create and take pleasure in his creation, perhaps we won't rear yet another tormented generation. Surely these gross ills of our society are not *required* by the mere fact of exist-ence. Surely we can contemplate the *possibility* at least of improve-ment, and just as surely we can look to the school, the institution in which most of us spend a major part of our early lives, as perhaps the prime agency of that improvement. If, on the other hand, all we can hope to anticipate is more of the same, there is no hope.

But the schools are creatures of the society. We seem to get what we deserve. Which is to say that the institutions of a society are rarely better than the society itself. Yet it is feasible to ameliorate the society through its institutions. From time to time in history men have managed. If Congress, for example, is commonly a playing field for every kind of knavery, it does occasionally rise to some great moment and give us direction to something better. Likewise, we have had our outstanding prelates and presidents. So with our schools. Indeed, *so must it be* with our schools, for there is no human enterprise that offers such promise for man as the enterprise of education.

However, I hardly think it necessary to make the case for "education." What I mean to do is to make the case for a kind of education that has the potential for doing all that we might wish education to do. It is true that every few years a new theory of education comes along that promises much, but, alas, delivers little. For those who are interested there are shelves full of books expounding, and shelves full of books demolishing, these theories. I have no wish to embroil myself in these battles. All I will say for the present is that the approach to learning set forth here has the great advantage of hindsight and practical experience. My attention is on the student in the classroom. My techniques are drawn from many sources, but most of all from successful classroom practice. If a certain kind of thinking is sound in areas outside education proper, such as the sciences, there is every reason to expect that the same kind of thinking will be sound in education. If a logician can solve certain kinds of problems with certain techniques, then a child should be able to solve similar kinds of problems with similar techniques. Furthermore, discovering the techniques themselves will prove educationally valuable, the "whys" and "hows" always reach more profoundly into our thinking than do the "whats." If Dr. John Lilly can make enormous progress in understanding the alien mind of the dolphin through the research technique of model-building, the child should be able to make enormous progress in understanding the more familiar world in which he daily lives via the same technique. But, one demurs, these are only propositions: if . . . then. . . . Once they are tested and proved—as they have been—they are no longer only propositions.

One trouble with traditional "teaching methods" courses is that the "methods" are based on the same kind of half-baked "research" that Dr. Chall condemns in the field of reading. One is taught, for example, that a child below first grade shouldn't be taught to read because he is incapable of the fine eye-muscle control necessary for letter discrimination. (I say "taught," when in fact the notion is presented as something close to a divine commandment.) Of course, this is arrant nonsense. As early as forty weeks, the child, according to Drs. Ilg and Ames (in The Gesell Institute's *Child Behavior*, p. 29), and in any parent's observations, can not only "poke precisely at tiny objects with extended forefinger, but he can grasp these same tiny objects precisely between thumb and forefinger." This requires not only visual acuity of a high order, but depth perception as well. Dr. O. K. Moore's typewriter-based reading/writing program likewise puts the educational fancy to flight with fact. Perhaps 85% of the many teachers I have talked with about teaching problems have told me that their methods courses were useless, that they gave the teacher "very little that was really useful for the classroom." The program here is useful. The philosophy and techniques are field-tested. They work. This is not a case of the theoretician remote from the classroom.

The issue, insofar as teacher education is concerned, is not that methods courses are bad *in principle* (an impression left by the numerous attacks on what has been clumsily termed "education-ism"), but that they are bad *in practice;* that is, the practices they engender. No matter how well informed one may be in a subject, he is not by virtue of either superior intelligence or vast specialized knowledge *automatically* equipped to do a good job in the classroom, unless by teaching we mean nothing more than holding a public dialogue with oneself about matters which especially interest one. I venture to say that relatively few researchers in any field could do well in *teaching* their subjects to a group of youngsters, though the youngsters might very well learn something, perhaps a good deal, from watching the researcher research, at least if the research made use of laboratory hardware. Research into the provenience of medieval drama might be less than interesting to watch. It is no more than a betrayal of ignorance in one who thinks that a classroom is not a special kind of place where special kinds of relationships must be developed and special techniques used to accomplish worthwhile ends. I doubt whether a biologist, for example, would deny the need of a great deal of training and practice in laboratory technique, even though laboratory technique is not the "subject" of his studies as a biologist. Of course, it would serve the fledgling biologist ill were his training in laboratory technique not based on the use of the microtome and the other exquisite tools of the laboratory, but based rather on the use of the butcher's cleaver. Thus, we have been teaching our teachers to do the wrong things and they in turn, predictably, have been "teaching" their students the wrong things the wrong way. The methods of teaching have grown out of the "Education" curriculum; the materials to be taught have been programmed into the curriculum largely through the agency of the textbook.

The question is not *whether* "methods" but *what* methods. Can we, after all, say that the academic care of children (not graduate students, mind you, but children) is any less exquisite a task in its way than the preparation, say, of tissue sections for microscopic examination? *Methodology* is an eminently respectable word, it would seem, in every area but education. Strange. Yet not so strange, for the educationists have contributed mightily to their own lack of academic respectability. This is most unfortunate and has made for a needless and hurtful barrier between the "professional educator" and the "academician." Indeed, there are few professors of any kind who call themselves, plain and simple, teachers. (Perhaps that's as it should be, for relatively few professors *are* teachers, but, then, relatively few teachers are teachers.) There are likewise few professors outside of education departments who have a noticeable—to say nothing of a notable—interest in teacher education. On their side, the educationists have commonly busied themselves with one brand of trivia in the name of "education," while on their side the academicians have busied themselves with another brand of trivia in the name of "scholarship." On both sides I exempt those few who have made genuine contributions to knowledge. The sins of the educationists have been sufficiently displayed of late to warrant their being omitted here. But, in the interests of balancing the view, I quote Professor Graham Hough, British literary scholar, on one of the academically "respectable" subjects:

> At its best English literature as a university subject attracts the perceptive, the devoted, the enthusiastic; at its worst it becomes the bolt-hole of those who can't do mathematics and are too lazy to learn a language properly. It is not at all easy to fail a university course in English completely, so the English faculty contains an un-

usually high proportion of layabouts and persons working at half pressure. ("Crisis in Literary Education," *Crisis in the Humanities,* p. 102.)

For a detailed picture of the educationist-academician schism, see, for example, Myron Lieberman's *The Future of Public Education,* or visit your nearest university.

To some who read these pages, that old bogey, Progressive Education, may seem to be lurking hereabouts. Like so many bogies, this one turns out to be something quite different in fact from its vision in fancy. E. Paul Torrence delineates the precepts of "Progressivism" as follows:

1. Individual differences among children must be recognized.
2. We learn by doing and by having a vital interest in what we are doing.
3. Education is a continuous reconstruction of living experience that goes beyond the four walls of the classroom.
4. The classroom should be a laboratory for democracy.
5. Social goals as well as intellectual are important.
6. A child must be taught to think critically rather than to accept blindly.

("Scientific Views of Creativity," *Creativity and Learning,* pp. 86–87.)

These precepts are certainly beyond cavil. Yet the hue and cry over "progressive education" is still on in some quarters (the critics are strange bedfellows: educational elitists on one hand and troglodytes on the other). The curious fact is that "with a few notable exceptions, what we call progressive education was *never tried.*" (Joseph Featherstone, p. 13, emphasis added.) "Education," Featherstone continues, "that treats people as individuals has become a cliché without ever being a reality. . . . What wisps of the vision of education as individual growth trailed into the public schools were largely rhetorical. . . . Along with the new rhetoric . . . went an increased emphasis on administration; *there was no basic change in methods of teaching or classroom organization.*" (P. 14, emphasis added.) To which observations we can add Paul Goodman's: "On the whole, the history of progressive education has not been a cheerful one. Its ideas and methods have been stolen and bastardized precisely to strengthen the dominant system of society rather than to change it." (*The Community of Scholars*, p. 211.) So much for "progressive education," "Progressivism," "Dewey-ism," or what you will. It was the talk of the educationists and the talk of the enemies of the educationists, but it never really happened. The *real* failures of education were mostly overlooked, or ignored. What a pity no one bothered to write a book like *Our Children Are Dying* back in the heyday of the "great debate."

I shall not call the approach to education outlined here "progressive," for the word is debased coin. It is probably best not to stigmatize it with a name, though the word *creative* does appear in the title and will be used many times throughout the book. Yet *creative* seems to be going the way of *progressive* and *relevance* and other transiently fashionable tokens. Why fret over labels? Our thinking is too much governed by them in any case. We fail to see what lies beyond the word. I shall be satisfied to breathe a little new life into *education*. There is, however, not much time. Death, as Jonathan Kozol so eloquently reminds us, comes at an early age! The assertion that while politicians talk people die is as true of the classroom as it is of war.

The school textbook served to take up the slack between what the teacher was prepared (*i.e.*, competent) to teach and what the curriculum planners (who were often the textbook writers) thought should be taught. As we have noted, teachers traditionally have not been prepared to teach very much. Thus they were, in a sense, creatures of the curriculum and textbook. The inbred nature of the educationist establishment effectively kept the teacher in a state of thralldom which only recently he has begun to break free of (with a good deal of help, ironically, from those students who are increasingly unwilling to buy the established nonsense). An approach to teaching that allows the teacher to get out from under the dead weight of that establishment can be, I think, a significant contribution to the growth of the profession—particularly so in a time of such desperate need for humane and imaginative solutions to the most frustrating and perplexing problems we have ever faced. Rote memory, pre-digested "knowledge," pat answers, standardized busywork, and other forms of intellectual sloth and vacuity—the methods and legacy of the textbook—do not make an education for survival. Many of the textbooks being rushed into print to meet the new demands for relevance do attempt to be relevant (after their fashion); but textbooks are textbooks, and the system of education they represent is the heart of the matter, not the addition of a few black faces in the illustrations and a few scraps of "minority group" literature. Nor do words like *discovering* and *exploring* in the titles represent anything more than the same old stuff tricked out in new finery. What the student will discover is that most textbooks are not worth exploring!

TEACHER AND CLASSROOM

Our schools are hung up on the notion that learning in the classroom is a by-product of order.

[John Holt, *The Underachieving School*]

Formal classroom teaching—the instructor standing up front, talking to the group, or even the first-grade room divided up into reading groups which the teacher listens to separately as she desperately tries to keep order—has disappeared from many infant and a number of junior schools. It has disappeared because it imposes a single pattern of learning on whole groups of children—thus forcing schools to "track," or to group classes by ability—because it ignores the extent to which children teach each other, and because in many workaday schools other methods are working better. Ordinary teachers, trained formally, take to the new role when they can see with their own eyes that the result is not chaos.

[Joseph Featherstone, *The Primary School Revolution in Britain*]

We encourage children to act stupidly, not only by scaring and confusing them, but by boring them, by filling up their days with dull, repetitive tasks that make little or no claim on their attention or demands on their intelligence. Our hearts leap for joy at the sight of a roomful of children all slogging away at some imposed task, and we are all the more pleased and satisfied if someone tells us that the children really don't like what they are doing. We tell ourselves that this drudgery, this endless busywork, is good preparation for life, and we fear that without it children would be hard to "control."

[John Holt, *How Children Fail*]

It is clear that a classroom of the usual size and composition is more adequately adapted to the perpetuation of a traditional culture—one based on ritual, incantation, and unquestioning acceptance—than it is to giving instruction in the disciplines of science and rational ethics.

[S. T. Kimball and J. E. McClellan, Jr.,
Education and the New America]

Teachers talk too much.

[John Holt, *The Underachieving School*]

THE SCHOOL, typically a set of cells communicating with each other through the corridors of a cell block, is probably the most irrational and arbitrary environment in which most of us will ever find ourselves. In our other environments we are relatively free agents pursuing activities (or not) in some "organic" way. At home we eat, sleep, play, make love, read, watch television, etc., according to some "natural" rhythm that each of us establishes within a more-or-less-agreed-upon framework. We can indeed bend our children to our will, but what they do under these compulsions is a "normal" part of the process/entity known as "family" or "home." At work, we fall into a coherent pattern based upon the logic of the work. We don't, that is, hop about from task to unrelated task at the clanging of a bell. Well, perhaps we do in the military, and surely we do in prison. And what is the school if not an archetype of both military and prison life. The classroom is our six-hour-a-day prison, to which we are consigned by law and in which we work for years at imposed and largely discrete tasks—for what end? In prison, in garrison life, in school we go through motions, we are "disciplined." And what have we, when we are done, to show for it? The only career for a soldier *qua* soldier is soldiering, which in honest-to-goodness peacetime means garrison life. The only career for an ex-con is his next (and predictable) term in stir (for that is all his "rehabilitation," *i.e.*, his prison activities and "discipline," has prepared him for). And the only career for a schoolchild is—what? We complain, do we not, that our high school and even college graduates can't speak or write articulately, can't "do" math, can't even keep their hair in order. Virtually every business of any size runs some sort of training program to bring its new employees up to at least company standards. For the past several years I have taught a course in "effective communication" to executive-level employees of state government. What have all those hours and years in the classroom really accomplished? Beyond a minimal literacy, not much. Are we turning out the intelligently informed citizens that a free society requires for survival? A canvass of one's neighbors in virtually any community on virtually any subject of import will reveal our dismal failures on that score. I fear that our "commitment" to education in America is verbal and financial, the easiest kinds of commitment to make. Indeed, other than marginal literacy and a ragbag of "facts," what do those twelve years of enforced education endow our children with? Perhaps those who manage to get through college are a little better off, but not much. Oh, yes, the diplomas and degrees are keys that open doors, but the status game is quite another matter. I am speaking of *education* and the *quality* of life. "It is said that our schools are geared to 'middle-class values,' but this is a false and misleading use of terms. The schools less and less represent *any* human values, but simply adjustment to a mechanical system." (Paul Goodman, *Compulsory Mis-education*, p. 21.) There are flashes of hope, to be sure—the Parkway Program of Philadelphia is one such—but they are all too rare when taken against the mass of schools in this country.

The American school today is an exotic growth, a strange entity typically American yet unrelated to life in America (even less to the world). It is so functionally removed from its society that its use even as a progenitor of values is attenuated to the point of inanition. Yet by some ironic twist, the school locus—the actual, physical school—is often the breeding ground of a demimonde that the school on the one hand witlessly engenders by virtue of its inanity and on the other hand tries to make believe doesn't exist. I speak, of course, of the hip pre-teen/teen culture that has found its perfect hothouse in the school. Talk about the generation gap!—the community thinks it's running the school; the kids know better. The parallels again with the prison world are both startling and instructive. The school is the place to learn the ways of the world: pot, pills, and the rest. Strategies for survival. Meanwhile, back in the classroom, busywork and boredom, discipline and detachment. All the noble aims and ideals of education lost, frozen, rotted out. Neat rows, neat books, but behind the glassy or unnaturally bright eyes, a world that has nothing whatever to do with attendance records and weekly exams.

The operational center of the school (as *school*, not "clubhouse") insofar as the child is concerned is the classroom with its complement of window walls (with venetian blinds), plasticized birch and tubular steel furniture, audio-visual oddments, chalkboards (being green these days instead of black), textbooks, and teacher, who is commonly a pleasant enough person but as commonly not a very good teacher. Not that he is necessarily to blame for being a bad teacher (or at least not a really good one). Our schools generally don't want really good teachers, because, among other things, good teachers make waves; they distrust the oily slickness of the "well-administered" school; they bug students, irritate parents, and discomfit their time-serving colleagues. What a school there could be with those teachers who have been sent on their way by "threatened" systems. The case of Jonathan Kozol *vs.* the Boston Public Schools is but one well-publicized example of institutional pin-headedness. (See Kozol, Bibliography.) But what's a teacher to do who has a family to support? If he understands, and some do, he goes along with the system while trying to damage his students as little as possible.

So here are the students arranged in their cells awaiting (frequently with genuine dread) their daily six-hour hassle with "authority." In the ideal society there would be no such thing as compulsory education. As I noted earlier, there are those who seriously question the need for it even now: "On the whole, the education must be voluntary rather than compulsory, for no growth to freedom occurs except by intrinsic motivation." (Paul Goodman, *Compulsory Mis-education*, p. 61.) "To keep kids in school who would rather not be there costs the school an enormous amount of time and trouble, to say nothing of what it costs to repair the damage that these angry and resentful prisoners do whenever they get the chance." (John Holt, *The Underachieving School*, p. 29.) But this is an argument for another day. Compulsory education is the way of things, and here is our school and its classrooms filled with semi-prisoners. There is small purpose in despairing of what we can do nothing about. Let us, on the contrary, turn our energies to what we can readily change, namely, what goes on in the classroom.

Though our first concern should be to decide what is worth both-ering about in education, let us forestall that question momentarily, for the best of ideas will die aborning in an environment unsuitable for their nurture, growth, and development. Let us at this point be content to assume that educationally important things *can* happen in the classroom, or at least in the tutelage of a typical classroom teacher (the school precincts are not, of course, sacred; we need *classrooms* far less than we might think). To be sure, the teacher who responds to the ideas set down here will no longer be the *typical* teacher, though I would hope that in time he will be. That is, I hope that a time will come when these "radical" ideas will be the commonplaces of education practice and when every teacher will be free to teach truly, free of the gartered-sleeve mentality of the front office.

Though nearly every anthology of English literature in current use reprints "The Rime of the Ancient Mariner" and though most English teachers drag their classes through what they fulsomely call "a masterpiece," "great literature," "beautiful poetry," etc., etc., I doubt that it occurs to many that the line, "And he blessed them unawares," is singularly apposite to the whole issue of learning, education, classroom ambiance. In all the conventional blather about "literature and life," a really pertinent conjunction is overlooked. The guilt-ridden mariner has innocently internalized his experience and has been changed (*i.e.,* educated) by it, for out of him is then drawn (*educere*) the truth which, in its manner, sets him free. But the truth never really sets us free, for it imposes obligations. And henceforth, mariner-like, we must go forth carrying its light. ("The torch is passed. . . .") If all this sounds arcane and precious and remote from the announced topic, I did not mean it to be so. By a wrench of the poetic imagination, Coleridge creates for us a fine metaphor of the ideal education. No one imposed a solution on the mariner. No one lectured him on his salvation. He stares hollow-eyed out at the strange silent sea. Hideous serpents writhe in the phos-phorescence. He is almost hypnotized by the weirdly fascinating sight. And then, by some kind of quantum leap of being, he blesses the serpents "unaware," *i.e.*, unself-consciously, and he is "saved." To be haunted evermore by the truth. And the truth does haunt, does it not? "It's not beauty to abruptly halt the growth of a young mind and to overlay it with the frame of an imposed culture. . . . The true conception of beauty is the shape of organic life. . . ." (Sylvia Ashton-Warner, *Teacher*, p. 31.) "The shape of organic life"—is this not what the mariner discovered? Cannot we and our children discover it too?

If the classroom is to play a positive (*i.e.*, productive, creative, or whatever, as opposed to a *positively destructive*) rôle in the lives of our children, it must generate an atmosphere which makes this possible. An atmosphere, in terms of transactional analysis, of "I'm okay and you're okay, too." We cannot preach the mealy-mouthed "democracy" of the "social studies" textbooks on the one hand and treat the students like members of a pressgang on the other, and expect anything in return but resentment, confusion, rebellion, and despair. What is a child to make of the typical repressive classroom *vis-à-vis* a typical social studies textbook title like *Our American Heritage of Freedom* (to say nothing of the truth of American history!)? And let us not be beguiled by the ingenuous faces, for the kids have simply learned to use our foolishness against us. We cannot talk seriously of "freedom," "love," "respect," "brotherhood," or any of the conventional virtues in an atmosphere so manifestly barren of them. And we surely cannot expect that through the tyranny (strong word? so it is, but that's because we're not accustomed to facing the truth of teacherly behavior) of the typical classroom we can truly engage our students to work toward worthwhile goals. Yes, we can compel them to *perform* after a fashion. The coercive classroom is no place for the *drawing out* that education must be if it is to be anything. Consider a small example from my observations of elementary school teaching: A first-grade child is struggling at the imposed task of printing something that the teacher has written on the board, something from a book, incidentally, not from the class itself. Obviously, this is a dull mechanical activity, which is justified to the child on the basis of its *future* utility (as if the child has any sense of future utility, but let that bit of pedagogic idiocy pass). The child finishes his task, but he has failed to proportion his letters according to the lines on the paper and has even written a few letters backwards. Instead of praise for sitting and doing what is for the child an asinine, empty task, the child is scolded for his "sloppiness." The message that the child draws from this experience, what he "learns," is that "making letters that look like the teacher's letters is important and I will be punished if I fail to do so. Yet copying letters is an empty task that is about as boring a way to spend time as anything I can think of. I conclude, therefore, that school is for the birds." (These are not the child's *words*, quite naturally, but his *feelings*.) The long-term ramifications of this type of experience are both obvious and catastrophic. Teachers self-righteously think that "negative attitudes" on the part of students are the fault of the students. It never, or hardly ever, occurs to the teacher that he and the system may be at fault, that the system itself builds the "negative attitudes" into the student. We find it extraordinarily difficult to question received ideas, attitudes, and systems. They are the "givens" of society and on that account must be right. But if we look around we discover the disconcerting truth that most of the "givens" have been proved all or partly wrong. Conventional wisdom is just that, conventional. The wisdom is far to seek.

How much *listening* does a teacher do? We are surely great, even compulsive, talkers. We spill out the verbal (if not the literary) equivalent of all of Shakespeare's plays every few days. When we do listen, it is to the answers we extort from the student to the questions we ask, the answers we already know and expect. If we get an unexpected answer, the student is "wrong." We create for ourselves and our students a dichotomous world in which everything is either "right" or "wrong," "correct" or "incorrect." Why, for example, should a fourth-grade teacher (in, incidentally, a very high-status public school) grow passionate (seriously) about the dictionary definition of *cape* as against *peninsula*? It strikes me as being a matter of uncommonly little interest to fourth-graders. If this be geography, then we have had enough of geography!

I recommend that we have a listening day each week, during which we listen to the students, not, I hasten to say, the plain or distorted echoes of ourselves. We might be surprised at what the kids have to tell us. *Teach Us What We Want to Know*, the published findings of the Connecticut State Board of Education's research program to redesign their health curriculum, is an instructive insight into the real world of the child's mind. ("Over 5,000 students from kindergarten through twelfth grade were involved in the study which accumulated a minimum of 8,000 pages of written material, almost completely in holograph form," Preface, p. vii.) The primary focus of this study is "health," but the range and depth of the questions are astonishing. In reply, for example, to the question "What do you want to know about the body?", kindergarten through second-grade children responded with such questions as:

> How does my body get made?
> How does my heart beat?
> How does God get your heart in there?
> How do you get bones in your body?
> What makes the bones? If they are bones, how come they can grow and not stick through our skin?
> What makes blood?
> Why do some things taste bitter and some sweet and some things smell awful?
> What makes people cry and laugh?
> What makes you remember?
> What makes people smart? (Pp. 7–8.)

These are but very few of the questions that occupy the thoughts of youngsters. Were teachers to spend more time in honest listening and concomitant honest exploration, perhaps the classroom would be a place where our children would more gladly go.

In *Learning, Language, and Cognition*, Arthur W. Staats makes the following (unfortunately rather pallid) suggestion:

> Education is compulsory because many children would not attend otherwise. With proper use of the reinforcers [*i.e.*, behavioral reinforcers such as praise, tokens, toys, etc.] available, however, it would probably be possible to construct an experimental school situation to be positively reinforcing to the extent that children would go, with few exceptions, on a purely voluntary basis, as was the case in the child research that has been cited. (P. 550.)

I say "pallid" because we haven't time to dawdle. If the principle is sound, as it has proved to be, then it should be implemented as soon and as widely as possible. What Staats is saying is that the school should provide an environment which encourages the child to learn, which is to say, an environment wherein genuine learning can take place. Alas, Staats' view of learning (an "orthodox" psychologist's view) is not a very enlightened one. If the child can repeat what might be called "learning bits," whether orally, graphically, or manually, the psychologist seems to be satisfied that "learning" is taking place. One of the problems that arises from the behavioral scientist's attack on questions of learning is that, by virtue of the need for statistical data, "quantification" becomes the desideratum of learning, that is, learning is reduced to a kind of nut-gathering. This, of course, is not what I mean by learning, but one cannot take issue with the principle enunciated by Staats that learning must be reinforced. The use of tokens, etc., in the "real life" situation of the classroom may, however, generate problems not anticipated in isolated-child experiments. *This* type of reinforcement (not so very different, after all, from grades, one of the disaster areas on the educational landscape) may produce a new set of inhibitory tensions. I am not convinced that in social contexts (which is what a classroom is), our "free-enterprise" competition for gain is educationally useful. Children are easily goaded by competition into being cruel and abusive to each other. I don't think that we want the classroom to continue to be an arena for hostility-and-insensitivity training. Lest I seem to be arguing against myself, however, the principle of reinforcement in education is surely a sound one. It merely remains for us to work out the mode of reinforcement that best serves the child in a context of children.

One answer lies in the "self-concept" theory of learning:

> The [self-concept] theory proceeds from three assumptions: (1) man is purposeful, (2) man is becoming, and (3) man is aware-ing. All behavior is seen as a process of expressing the self. An individual develops a concept of adequacy and a concept of perceived-self. To some extent these overlap, but in many ways are discrepant. These discrepancies must be harmonized by the individual's strivings to become adequate. This motivation takes the form of action as the individual defines what action is appropriate to his definition of adequacy. Consequences of these actions are evaluated and lead to modifications of behavior. This leads to the definition of learning as being the changing of relations between a self and its perceived-world as the self is expressed in striving to become adequate. (Walcott H. Beatty and Rodney Clark, "A Self-concept Theory of Learning: A Learning Theory for Teachers," Report prepared in 1961 (revised 1962) for the Teacher Education Project of San Francisco State College.)

In essence, this is a *self*-reinforcing learning program, wherein the teacher's task is to stimulate and challenge the student, to set (with patience and understanding) goals of adequacy, remembering, as the authors write, "All that each of us is knowing integrates with what we have been knowing. We cannot have new knowledge except as what we know tells us what new knowledge is. Each man constructs his knowledge, but this is an integrative, not an additive process. In each new experience there must be elements already in the aware-ing process if the knower is to integrate the newness." (P. 162.) The following observations by Jerome Bruner on the role of the teacher in engendering the will to learn speak precisely to the point:

> [What] the teacher must be . . . is a day-to-day working model with whom to interact. It is not so much that the teacher provides a model to *imitate*. Rather, it is that the teacher can become a part of the student's internal dialogue—somebody whose respect he wants, someone whose standards he wishes to make his own. It is like becoming a speaker of a language one shares with somebody. The language of that interaction becomes a part of oneself, and the standards of style and clarity that one adopts for that interaction become a part of one's own standards. (*Toward a Theory of Instruction*, p. 124.)

The classroom is more than anything else a state of mind, the merchandisers notwithstanding. (Padding a cell doesn't make it any less a cell.) If, by virtue of the activities which go on and the attitudes which are expressed in the classroom, the child feels that this is the right place for him to be, then we have a classroom worthy of the name, a place for education. But all the carpeting, closed-circuit television, overhead projectors, felt boards, pastel-colored furniture, self-regulating light controls, and restful green chalkboards in the world will make no difference in an atmosphere of compulsion, rigidity, "discipline," and mindless busywork. Though we protest otherwise, our words and actions betray our fundamental distrust of and disrespect for our students. "We give a child the enormously compendious command, 'Don't be so careless!' without reflecting that it is about as useful and specific an exhortation as if one should cry to us, 'Do be more virtuous!'" (Dorothy Canfield Fisher, *Montessori for Parents*, p. 147.) Not only is the exhortation useless, it is disrespectful, disrespectful at a time when the child is trying to discover his worth and individuality. An adult can shrug off the admonition to "be virtuous" as being plain silly; but to charge a child with, for example, "carelessness," especially in a situation he has been coerced into, is not only stupid and thoughtless, it is cruel. And "carelessness" is perhaps the *least* of the frightening and threatening charges that we daily fling at our children.

THE "educational" issue that looms largest in most classrooms is "discipline." By *discipline* I mean, of course, *classroom behavior,* not *intellectual discipline,* for there is relatively little of the latter in our schools. (Memorizing and parroting do not equal intellectual discipline!) In some schools I have visited, 75% to 90% (and more!) of the teachers' time is spent on classroom discipline. I marvel at how any teacher can face that type of non-productive tension day in and day out. I likewise marvel that the students in these environments don't burn the schools to the ground.

> A professor of psychology, at a college where many of the students do practice teaching in a nearby medium-sized city, told me not long ago that one of them, when she went to a school to teach, was handed a stick by the principal and told, 'I don't care whether you teach them anything or not, just keep them quiet.' " (John Holt, *The Underachieving School,* p. 16.)

A repressive system, whether it be national or local, is equally repugnant. (Let the super-patriots take note: There is little logic in attacking "totalitarian, freedom-repressing communism"—or whatever the current rhetoric is—on the one hand and supporting a totalitarian, freedom-repressing system of "education" on the other. The major difference between a free man and a slave is the source of his discipline. Disciplined from without, he is a slave, from within, he is free.)

"But," says the reader, "I know of no teacher who uses sticks to maintain discipline. The example is atypical and is being unfairly used to stigmatize our schools." I would answer that in the first place, the example is not so out of the ordinary as we might wish for the sake of conscience to believe. Jonathan Kozol's experiences (grimly recounted in *Death at an Early Age*) suggest that at least in one part of the country, the stick (and worse) is well known. And it is not unknown elsewhere. In the second place, my point is less dependent on the issue of corporal punishment than on the attitudes which underlie it and which may be manifest in less dramatic but in no less damaging ways. There are worse punishments than violation of the flesh. I speak of damage to mind and spirit. Furthermore, aggression begets aggression; and for those who doubt the truth of this truism, at least insofar as it applies to the classroom situation, one should read Kounin and Gump's "The Comparative Influence of Punitive and Nonpunitive Teachers upon Children's Concepts of School Behavior" (*Journal of Educational Psychology*, 1961, 52, 44–49), which is a most valuable contribution to good sense in the question of school discipline. The three hypotheses of the study are clearly supported by the findings:

1. Punitive teachers will create or activate more aggression-tension than will nonpunitive teachers.
2. Children with punitive teachers will be more unsettled and conflicted about misbehavior in school.
3. Punitiveness of teachers will detract from children's concern with school-unique values. (Pp. 259–60.)

Hence, we would do well to rethink our conventional attitudes concerning classroom punishment (corporal or otherwise). Though the expression "Spare the rod and spoil the child" is rarely heard these days, there are many who believe that it does represent the better part of wisdom insofar as child rearing and education are concerned.

> If punishment were ever successful, there might be some argument in its favor. True, it can inhibit through fear, as any ex-soldier can tell you. If a parent is content with a child who has had his spirit completely broken by fear, then, for such a parent, punishment succeeds. (A. S. Neill, *Summerhill*, p. 169.)

The motion picture *If . . .* is a profoundly shocking parable that bodies forth the terrifying results of disciplinary education. But we needn't pile up statistics to appreciate what punitive education does to our children. Prating about the "good old days" is the idle chatter of the ignorant.

In The Nongraded High School, a book of considerable significance to educational change in America, B. Frank Brown writes:

> When we began to ungrade the high school at Melbourne [in Florida], one of the earliest observations of the effects of change was a difference in the attitude of the student toward learning. Almost overnight, students began to take the initiative for their education away from the teachers. Not only did their attitude toward

learning improve, *but their behavior at school underwent an amazing transformation.* The need for teachers to monitor in the halls, the cafeteria, and bus-loading areas diminished; *finally this problem disappeared completely as an administrative function of the school.* As scholarship began to slip out of the shadows, students started assuming greater responsibility for their conduct and teachers found themselves wisely using the leftover monitoring time to develop a better brand of education.

Student behavior and attitudes continued to change so greatly at Melbourne High that by the middle of the third year of gradeless education, the school was able to abandon its truancy regulations. *The problem of truancy diminished to the point where it finally eliminated itself.* The function of the Dean of Students shifted from one of disciplinary administration to counseling. There are still occasional discipline problems at Melbourne, but all of them originate in the classroom. *The indication is strong that even these are generated by the teacher rather than the student.* (P. 62, emphases added.)

Educational reform cannot, of course, succeed through random expediencies. Here we see that a radical revision of the educational structure underlay what was a serendipitous by-product. Yet the Melbourne High program does teach us something of great importance, namely, that, when the student is *in fact* considered, problems (like discipline) are suddenly no longer problems. Thus, in lieu of root-and-branch reform (like the nongraded program, a reform sufficiently radical to preclude its being widely adopted in America for a long time to come), we can at least modify our classroom practices to achieve somewhat the same ends. Hence, for example, intra-class "ability grouping," which is *de facto* tracking and which at a very early age creates the "dummy-smarty" syndrome, should be abandoned. The great "promise" of tracking has failed to materialize (despite its encouragement by prestigious educational reformers whose ideal school system is something on the order of a high-speed, high-powered sausage-stuffing mechanism, the aim of which, incidentally, was to overgo the Russians). On the contrary, the promise has turned out to be a disaster, the results of which are narcissism and self-hatred (depending upon whether one is a "smarty" or a "dummy") engendered by predictable teacher attitudes toward "achievers" and "non-achievers." (Just what is being "achieved" or "non-achieved" is rarely the issue. The central concern of this book is precisely with this point.) These attitudes in turn breed a variety of psychological, disciplinary, and educational problems. The natural assumption is that the supposed "dummies" are bad and hopeless, and the best to be done with them is to keep them in line with good doses of discipline: "Many people in Boston are surprised, even to this day," writes Jonathan Kozol, "to be told that children are beaten with thin bamboo whips within the cellars of our public schools and that they are whipped at times for no greater offense than for failing to show respect to the very same teachers who have been describing them as niggers." (*Death at an Early Age,* p. 9.) Whereas the "smarties" are the great (usually white) hope of the society and should be lavished with all the riches the school has to lavish (which, in most schools, isn't so much!). Thus the low trackers are given idiot work and are in effect told that they are idiots (and bad ones at that) and the high trackers are given idiot work of another kind and told that they are doing "rich" and "significant" things (workbook exercises, for example). And, of course, the majesty of the whole great system intimidates or impresses the community and another generation of children is run off the assembly line, or what Fred Allen (writing on another subject) called "the treadmill to oblivion." Intra-class ability grouping in the early grades, then, and tracking in the later grades are both forms of the same destructive system. I should think that no honest teacher would countenance such a system. The fact that so many do, indeed, that so many think it to be a good system speaks ill of our educational enterprise. And we are brought back to dismal reflections on the quality of teacher education.

To discipline problems arising from other sources, one may perhaps apply an Alexandrian solution. On the theory that a classroom is a place for quiet and order, then anything that a student does that steps outside this narrow frame is counted cause for disciplinary action of some kind (commonly, tongue lashings and angry shouts of "Quiet!"). If we simply shift our focus, then much we have considered cause for disciplinary action in the past will just vanish. One may argue that by looking the other way, as it were, we have solved no problems. That may be, but I am not suggesting that we look the other way. I am suggesting that we modify our notions of classroom decorum away from the present repressive ideal. What child of any spirit will not challenge repression? Education is not medicine, nor is it a form of penal servitude (though our educational institutions have long seemed bent on making it so). In the British new-plan schools, "The rooms are fairly noisy—more noisy than many American teachers or principals would allow—because children can talk freely." (Featherstone, p. 4.) Hence, the need of scolding (*i.e.*, disciplining) for noisiness disappears. Noise is no longer on the Index. The result of this type of freedom is *not* the chaos that the American teacher naturally imagines. Chaos comes to the classroom primarily through non-engagement on the part of the student. When one is engaged, one is disciplined in the best possible way—from within. Our usual classroom activities are only rarely engaging. And when they are, what discipline problems arise? Watch the most obstreperous boy in school when he is attending (in all senses of the word) to his bicycle: fixing a flat or replacing a part or attaching an accessory. Concentration, discipline, and (very probably) skill in abundance! Does this mean that we have to provide broken bicycles for our problem kids to work on? Not precisely (though it isn't a bad idea), for there are "appropriate" classroom projects that will engage even the unruliest of kids, and there are teacher-created classroom attitudes that will neutralize the urge to rebellion.

In *Montessori for Parents*, Mrs. Fisher conjures up a "Puritan ancestor" who asks, "But where does the discipline come in here, if it is all automatic and unconscious?" Mrs. Fisher devotes a chapter to the answer, but the following comments will here suffice:

> The most obvious [answer] is the retort brutal, i.e., that a great many generations have experimented with that simple method of training children, with the result that family life has been considerably embittered and the children very poorly trained. In other words, the practical experience has shown it to be a very bad method indeed and in use because we know no better one. (P. 153.)

Though we would protest otherwise, our actions with regard to discipline and obedience (which is the goal of discipline) announce that what we want to do is to break the child, as we break a horse, to literal, unquestioning obedience. But the desire for acceptance and approval is sufficiently strong that it will flourish if the classroom is a genuinely loving place. (I write the word *loving* with some reluctance because it too has become debased—the word, of course, not the reality it is meant to represent!) Most schools are not such places. The degree to which children can develop "lovingly" in an enlightened school environment is revealed in Marion Nesbitt's *A Public School for Tomorrow,* a warmly written portrait of the Matthew Fontaine Maury School of Richmond, Virginia.

> A psychology of learning compatible with our way of life must be creative. As free Americans we do not wish to be conditioned and manipulated to respond to preconceived answers. We wish our children to be deeply involved in the process of learning and to understand well the meanings involved. (P. 148.)

Self-discipline arises from commitment. Commitment is possible only when one feels that one belongs where he is and is doing what is important to him. There are probably few convicts who feel committed to prison life, despite the fact that they have been committed to it by society. The sense of belonging will develop only when one is in a situation in which one feels worthwhile and engaged in activities that one feels are worthwhile. The convict is surely not made to feel worthwhile, and he understands all too well the worthlessness of his prison activities. For the student, then, the classroom must be made integral with the texture of life. The traditional discontinuity between school and the rest of the world must be ended. Occasional visits to the firehouse and police station provide for the child little more than a welcome relief from the daily (frequently deadly) classroom routine. The "educational" value of such trips is minimal, although a commendable (however attenuated) urge to be "relevant" undoubtedly lies behind them. There are, as we shall see, more realistic (*i.e.,* educationally productive) things to be done.

It is commonly assumed that the young child has little or no ethical sense. Therefore, the reasoning goes, acceptable patterns of behavior have to be imposed on him. But, as we have seen, the imposition of pattern runs, as it were, against the grain and creates more problems than it solves. (The teacher who believes she has the problem licked because she can point to her class of "little angels" sitting in quiet order is surely naïve. She need but follow her angels on their academic career to discover how naïve. Teacher scuttlebutt, let me repeat, is preeminently concerned with "discipline problems.") It is interesting that the child unwittingly programs himself in the most complex of human systems, namely, language, without any conscious pressure or even effort on the part of his elders. That is, no coercion or disciplinary action is required. Perhaps "socialization" (other than linguistic) is different. Nevertheless, Maria Montessori, A. S. Neill, and others have demonstrated that the child can be brought to a comfortable degree of ethically acceptable behavior exclusively through the process of inculturation, wherein the desired behavior is made the business of the class, not a private war between teacher and child. "For thirty-eight years, I have seen nasty, cheeky, hateful children come to the freedom of Summerhill. In every case, a gradual change took place. In time, these spoiled children have become happy, social, sincere, and friendly children." (A. S. Neill, *Summerhill,* p. 161.) None of this is news, of course, but the easy expedient of traditional discipline is the usual classroom practice. (I know, for example, of "enlightened" suburban schools in affluent communities in which "naughty" children are made to stand in the corner. Recourse to this updated form of pillorying bespeaks loudly the ineptitude of the teacher.) The overriding force in discipline is, as I have said, student commitment to classroom activities. This sort of commitment does not result from threats, harangues, admonitions, or any other of the conventional pressures of the classroom. (Likewise, the residual effects of pulpit oratory are close to nil. Who has ever "mended his ways" in consequence of having been exhorted to do so?)

MUCH has been written on the aesthetics of the school and classroom, and there is no gainsaying the value of pleasant surroundings. Cows, I am told, produce more freely in clean, well-lighted, music-filled barns. Yet the experience of many teachers suggests that it is the *climate* of the classroom rather than its overt design that makes the big educational difference. (Perhaps the mood and expectation of the farmer are what make the real difference in the case of the pampered cows.) Further, one might question whether the currently fashionable glass, chrome, and plastic "ideal" classroom is really all that aesthetically pleasing. We Americans are prone, I think, to equate beauty with (a) newness and (b) slickness (both of which are set as desiderata in advertising on the subject, though slickness is not called that). But with a curious inconsistency, we buy "colonial," "traditional," and "provincial" houses and furniture.

Not that I am advocating a speciously traditional decor or a return to the colonial schoolhouse. Rather, I am simply raising the question of what does constitute an aesthetically pleasing environment. The majority of Americans surround themselves with some form of fake-traditional "coziness" whilst sending their children off to fake-modern architectural horrors to sit in classrooms of indifferent aesthetic value. I should think that some exploration by students and teachers of the aesthetic environment with some options available for modifying that environment (beyond putting up drawings and travel posters) would be educationally valuable. Aesthetic sensibility can be developed at a very early age and some formalization of this in the classroom might help to produce a generation of adults who would be loath to surround themselves with either the cutesy-cozy ugliness of "colonial," etc., or the plasticized, gold-flecked ugliness of discount-store "modern." If there is a pre-college program in America which addresses itself to the quality of the man-made physical environment, I am unaware of it. Community design, object design, architectural design are all proper matters for classroom discussion at every level, and the classroom itself should be equipped (even if only attitudinally) to explore these matters so vital to the quality of life. Here is "relevance." Here is a connection with the circumambient world. If a child is made aware of the aesthetics of living, from the time of his earliest school experience, he will, by the time he has reached the age of community responsibility, be ready to act in concert with the community to change that which needs change. (Would an aesthetically literate public have tolerated what has become the typical American housing development?) And he will be far less likely to fall for the cheap and meretricious. (As I write, however, I must struggle to overcome the sense of despair that comes of my knowledge of the speed with which we are despoiling our total environment, perhaps beyond recovery. Could a genuinely relevant education two or three generations back have sensitized us as a nation sufficiently that we would have never allowed ourselves to reach our present crisis? One cannot say, but one can anticipate.)

We should not forget that the only practical way of judging the quality of our educational programs is by examining the actions of its products. Can anyone be satisfied that the country is moving along in good order? Any assertion that we are can only prove that our education has been largely a failure. The colossal disorder itself proves it. It's no good to point to our fantastic gadgetry, our moon-flights, and the like, for these serve only to underline our plight. We do all these marvelous things and at the same time heedlessly make our planet physically and socially uninhabitable. We surround ourselves with tasteless junk, give credence to anyone with a good line, and confuse show with substance. I am, in a sense, digressing, but the point that brought me here is that if we continue to fail in the classroom, we shall surely fail in the world.

THE polarities of the classroom are student and teacher. The title "teacher," the state "adult," and the symbol "desk," all serve to support the teacher as the dominant polarity, the authority, the boss, the dictator. Despite the teacher's oft-professed sense of inconsequentiality (a sense produced, of course, by the next hierarchical level, which, however, is being challenged—with considerable success— by the teacher through union organization), he is, insofar as his students are concerned, a figure of great and seemingly absolute power. And since few human beings at any age enjoy being held in another's power, students resist in such ways as they can manage. (One might fairly ask where the student's union representation is.) Is there not more than a touch of arrogance in the tacit assumption that, though teachers, who teach voluntarily, merit the amelioration of their conditions of employment through the mediation of an extra-institutional organization, students, who are compelled to be in school, are entitled to nothing and, indeed, are subject to a variety of punitive actions if they move to reject this or that in their educational environment? One can reply that the parents serve the child's interests. But that, as we all know, is baloney. What influence does a parent have on a school system? Parents can sew curtains, sponsor bake sales for the class trip, and donate books to the school library, but what goes on in the classroom is for all practical purposes beyond their power to control. Of course, parents can be worked into an irate mob and raise a great deal of hell about touchy subjects like sex education and sensitivity training, but these are still at the periphery of the real issues of education. The parallel with prison—and the military—holds: convict, soldier, student, all without organization and representation, though the former do have their chaplains! In a proper classroom, the separation suggested by the term *polarity* will not be allowed to happen.

And it will not happen if the teacher understands what he is supposed to be doing. In the process/problem-solving/inquiry-discovery classroom, the teacher must in fact do several things:

1. He conceives and plans. But his planning must be far more flexible than the usual "unit" and "lesson plan" system now in general practice. Planning other than of the broadest kind prior to initial explorations with any given class is unrealistic and unproductive. Detailed advanced planning supposes a curriculum, and unless the curriculum is itself concerned with the process of learning, it is largely fraudulent, for the curriculum developer assumes that he can predict the needs and intellectual behavior of each student and each class without having met either student or class. The long-standing habit of traditional school curricula leads us to believe that certain "learnings" are *sine qua non,* which of course is nonsense. I can readily conceive of an early-grade educational program in which reading, for example, is either done not at all or done only by the way. In fact, such a program might in the long run serve the cause of literacy far better than present programs with their obsessive concern for reading.

2. He introduces. Only in the flexible program is the teacher really free to push the right button at precisely the right time. There are occasions when an entire class is ripe for the challenge the teacher wishes to offer. By the same token, the teacher must be ready to deal with the critical moments of each student. Never should the teacher feel or be obligated to require all students to do the same thing at the same time. There is nothing sacred in anything the teacher might wish to introduce, and it is entirely possible that the class or the individual student will be as wise in the choice of things to do, avenues to explore, as the teacher. Perhaps wiser, for the student knows better what is inside himself than the teacher can ever know.

3. He questions. There is no use in the teacher's pretending to be universally knowledgeable. No one is, and it is silly to pretend otherwise (even though our conventional educational patterns

make the teacher appear to be a walking encyclopedia). What the teacher should have is wisdom born of experience, appreciation of the process of learning, respect for the student, and a reasonably well stocked and agile mind. He is in the position of being able to offer sensible guidance, not "the" answers to all questions. Indeed, he is himself a questioner, and the classroom is a place for asking questions and devising means of answering them. The teacher seeks answers right alongside the student. To ask questions of the student to which the teacher already has "the" answer is to play a foolish game that has little relationship to the purposes of education. An extreme, though not uncommon, form of this game is the question-answer pattern that goes: "What are Japan's principal exports?" Student: "Textiles and electrical products." Teacher: "Wrong. Textiles, textile machinery, and toys." Student (inwardly): "Ugh!" This type of information (*i.e.,* "garbage-pail of knowledge") is perhaps losing favor even among the most hard-shelled traditionalists, but the pre-answered question is likewise a staple in such exercises as that of "interpreting" a poem, wherein the student must come up with the "interpretation" the teacher has already decided on or he will be accounted wrong. This is not the kind of questioning that the new teacher will do. This is not searching in the true sense but more like hunting hidden Easter eggs. As the student's skill in data-gathering and data-manipulation grows, he has every hope of arriving at as sensible solutions as those of the teacher. It is the job of the teacher to make himself increasingly unnecessary to the student. That is, the teacher should help the student to reach a degree of intellectual self-sufficiency such that the student will be challenging himself and finding his own way to meet his challenges.

4. He expedites. In a sense, the teacher is like an executive or project chief. He keeps the operations of the classroom flowing (toward, we would hope, some worthy goal, a goal that can perhaps be anticipated by the class at large and reexamined from time to time along the way). He channels the intra-class movements and helps to shape the "equations" of this sort of enterprise.

5. He encourages. Encouragement can be of many kinds: reward,

stimulation, performance. Like the conductor of an orchestra, he tries by a variety of means to draw all that he can from each student. But unlike the conductor, he is not the leader absolute. And he cannot separate himself from the class as the conductor does from his orchestra. The ultimate reward must of course be the reward the student accords himself, the pleasure of taking pains to achieve something worth achieving. But he will not very likely ever get there without the warmly encouraging presence of the teacher.

6. He learns. Teaching and learning are not two things, they are the same thing. And the teacher must approach his task with the full appreciation that he will learn as much from his students as they will learn from him. Because he has certain kinds of knowledge that they don't have doesn't mean that they are merely empty vessels waiting to be filled. There is a story about a white man who when dealing with a certain Indian chief drew a small circle in the dirt and told the Indian that the circle represented what the Indian knew. Then he drew a larger circle around the smaller and told the Indian that this was what the white man knew. Whereupon the Indian described with his hand a circle around the entire bowl of sky and told the white man that this was what neither of them knew. Of course, the Indian was being generous to the white man; he should have rubbed out the two circles in the dirt. Let us grant that we all know a great deal about lots of different things and that we all have something to learn from each other. A slum child will know more and more profoundly about ghetto life than an army of sociologists. There are all kinds of knowing.

The teacher need find no place in his many rôles for denial, punishment, insult, and distrust. He likewise cannot serve his students well if he accepts only the orthodox and conventional. What may seem on first blush to be an absurdity may in time prove to be the best possible answer. Teachers have the deadly and deadening habit of condemning out of hand what they are unfamiliar with, don't immediately understand, or can think of no precedent for. We are all ignorant. The difference between what a student is ignorant of and what a teacher is ignorant of is not as great as we teachers would like to believe. Beyond what any one of us knows, as the Indian in the story pointed out, there are worlds yet to know. We deceive ourselves if we equate education with the accumulation of data. I can do more with problem-solving techniques, a bit of mathematics, and an inquiring intellect than I can do with an entire encyclopedia committed to memory. We must overcome our insecurity in the face of uncertainty. Beyond the apparent certainty of, say, the multiplication table, certainty is only some degree of uncertainty. Heisenberg tells us that uncertainty is a scientific principle. Even the once so "simple" question of medical death is fraught with uncertainty. (Consider: not only is the medical profession unable to define death to its own satisfaction, but law and theology are equally muddled on the issue.) Our traditional certitudes never really were of much use; now they are a positive danger. Hence, the teacher always presses forward, is never content to settle for something less than can be further explored. The classroom is thus a laboratory wherein life itself can be probed and in which there is no easy predicting of results. Instead of going, as in the usual curriculum, from here to there, we go from here to——?

"But what will our children really learn?" It may sound too elemental to say that they will learn how to survive, but survival is the issue after all. And survival applies to matters other than chopping down the wilderness or learning how to live in the jungle. At any rate, there are other kinds of jungles than those of the tropics or even of the city streets. Let us say that supporting the idea of "survival" are the capabilities of solving problems and making decisions. These in turn subsume awareness, self-realization, responsibility, "humanization," and so on. Reading and writing and the other school subjects are functional by-products of this kind of education. They spring (ideally) from discovered needs and are far more meaningful and far better acquired as a result. Anterior to the whole educational process is what might be called the "ethics of discovery," the attitude of teacher and community toward education. I choose the word *ethics* because, without a sense of the ethical basis of democratic education, the enterprise degenerates into a series of mechanical strategies—as it in fact has long since done under the traditional regimens.

We have spoken of the various rôles of the *teacher*, but beneath these rôles is the *person*, and a great deal of what succeeds or fails in the classroom must be charged to that person. "Interactional analysis," the study of what happens when people interact, demonstrates convincingly that "the method is the message." By this is meant that what the teacher *actually* does (as opposed to what he is *saying* or what he *thinks* he is doing) is what the student really responds to. Hence, by a variety of often non-verbal signals (glances, finger-pointing, etc.) the teacher tells the class that what he wants is the *appearance* of attention, this appearance being a conventionalized pose that we have come to associate with the *idea* of "attention." The question of whether anybody is in fact paying attention to the content of the teacher's remarks (on, say, the tradition of the pastoral novel) becomes irrelevant. Or consider the teacher who has just astonished himself with an elegant exegesis of *The Windhover* and is radiating pleasure at the smoothness of his delivery, the trenchancy of his reasoning, and the brilliance of his wit, all tossed off the cuff, as it were. The *real* message, especially after he says, "There, now, that was easy, wasn't it?", of his performance *is the performance,* which tells the student that (1) any dimwit should be able to toss off an analysis like that and (2) if the student can't do it, which of course is the case, he is a dimwit. Thus, when the teacher, still aglow, asks the class to do the same for the poems in the textbook, he draws a blank, not realizing that no one in the class is willingly going to deliver himself up for the knucklehead award. A video tape recording of a class in action can inform and chasten us in a most useful (though initially threatening) way. We shall do our best as teachers when we properly interlock all of our "messages," for only then will the classroom have the attitudinal coherence necessary for accomplishing the kind of learning we would profess to desire.

Thus the classroom is a place in which, *because of the nature of the place itself*, the student should feel he belongs. Though under current laws he must go to school for a considerable part of his youth, he should, if asked, assert that school is where he'd want to be anyway. Though the pre-college teacher has a captive audience, he will do best if he but treat that audience as though it were in his class voluntarily and free to leave when the classroom fails to do its proper job.

We don't live in anything like a perfect world, and it is useless to hope that things will ever be entirely (perhaps even close) to our liking. Only rarely does a teacher have the opportunity to start afresh in a new school free of the inertia of tradition. For most teachers, the school and its ways are given, and he must fit himself in as best he can. Yet the potential for change and growth is always in the air and it need take no more than a very few energetic people to send the school off in a new (better) direction. If we cannot have it all our own way, the alternative is *not* to do nothing at all. In lieu of anything else, the individual teacher can bootleg excitement into his own classroom. School functionaries are generally responsive to what "works," especially if it doesn't cost anything. And what works often catches on with the more cautious. (What a pity that teachers feel they must be cautious; if we are the "professionals" we profess to be, then we should work *professionally* and not fearfully.) A small beginning is better than no beginning. If one cannot change the system instantly and single-handedly, one can change something that may in time force larger changes, and so on. In short, one can be subversive. And why not? The fact is that more and more schools are starting to thaw out. Every educational technique in this book is in use somewhere in some form. The shame is that so many young people continue to lose the great learning years to parochialism, small-mindedness, brainless conservatism, and ineptitude (and lots of other bad things).

Robert M. Hutchins once said that a university (any and all universities) should be burned to the ground every fifty years (though he seems to have pulled back from that sort of explicit radicalism of late, just as Professor Hayakawa seems to have abandoned the fine ideas of the book that made him famous—sad how our gods betray us!), by which seemingly outrageous metaphor he means, I think, that as soon as the vitality of what should be the center of vitality begins to fade, we should question everything about it including its premises and reshape it consonant with our findings. Hence, the public, the school officials, the teachers, and the students should constantly subject their institution to the closest scrutiny and never allow themselves to feel that anything about an institution is "sacred"; *i.e.*, beyond criticism, immune to change. Change is the one constant of existence. Where we fight change, we fight a rearguard and ultimately losing action, and we lose precious time in the process. The student who asks, "Why?" is the ally of education. The teacher who refers him to the authority of habit (received beliefs, rules, traditions, and what not) is its enemy. Ours *is* to reason why.

 LANGUAGE

Language is one of the points of intersection in that network of habit and choice which is the pattern of our human doings.

[W. F. Twaddell, "Meanings, Habits and Rules"]

The blab blab, which has nursed the blabs of blabs, call upon you for the blab blab which you, in whom flows blab blood, will not fail, and which will echo down the blabs of blab.

[Stuart Chase, *The Tyranny of Words*]

One great use of words is to hide our thoughts.

[Voltaire]

Monolingual persons take language so much for granted that they often forget its arbitrary nature and cannot distinguish words from things.

[Yuen Ren Chao, *Language and Symbolic Systems*]

How every fool can play upon the word!

[*The Merchant of Venice*, III, v]

In the schools misconceptions of Standard English have produced "school-marm English," taught as if it were a dead language, like Latin. In particular teachers have treated spoken English as simply an inferior form of written English, instead of a properly independent form, and assumed that "colloquial" means corrupt. They have taught their students never to write in the natural way they talked; they have even tried to make them talk in the way they were supposed to write.

[Herbert J. Muller, *The Uses of English*]

Perhaps the best safeguard against such hazards as language involves is a sound understanding of what language is and does.

[O. Hobart Mowrer, "The Psychologist Looks at Language"]

TEACHING is communicating, and teaching is about communicating. The teacher talks and "communicates" thereby. The teacher talks about some sort of textual materials, which are themselves communications. It is a complex and, when talked about, confusing process, for as Professor Chao (quoted above) says, we take language for granted. When, therefore, our attention is drawn to what is generally "background" for us (compare imaginatively the visual perception of a tribe of beings who see only yellow—ordinarily, they would have neither a notion of color in general nor yellow in particular), we are likely to become confused (a fact that does not, to be sure, interfere greatly with our *use* of language). Once we have started to grasp the nature of language, however, the confusions lessen and we are far better equipped to understand the process of communication and to communicate more effectively.

Language is what we teach no matter what we teach, and the exploration of language is not the exclusive province of the "language arts" teacher, though he is perhaps more professionally concerned with manifestations of language than is, for example, the mathematics teacher. What follows in this chapter is an overview of the *study* of language as a "subject" (linguistics), and an examination of language as a phenomenon. Any teacher will be more effective with some formal background in language study. But for the English (language arts) teacher, this background is the core of his (unfortunately rather vaguely defined) discipline. The subject, "English," is usually thought of as an amalgam of "grammar" (a term we shall presently look at in detail), composition, and literature (in the elementary grades, "language arts" subsumes reading, English—*i.e.*, "grammar" and punctuation—spelling, handwriting and *no* literature). "The so-called 'language arts' designation exists in name only, for there has been little attempt to unify the study, and each subject continues to be taught separately. The use of the term 'language arts' in elementary school curriculum may, therefore, be a dangerous deception." (I. M. and S. W. Tiedt, *Contemporary English in the Elementary School*, p. 5.) What "English" *should* be, however, is the study of language—composition and literature being but two of many manifestations of "English." "Grammar" is meant, presumably, to take care of the language side of the subject, but this too plays English false, as we shall see.

The energies of science are largely concerned with identifying, classifying, defining, and describing—with, that is, *discovery*. And what the research scientist does *vis-à-vis* the phenomenal world, the linguist does *vis-à-vis* language. In the following pages we shall probe about in language rather like a biologist probing about in a specimen.

Although linguistics (as a more-or-less self-contained discipline dependent upon scientific methodology) did not emerge until the nineteenth century, man has long been interested in the phenomenon of language and has long attempted to pluck out the heart of its mystery. Perhaps the oldest linguistic experiment on record is the one reported performed by the Egyptian king Psammetichos, who, in an effort to determine the most ancient and therefore the parent language of man, caused two infants to be reared in isolation until they spoke for the first time. The noises they finally uttered sounded roughly like *bekos*, the Phrygian word for bread. The conclusion was obvious; Phrygian was the most ancient of languages because untutored infants unexposed to any other language drew upon their "instincts" and produced a word in the "parent language." This is not very scientific by our standards, but it does have a scientific spirit which is admirable. The Book of Genesis approaches the question of language in quite a different way and arrives at equally absurd results. But, once again, man is simply trying to come to grips with this most fascinating of his creations. The primacy of language is so strongly felt that in the Gospel of St. John, the evangelist opens with the stunning assertion, "In the beginning was the Word" (*En arche en o logos*). All creation, it would seem, springs from language. Such a view informs that modern Johannine testament, *Finnegans Wake*.

As we might have expected, it was the Greeks who, in the Western world, first attempted to come to grips with language in an orderly, intellectual, and philosophical way; and they did such a remarkable job that the principles they laid down (beginning with Plato, insofar as extant documents can tell us) have dominated Western thinking on language at least until the nineteenth century. Somewhat earlier than Plato's comments on language (in the *Cratylus*) is the work of the Indian grammarian Panini, whose Sanskrit grammar has been called one of the most stunning of all the monuments to the human intellect. But it was the Greeks, and the Romans after them, who shaped the course of language study for centuries to come. Because it was the Greek view of man and nature, *i.e.*, of reality, upon which the western world founded its systems of thought or from which its systems of thought sprang, the Greek pronouncements on the nature of language were not only accepted by Roman and post-classical civilization but were accorded the status of "truth." Even in the Christian Middle Ages, Aristotle was "the Philosopher," as though there were in reality only one worthy of the name. This veneration of Aristotle, and later of other classical philosophers, Plato in particular, gave the Greek grammars and the works founded on them unimpeachable authority. Over the centuries, linguistic data accumulated greatly, but the philosophical foundations (and biases) were almost purely Greek.

Unfortunately, Greek and later assertions regarding language (and regarding the phenomenal world in general) were largely speculative, deductive, and normative (without, alas, a clear sense of what the norms were). In summarizing his discussion of the most influential of the early grammatical works, that of Dionysius Thrax (*c.* 100 B.C.), Father F. P. Dinneen writes

> The questions he raised and the order in which he treated them have been little improved upon for more than twenty centuries. . . . [I]t is not unfair to say that many traditional grammarians who do not employ structural methods are still, to a large extent, translating languages into Greek, even though they may know no Greek. That is, they discuss modern languages in terms of meaning categories that are important as a consequence of Greek structure. . . . (*An Introduction to General Linguistics*, Holt, Rinehart and Winston, Inc., p. 105.)

There is unquestionably much of value in the twenty-five short paragraphs that comprise Thrax's *Grammar,* but, ironically, such advances in linguistic thought as his *Grammar* represents served also to stunt linguistic thought. Perhaps it was because the speculative habit early became the dominant habit of thought in the West, and even after empiricism overtook the West, language study continued along the old paths. The urge of the speculator (like that, interestingly, of the scientist) is toward generalization, for through generalization we see relationships, organize experience, make predictions (in the scientific sense), and contrive explanations. But not all generalizations are useful.

> There are two kinds of false generalization, which can be classified as innocuous and pernicious forms of error. The first, often found among empirically minded philosophers, lend themselves rather easily to correction and improvement in the light of further experience. The second, which consist in analogies and pseudo explanations, lead to empty verbalisms and dangerous dogmatism. Generalizations of this kind seem to pervade the work of speculative philosophers. (Hans Reichenbach, *The Rise of Scientific Philosophy,* University of California Press, 1951, p. 10.)

What Professor Reichenbach says of speculative philosophers in general is applicable *a fortiori* to the grammarians, who at their best posed interesting questions and offered shrewd insights and at their worst (from the vantage point of the twentieth century we can comfortably judge them) indulged in sterile intellectual exercises wholly divorced from the "real world" of language. There is of course little point in belaboring the ages for their failures. Suffice it to say that with the entrance of the study of language into science, we should be able to set aside the false generalizations of the past. Lest I appear to have overstated the case against the grammarians of the past, let me offer the corrective of the following comments by one of the leading linguistic theorists of our time, Professor Noam Chomsky:

> I think that we have much to learn from a careful study of what was achieved by the universal grammarians of the seventeenth and eighteenth centuries [in particular, that of the philosophical Port-Royal *Grammar* of 1660, by no means a "typical" work]. It seems

to me, in fact, that contemporary linguists would do well to take their concept of language as a point of departure for current work. Not only do they make a fairly clear and well-founded distinction between deep and surface structure, but they also go on to study the nature of deep structure and to provide valuable hints and insights concerning rules that relate the abstract underlying mental structures to surface form, the rules we would now call "grammatical transformations." What is more, universal grammer developed as part of a general philosophical tradition that provided deep and important insights, also largely forgotten, into the use and acquisition of language, and, furthermore, into problems of perception and acquisition of knowledge in general. These insights can be exploited and developed. The idea that the study of language should proceed within the framework of what might be called "cognitive psychology" is sound. There is much in the traditional view that language provides the most effective means for studying the nature and mechanisms of the human mind, and that only within this context can we perceive the larger issues that determine the directions in which the study of language should develop. ("The Current Scene in Linguistics: Present Directions," *College English*, Vol. 27, May, 1966, 588–89.)

From the standpoint of teacher and school, the central concern of "English" would seem to be the ever-burning issue of "correctness." This concern is a dominant feature of the grammar books of the Renaissance and later periods. It might clarify our thinking on the subject if we understand that it has been only since the invention of printing, which made possible cheap books which in turn made possible mass education (and the social hegemony of the upward-striving middle classes), that "correctness" was even an issue. Correctness in spelling, for example, was established as a convenience by printers, correctness for them being merely their way of spelling. As soon, however, as spelling was hardened into print, there, with relatively few succeeding changes, it stayed. It should not therefore surprise one to learn that modern English *spelling* is a fairly accurate representation of fifteenth-century *pronunciation* (that is, of certain fifteenth-century British dialects). It is, as we all know, a rather less than precise representation of modern American pronunciation. Only the French and Irish spelling "systems" are less in touch with linguistic reality. Bernard Shaw and others have long entertained us with the likes of *ghoti* and *ghoughtheighdough* (*i.e.,*

> f   i   sh   p   o   t
> *fish* and *potato:* laug*h,* women, na*t*ion; hiccoug*h,* thoug*h,* *Th*omas,
>   a   t   o
> *w*eig*h,* talke*d,* doug*h*),

and we all have our own painful memories of
spelling lessons. Who, indeed, is wholly at ease with English spelling? Shaw had a lifelong obsession with the subject and left considerable money in his will for the purpose of encouraging spelling
reform. (Nothing, by the way, has come of it and the money has
been used for other things.)

Prior to the late seventeenth century, there was either universal
agreement or universal unconcern regarding questions of usage (*i.e.,*
of "correct" language usage), for scarcely a word on the subject can
be found (in English, at any rate). It is true that there was the
"Purist-Inkhornist" controversy that raged (if "raged" is precisely the
word) during the Elizabethan and Jacobean periods over whether
English should incorporate or reject exotic (and often monstrous:
"potamophilous") words, but this was a narrowly focused issue and
not precisely germane to the work of the later prescriptive grammarians. (See *Hamlet,* V,ii, 11. 81–172, for Shakespeare's oblique
comment on the controversy.) But once the grammarians were established, they unblushingly issued directives on all aspects of English, blandly assuming that their private views of the language warranted the force of public ordinances, and, of course, they felt comfortably a part of a tradition stretching back to the great Classical
ages.

The pre-scientific study of language reached its climax for the
English-speaking world in the work of the eighteenth-century grammarians (James Harris, James Buchanan, Robert Lowth, Lindley
Murray, and others), who worked from two main assumptions,
namely, that (1) there was such a thing as universal grammar and
(2) it is the rôle of the grammarian to proscribe and prescribe linguistic behavior. Though certain contemporary linguists offer convincing arguments in favor of the idea of language universals, we
have as yet no such thing in hand as a "universal grammar" or even
a universal theory of grammar. To the eighteenth-century grammarian, Latin was the "universal language" which provided the
"universal grammar." (Professor Chomsky points out that the Port-
Royal *Grammar* was vernacular in orientation and cannot be fairly
charged with a Latin bias. This may be so, but it is not relevant to

the case. The fact is that the English grammarians of the eighteenth century were avowed Latinists and this is what informed their writing on English grammar.) The received wisdom of the age was that Latin was the perfect language and that the vernacular was to some degree or another a "fall from grace." But in lieu of a sound historical background and a rigorous methodology, the grammarians did have vigorous intellects and an impressive collection of whimsies and idiosyncrasies. This meant that much of what they said was forcefully and convincingly said but had little to do with the realities of the language. This forcefullness made the grammarians' way the "right" way, and there was an end of it. Lindley Murray (1795), for example, writes, "The *fifth* rule for the strength of sentences is *to avoid concluding them with an adverb, a preposition, or any inconsiderable word.*" Because school grammars from that time to this have in fact merely copied from each other, we are still told that one should not end a sentence with a preposition. If Murray had but done a little serious research, he would have appreciated that his proscription plainly flies in the face of normal English usage. Not only is the sentence-final position of prepositions a long-standing tradition in English (compare *What did you do it for?* with *For what did you do it?*), but the sentence-final position of adverbs is the most common adverbial position for simple (*i.e.*, one-clause) sentences (*e.g., He walked home quickly,* which, one can argue, ends in *two* adverbs).

Tied to a variety of misconceptions about language, lacking modern linguistic methodology, committed to the belief that linguistic virtue resided in Latin above all languages, Murray and his compeers were working, as it were, on the edge of darkness. They did have some "linguistic" materials to work from—the grammars of Latin, for example, which provided much of the terminology, and, alas, much of the confusion as well. The term "preposition" is a case in point. In Latin, the language feature called *praepositio* was in fact a pre-positioned (and rarely used) particle. Since the particles in English that could *translate* the Latin pre-positioned particles were called after the Latin designation, "prepositions," the argument was that one cannot logically put a *pre*-position in a *post* position. A semantic quibble. (To his credit, Murray did not try to convince by such specious argument, but the "rule" stems from the argument nonetheless.) Likewise, the traditional names for the *tenses* of English verbs are the translated names of the Latin tenses. There are precisely six marked tenses in Latin. We are taught that there are six tenses in English. Are there? Well, however many tenses we have in English, six is precisely the wrong number. Furthermore, the traditional Latin schema provides us with an almost entirely erroneous set of semantic values for the English verb system. English of course does not derive from Latin (though there are still English teachers who retail the nonsense that it does) and cannot be very usefully studied as if it did. English and Latin are related—as distant cousins with a remote common ancestor (called by linguists, *Indo-European*).

In the nineteenth century, the beginning of the scientific age so far as language was concerned, a schism developed between school grammar-book writers and academic grammarians. The former simply took over the work of the earlier prescriptivists, though lacking their imagination and intellectual vigor, made minor changes in grammar-book format, and fobbed off their "grammars" to a rule-hungry middle class. (This is a fascinating byway in social history, but we must leave it unexplored here.) Advances in the study of all aspects of language went by them, generation after generation, and generation after generation of our children have been "taught" from grammar books that are substantively not a jot different from the first feeble copies of the originals. Yes, they are expensively printed, lavishly illustrated in four (or more) colors, and bound in the latest plastics, but inside, it's the same old stuff. Neil Postman and Charles Weingartner observe:

> In discussing the subject of grammar with dozens of parents, scores of teachers, and hundreds of students, we have been astonished to discover that most of them do not have the slightest idea where a grammar comes from. Even worse, most people seem unaware that grammars—that is, descriptions of the structure of a language—are invented and written by human beings. They seem to believe that a grammar is something that is just *there*, like the seasons, or the tides, or the stars. Such people are predictably confused by "modern developments" in grammar, since they cannot imagine "modern developments" in the seasons, the tides, or the stars. (*Linguistics: A Revolution in Teaching*, p. 45.)

The story of language study in the nineteenth century is well told in Holgar Pedersen's *The Discovery of Language, Historical Lin-*

guistics in the Nineteenth Century. Suffice it to say here, the philologers (as they were called) of the age, Erasmus Rask, Jakob Grimm, the *Junggrammatiker* ("Neo-grammarians"), Franz Bopp and others, brought language study to the level of a science and provided a sturdy foundation upon which the modern linguists could build. Theirs was a new orientation toward language study, a philosophy free or reasonably free of the prejudices of the past. Language study moved, as it were, from astrology to astronomy. Not, let me repeat, that the Greeks and their intellectual descendants performed without distinction and failed to cast significant light on language. On the other hand, had we continued along the same paths and followed the same methods as the pre-scientific grammarians, we would today know little more about language than was known several hundreds of years ago, and much of what we would know would be of little use.

> The true followers of the classical and scholastic [*i.e.*, early academic and philosophical] grammarians are not those who seek to preserve intact the whole framework of classical grammar, but rather those who carry out free and critical inquiry into the role and nature of language within the context of present-day scientific thinking, and with the more extensive knowledge of languages and cultures that is now available. (John Lyons, *Introduction to Theoretical Linguistics,* p. 18.)

The nineteenth century was chiefly concerned with language history and language relationship, that is, with discovering sources and delineating linguistic "family trees." But twentieth-century interests have been directed mainly toward matters of form, structure, and theory, in short, toward discovering the "nature" of linguistic phenomena. Hence, the thrust of linguistic work has been away from "philology" and toward formal linguistic analysis. One of the important lessons learned from the historical (as opposed to the pseudo-historical) approach to language study was that change is a fact of language and that terms like *corruption* and *decay* can be only metamorphical, not pejorative. One can speak of the "decay" of inflections in English without at the same time suggesting that something "bad" happened, *decay* simply meaning that the English inflection system has been undergoing a reduction from the relatively full system of the Old English period (*c.* A.D. 450–1100) to the vestigial system of present-day English. The linguist can describe

change and even attempt to account for it, but he cannot fin
sound basis upon which to qualitatively evaluate change. Ques
of "good" and "bad" have perhaps a proper place in discussion.
rhetoric (the artful use of language, the "aesthetics" of composition),
but not in the scientific examination of language. A sociolinguist,
of course, might wish to record that certain segments of a population
prefer this form to that form and that a variety of social controls
exist which direct language usage. But the question of whether
the loss, say, of the distinction in common speech between "imply"
and "infer" is good or bad must be outside the linguist's purview,
when he functions as a linguist. When (or if) he functions as a
rhetorician (a teacher of writing perhaps), he can set whatever
standards he wishes (so long, I expect, as they are within some
existing frame of usage).

In very broad terms, linguistics in the twentieth century has devoted itself largely to describing language; *i.e.*, with examining the
structures and processes of language. This direction in language
study was pointed first by the Swiss linguist, Ferdinand de Saussure
(1857–1913), whose lectures on language provided the science with
both concepts and terminology that have proved basic. Of particular interest are the distinctions he draws among the three levels
into which he analyzes the phenomenon of language. The inclusive
term is *le langage*; *i.e.*, the idea of human speech, language as man's
special mode of communication. It is with this level that the student
of human origins is mainly concerned, for it is at this level that language is most directly "attached" to intellectual function, that is, to
the symbol-making function that can manifest itself in graphic symbolism (the cave paintings, for example) or in linguistic symbolism.
The other "languages" of de Saussure are more directly within the
purview of the linguist proper. *La langue* (again, "language," but
applied to language systems such as English, German, Chinese, and
so on) is language at the communal level. It is in a sense an abstraction, being the sum of all its speakers and existing as a "thing"
nowhere apart from its uses; its uses, then, being the third "language," *la parole* or individual human speech; *i.e.*, individual speech
acts. *La parole* is the only physically demonstrable manifestation
of either *le langage* or *la langue*. We can say, therefore, that human
beings have language (*le langage*), Americans have *a* language (*la
langue, viz.*, English), which is realized through speech (*la parole*).

Thus, while there are scholars who address themselves to the philosophical question of language universals (*le langage*), they must first deal with actual existing languages (*les langues*), which can be known only through their use by individual speakers, through, that is, *la parole*. While we all speak language, it is *a* language we speak; but a language is only manifested at any moment as particular bits and pieces of speech (or writing, which, after all, is merely displaced speech). It might be argued that once any language is schematized, it "exists" apart from its speakers. But a grammatical description of a language does not equal the language any more than a road map equals the actual territory.

One obvious value of de Saussure's schema is that it enables us to see what we are looking at and helps us to avoid unwitting shifts of attention from one reality to another. If we are thinking of *la langue*, we shall be concerned with a large abstraction beyond the control of any one individual but exerting fairly rigid controls on him. If we are thinking of *la parole*, we shall be concerned with the specific phonetic, morphological, and syntactic productions of a given speaker. We can never, of course, fully know a language. We can know only the generalizations drawn from a finite body of data. There is, in fact, no such thing as a complete description of a living language. By the time such a description could be concluded, the sum of all the usages of the language would have changed it in a variety of ways. Hence, no grammatical work can honestly claim to be *the* grammar of English or Italian or Arabic. Even Jespersen's lengthy and seemingly exhaustive study of English is incomplete and already dated. One can conceive of a "complete" *theory* of grammar, but not a complete grammatical *description*.

Linguistics in the twentieth century owes a great debt to de Saussure. Perhaps his most significant "ideological" contribution to the field is the importance granted to the spoken language by his tripartite analysis of "language." He made it clear that everything about language ultimately devolves on the fact of people speaking. Virtually all students of language prior to de Saussure took for granted the precedence of the written word over the spoken word, which was considered merely ephemeral and often perverse insofar as the "logic" of language was concerned. It is unfortunate that this pedagogical bias in favor of the written language persists even to the present day, for it contributes mightily to what one observer has called "our national mania for correctness," the curious consequent of which is our national distaste for and ineptness at writing!

The "structuralists," who followed de Saussure (the most notable of whom was Leonard Bloomfield), focused on speech as the primary linguistic activity. And for those linguists who turned their attention to the languages of non-literate cultures (*e.g.*, the Amerindian), speech was the *only* linguistic activity. These workers applied themselves to the task of *describing* the languages they found, seeing language description as the basic function of the science. Since their aim was to discover the structure of any given language and to describe what they had discovered, they have been variously called "structural linguists," "analytical linguists," and "descriptive linguists." The last term, according to some, is more inclusive and less "precise." Be that as it may, the structuralists (or descriptivists) developed certain fairly well defined and workable techniques for the tasks they had set themselves, one very practical result of their work being the recording and describing of a number of rapidly disappearing exotic languages. Another result has been the gradual freeing of school grammar from the straitjacket of traditionalism. Although, a great many school grammar textbooks in current use are still mainly traditionalist, an increasing number include at least some structural materials. The practical results, of course, are very little different, for the overriding issue is the use of the textbook and the pedagogical evils attendant thereon. However, the point here is that some of the work of modern linguistics has found its way into the awareness of the classroom teacher.

The most important general principle to emerge with twentieth-century linguistics is that linguistics is (like all sciences) *descriptive* not *prescriptive*. The linguist may note that there are, in a given speech community, several levels of usage (he is bothered by the pejorative potential of "levels," but the word is a convenient shorthand); but he does not see it as part of his job *as a linguist* to say that one is "better" than another. This type of judgment is the business of rhetoricians and English teachers (which linguists may also be, but the functions must be kept well defined). That is, one may set up aesthetic and other standards (as representative views of a particular segment of the society, say, the "educated," for standards which are purely idiosyncratic are either the work of the artist or have a very low coefficient of survival). The charge that linguists say, "Anything goes," is a perverse misreading of the situation. Approval or disapproval has nothing to do with description. One might just as well imagine a physicist approving or disapproving of the micro-wave spectrum. The modern linguist (in composite) has set himself the work of finding out all about language. In his socio-linguistic guise, he can report that this or that locution is disapproved of by this or that segment of society. When he steps out of the magic circle of science and becomes a classroom teacher of English composition, he will surely urge upon his students those language practices that are in general use by members of that dialect of language we call "standard" or "educated." The teacher is, after all, the purveyor of a dialect. The teacher who grasps the nature of language and who understands the operations of language will be in a far better position to instruct wisely than the teacher who knows little more than a few (often arbitrary and irrelevant) "rules." I shall explore this question in some detail below under "Correctness."

Until the fifties, various forms of structuralism dominated the linguistic scene. But the publication in 1957 of Noam Chomsky's *Syntactic Structures* (a book indebted in some measure to the work of Zellig Harris) opened a new linguistic epoch. Almost overnight, structuralism was eclipsed by a conception of language analysis called *transformationalism* or *transformational-generative grammar.* Whereas the structuralist attempted to describe and classify given utterances, the transformationalist attempts to describe the *process* whereby an utterance comes to be (linguistically speaking). Hence, one can say that the structuralist view of language is predominately static while the transformationalist view is dynamic, *being* versus *becoming.* But linguistics is not a game of "Can you top this?" The inevitable synthesis is already beginning, wherein all the useful findings in the field will undoubtedly find their proper place.

An educated man should be able to think rationally and incisively about his environment and about his human situation. Yet the ideal of the educated man is seldom approached in one of the most significant facets of his life: language. Adult Americans are badly informed about language and endemically prone to naive reasoning on any linguistic question. Moreover, they have no better insight into their own English tongue than into language in general, and this is, perhaps, the most serious failure of liberal humanistic objectives in American education. (H. A. Gleason, "What Grammar?" *Harvard Educational Review,* Vol. 34, No. 2 (Spring, 1964), p. 267.)

The primary cause of our linguistic naïveté (despite the fact that we spend more time in school on "English" than on any other subject) resides in the nature of conventional "grammar" teaching, which focuses on a hodgepodge of linguistic isolates (functionless definitions, usage prescriptions, and the like) that never fall together into a comprehensive theory of language. (It is doubtful whether many English teachers can even make anything of the term, "theory of language.") Despite what seems to be an orderly presentation of material in the typical school grammar, no distinction is made between the concepts of *la langue* and *la parole* (approximating *competence* and *performance,* in Chomskyan terminology; the former the "programming," as it were, and the latter the "display" or "output"), or among grammar as structure, grammar as the study of structure, and "grammar" as usage. (*"Ain't* is bad grammar.") The result of eight to ten years of pre-college "grammar" study is precisely the ignorance of language to which Professor Gleason points!

The general direction of linguistics is toward a theory of language, just as the general direction of physics is toward a theory of reality. Though the scientist works with particulata, he works within or toward the abstract principle. In the paragraphs following, I shall present a brief picture of language from the point of view of the linguist. In my judgment, no teacher is fully competent to teach who doesn't have at least this minimal understanding of the nature of language, and an English or "language arts" teacher without it is downright incompetent.

We should, in the first place, appreciate the fact that language is a social phenomenon (hence, linguistics is properly a social or behavioral science), and as such is not antecedent to man or even to society. Language, that is to say, is not found apart from man. Further, "languaging" is an interested behavior: We talk to communicate, even when we talk to ourselves. We communicate to signal other human beings for the purpose of accomplishing a variety of ends. We may simply want to notify others of our existence or presence (the *contactive* function). We may want to cause something to happen (the *hortatory* or *directive* function). Or we may want to get or give information (the *ideational* function). These functions encompass greetings, commands, prayers, incantations, questions, and statements—in short, all the things we do with language. (The exclamation—*Oh! Ouch!, etc.*—is a conventionalized displacement of the animal *cry* or *call*, communication types quite different from the strictly human *word*. These terms—*cry, call, word*—represent the distinctions the psychologist G. Révèsz makes between human and animal communication in his *Origin and Pre-history of Language*.) Linguistically impoverished children become societal (to say nothing of psychological) failures in a variety of ways: failing at verbally-oriented IQ tests, failing at self- and interpersonal communication.

The central fact of language as "entity" is its systematic nature. When a language is in normal use, it is *a* system. Under the analytical scrutiny of the linguist it is seen to be a congeries of interlocking systems, the number and complexity of which are not yet fully known (hence the variety of language theories currently under development). Further, these systems are, despite the broadest kinds of similarities among languages, arbitrary; that is, no *particular* configuration is required by the fact of language. The practical result of this arbitrariness is the extraordinary variety of linguistic systems throughout the world of natural languages. Indeed, one of the principles of *structural* linguistics is that each language must be described in its own terms. That is, English is English, not a form of some other language, not, despite the traditional grammar books, a form of Latin. This is not to say that comparative studies of languages are not valuable, but comparative study is quite different from the study of the structure of one language in terms of another.

That language systems are arbitrary is easily shown, but let us first examine the nature of these systems. If we hear a foreign language being spoken with which we have no familiarity, all we will note about the stream of speech is its sound quality and its "foreignness." The sound or *phonetic* expression of a language is the actualization of its *phonology*. The sounds we hear are physical realities, the phonology is the abstract system into which these sounds are ordered and from which they proceed whenever anyone speaks. Individual actual speech sounds (called *phones* and shown in brackets, [ ]) are complex acoustical entities made up of a number of acoustical *features*, most of which we are normally only dimly aware of. (Incidentally, because a feature is a feature only in terms of the possibility of its non-occurrence, linguists, when assigning features to phones, assign their opposite, or non-occurrent, features as well. Thus any vowel is [+vocalic] + [−consonantal].)

From the standpoint of linguistic (as opposed to acoustical) analysis, phones are the raw data from which a phonological description can be derived. (It has become conventional to think of the phonological system as the first system to describe in examining a language, and the first one to study in an introductory course in linguistics. The precedence of phonology—even its more-or-less "independent" existence—is, however, being called into question by current theoreticians; but this is an issue that need not concern us here.) Briefly stated, the phonology of a language is its system of sounds that to the native user of the language *contrast distinctively*. In the course of a lifetime, every speaker of any language probably utters at least once every sound of every language. Obviously, only a few of these myriad sounds are *regularly* used by the speakers of any one language. English, for example, doesn't have the uvular [r] that is so characteristically French, although at one time or another we (as speakers of English) have uttered that sound if on no other occasion than that of making a "funny" sound to amuse a child. But all we've really said so far is that one can only rarely find French-sounding phones in the English-speaking world. We still haven't got to the phonology. The reasoning, nonetheless, is similar. Strange-sounding "r's" are not *distinctive* in English; that is, they are taken simply as unusual or foreign ways of making an [r]. Now if we listen carefully to a native speaker, we will discover that he actually produces, in normal speech contexts, a variety of "r's" (taking [r] merely as an example). However, since these different kinds of "r's" are considered by speakers of English as being [r] and nothing else, we respond to them as if they were all literally alike. In contrast, a number of East Indian languages use two varieties of [r]-like sounds that are not responded to as if they were "the same." Thus a word with one of these "r's" means one thing whereas the substitution of the other [r] in the same word-context results in a new word, not a different pronunciation of the same word. This means that the sounds we English speakers lump under the general category of [r] are not necessarily lumped under a single category in other languages. Or to look at it another way: *rip* is *rip* to a speaker of English so long as the initial sound of the word conveys an [r]-like quality to the listener (and remember that with electronic devices we can demonstrate that there are dozens of distinguishable [r]-like sounds), but if the speaker slips far enough out of [r] to reach [l], the listener will take the word as *lip*. Hence, in English, no [r]-like sounds *contrast* with each other, but [r] and [l] do indeed. In some languages, speakers are as indifferent to the presumed contrasts of [r] and [l] as we are to the presumed contrasts of the various "r's." In English, therefore, all the "r's" belong to a single *class* of sounds, a *phoneme*, in particular, the phoneme /r/. In another language, two classes of sounds might be required to account for the behavior of [r]-like sounds. The phoneme (shown in / /) is, then, an abstraction representing a variety of actual sounds or phones, called now *allophones* ("variant sounds") of the phoneme. In simple terms, the phonology of a language is its stock of phonemes and their distributional patterns. What the language has done is to gather a vast number of actual sounds into a small number of classes, and it is the classes that we respond to linguistically, even though it is each unique sound that we physically hear. What a phonetician might transcribe in a variety of ways depending upon the particular pronunciation of a particular speaker, the linguist (as phonologist), once the phonology is established for any dialect, will write down only one way. The phonetician is concerned with actual pronunciation (acoustically speaking), the linguist with what might be called idealized or abstracted pronunciation. With a phonetic transcription, a phonetician can produce a creditable imitation of the speaker's pronunciation. A phonemic or phonological transcription simply reveals the classes of sounds that speakers of that dialect respond to.

In addition to *segmental phonemes*, e.g., /p/, /b/, /t/, /d/, etc., English (as our specimen language) phonology includes a small but very important stock of features that are called *supra-segmental phonemes* and operate in conjunction with the segmentals. These features are the components that comprise the "sing-song" of language (the *intonation* system, which, in its totality, is a *meaning* system and properly a *morphological* phenomenon, of which more later). *Stress, pitch,* and *juncture* are the terms usually assigned to the supra-segmentals and reflect the acoustic realities respectively of *loudness, tone level,* and *pause* (an oversimplification, for juncture is really a collection of features, but *pause* is the word that in brief gives the best general idea of juncture). A comparison of *insult* in the following utterances will reveal the rôle that loudness plays at the phonemic level:

(1) Did he *insult* you?

(2) Indeed, he heaped *insult* after *insult* on me!

The first *insult* is, of course, a verb; the second a noun. The verb is pronounced louder on its second syllable, the noun on its first: inSULT *vs.* INsult. There are other very minor differences in pronunciation, but the significant contrast lies in the stress difference; that is, stress is here a distinctive sound feature, hence a phoneme. One might argue that the contrast of initial/final stress is *morphological* in that it seems to signal the *meaning* of "noun" (initial) or "verb" (final): CONtrast–conTRAST, ADdress–adDRESS, COMbat–comBAT, etc. In other contexts, however, increased or decreased loudness signals a "difference," but not any one assignable difference (as the noun–verb difference):

(1) Is Jack TYPing?

(2) Is JACK TYPing?

The first question is concerned primarily with typing, the second primarily with Jack. Hence, we have signaled a difference in meaning, but the loudness contrast associated with "Jack" carries in itself no identifiable meaning. We shall pursue this point further when we get to morphology.

Usually associated with an increase in loudness is a rise in pitch (tone) level. English is spoken on a scale of four distinctive pitches, pitch 2 being the normal pitch level of any speaker. On a true musical scale, of course, this "normal" pitch would be quite high for some and quite low for others. But where it lies on the musical scale is of no consequence. What matters are the contrasts afforded by the linguistic pitch system. Pitch can be readily perceived in, for example, a question that is made from a statement:

(1) She's an attractive $^{GI}R_L$.

(2) She's an attractive $_{GIRL}$?

Incidentally, contrary to the "rule" retailed by English teachers that the voice rises at the end of a question, it does so only for certain kinds of questions (and if the English teacher would merely *listen* to his own speech and that of his peers he would realize this!). In general, questions which are signaled either by the inversion of subject and verb or by a question word, follow the same intonational pattern as normal declaratives: /2–3–1/, *i.e.*, normal pitch rising (usually on the penultimate syllable of the *intonational clause*—a one-clause sentence, for example) one step to /3/ and falling two steps to /1/ (at which level the voice usually trails off to silence, the "trailing off" being a part of the *juncture* and conveying a sense of pausing). Pitch /4/ is usually reserved for anger and excitement and is really an intensification of /3/ insofar as the idea of contrast is concerned. An amusing illustration of the use of pitch is given by Professor Gleason in *An Introduction to Descriptive Linguistics*:

(1) What are we having for $^{dinner, Moth}$er?   (pitch dropped)

(2) What are we having for $^{dinner, mutton?}$ (pitch held)

(3) What are we having for $^{dinner, Mother?}$ (pitch held)

The "rule" of rising intonation has the curious effect of having no effect on the student when he speaks in normal conversational situations, but turns him into a kind of zombie when he reads a passage in which questions occur. (In fact, the ineptitude with which our youngsters read *anything* aloud is a national disgrace!) This is but one point upon which some hard knowledge about the language would serve teacher and student alike very well.

Two classes of juncture have been identified in English, an *internal transitional juncture* (also called *open transition* and *plus juncture*), marked in transcription with a /+/, and the *terminal junctures: sustained* /→/, *rising* /↗/, and *falling* /↘/. The internal juncture is commonly but not invariably a word-boundary marker and is phonemic by virtue of its rôle in distinguishing such pairs as

(1) I + scream   ice + cream
(2) beef + or + pork   before + pork
(3) Plato   play + dough

Of course, stress variations are likewise involved in these contrasts, a fact which reminds us of the interlocking nature of the intonational system. The precise phonetic value of the internal juncture changes from environment to environment. In the often-cited pair: night + rate *vs.* nitrate, the juncture seems to be a very slight pause achieved by withholding aspiration from the [t] of *night.* The aspiration is clearly heard as part of the pronunciation of the first [t] in *nitrate.*

If someone says, "Having missed my bus—" and then stops, we wait expectantly for the speaker to "finish" the sentence. Our expectation is prompted by two signals, the grammatical structure (participial phrase) and, more immediately, the sustention of the voice at the end of such a structure. This sustention is a *terminal* juncture (sustained /→/) and characteristically marks the end (terminal) of introductory clauses and phrases (which are *subordinate* sentence elements, not independent elements) and the boundaries of non-restrictive modifiers:

(1) Having missed my bus /→/ I took a cab
(2) When I heard who had won the election /→/ I laughed
(3) The wire wheels /→/ particularly /→/ interested him. (Contrast: *The wire wheels particularly interested him.*)

The rising terminal /↗/ is found, as we have noted, at the end of certain kinds of questions, generally those which have no other marker (such as a question word or an inversion of subject and verb).

(1) You're a bellydancer /↗/ ?

In a sentence like the following, there is an interesting elaboration of a simple question which requires both a question word and the rising terminal. Intonationally, the sentence contains two clauses, hence one can argue that in accordance with the principle that a question word generally obviates a rising terminal, the second "clause" (usually no more than a word or two) requires the rising terminal because it contains no question word.

(2) What are you reading /→/ Beckett /↗/ ? (= *Are you reading Beckett?* Contrast with *Are you reading, Beckett?* in which both intonation clauses in the transformed version end with a rising terminal and establish the phonemic value of the rising terminal.)

The sentence end is most commonly signaled by the falling terminal /↘/, to which our attention is consciously drawn when we overshoot a period in reading aloud and go back to the last word of the sentence we have failed to end properly and say, "period." Virtually all declaratives and most questions close with a falling terminal:

(1) What's the solution to this problem / ⩘ /
(2) The solution is simple / ⩘ /
(3) Can you help me with it / ⩘ /
(4) I'll be happy to / ⩘ /

Even though the child has a very well developed "sentence sense" long before he starts his formal education, teachers are forever fretting about the child's purported lack of sentence sense. The problem arises from the failure of the teacher to relate the child's generally well-formed speech habits ("language feeling," *Sprachgefühl*) to a new (for the child) language medium, namely, writing. There is a tendency on the part of teachers to (1) think of the written word as somehow "more important" than the spoken word (a consequent of traditional attitudes in language study) and (2) disassociate the written word as much as possible from the spoken. (Note how the term "colloquial" has popularly come to mean "slangy," "below standard," and so on, whereas to the linguist and lexicographer it means nothing better or worse than "conversational.") The teacher who understands the operations of the intonational system and who can perceive its echoes in our writing system, will find that many "problems" in "sentence sense" will quickly evaporate. If the student will read aloud his sentences (or non-sentences), he will soon discover where his written punctuation has deviated from his spoken punctuation, *i.e.*, his intonation. One can say as a rule of thumb that when the voice drops, we have come to the end of a speech segment, and in most cases such a segment is a free-standing utterance, a proper sentence, or a response to a yes/no question ("Yes," "No," "Maybe," etc.). The teacher who would demand of a student that he write a fully predicated answer to a yes/no question is out of touch with how the language is normally used. Unfortunately, this is commonly the case, despite the fact that the teacher himself is a "normal" user of language. The anomaly arises from compartmentalized thinking, a sickness that pervades the educational enterprise.

I have made no effort here to provide a detailed picture of English phonology. Numerous introductions to English linguistics do the job well. (In brief, English uses 24 consonants /p,b,t,d,k,g,č,j,f,v,ө,ð,s, z,š,ž,m,n,ŋ,l,r,w,y,h/; 9 simple vowels /i,e,æ,ɨ,ə,a,u,o,ɔ/; 2 semi-vowels /y,w/; 1 open transition /+/; 4 stresses / ′ ˆ ` ˘ /; 4 pitches /1,2,3,4/; and 3 terminal junctures /→ ↗ ↘/.) My purpose in the preceding section on phonology and the following sections on morphology and syntax is to sketch in some of the highlights of English structure and point a direction for classroom explorations in language. Ideally, the language data presented here (or in any source book on language) should be discovered by the student; but, of course, he requires the stimulation of a knowledgeable teacher! Our usual classroom approach to the study of our own language is deductive and authoritarian; that is, we present the student with rules, paradigms, definitions, and so on, and demand that he memorize and attempt to apply them (and since their range of applicability is narrow outside the rigged workbook examples, the game seems hardly worth the candle). This is a form of anti-intellectualism and cannot help but repel the student. Language is a subject like any other and can (and should) be studied as such and not as holy writ replete with a schedule of "Thou shalt nots"!

By themselves, phonemes are merely "bundles" of sounds (the whole bundle, the phoneme, being an "entity" that we have been psycholinguistically conditioned to "hear") free of meaning, though by the contrast of phonemes we distinguish meanings. (The contrast arising between /r/ and /l/ distinguishes for us *brush* and *blush* and enables us to respond to two meanings.) But when they are brought together according to the various patterns of the language, they disappear, in a manner of speaking, into units of meaning. The most obvious of these units is the *word,* ironically one of the most elusive of linguistic constructs. Indeed, linguists have long been shy of even trying to define the term. In a discussion of *word,* Professor Robert A. Hall, Jr., writes

> . . . we have normally put the word in quotation marks to show that we regard it as an expression which, although widely used, is not to be taken seriously as a useful concept in linguistic analysis. A *word* is popularly thought of as "a separate independent element of language," and as one which is written with a space before and after it. However, the concept of "word" has no universal applicability in linguistic analysis. (*Introductory Linguistics,* p. 133.)

Almost any page of a dictionary would seem to confirm Professor Hall's evaluation. Is, for example, *free-for-all* one "word" or three?

A more amenable concept is that of *meaning unit* or *morpheme* (*morphë*, "shape"; *eme*, "irreducible linguistic unit"), for this will help us account not only for words but also for meaning units which are not words.

Key is one word and so is *keys*, yet *key* is a single meaning unit while *keys* is a double meaning unit. If we delete the *s* (phonologically a /z/) from *keys*, we will at the same time delete the meaning "more than one," for that is what the /z/ attached to words like *key* means. We are now left with two items, a unit, *key*, with its meaning, and a unit, /z/, with no meaning in isolation (saying /z/ by itself does not convey plurality, though it might convey the [stylized] sound of a bee in flight). *Key*, then, is a *free* unit, /z/ a *bound* unit; both are morphemes and *keys* is a two-morpheme unit. Contrast the following utterances:

(1) The teacher*s* talk
(2) The teacher talk*s*

In (1), the plural-marking morpheme occurs with *teacher* and the verb is unmarked. In (2), *teacher* is unmarked and the verb carries a bound morpheme meaning "third person singular." (In these examples, incidentally, the *spelling* is consistent with the pronunciation —"s" = /s/ not /z/, and both noun and verb are modified by the addition of /s/.) Note, however, that in (1), the /s/ means *plurality* and in (2) it means *singularity*. We are, in fact, dealing here with two *different* morphemes despite their phonemic identity. These morphemes (plus a small handful of others; *e.g.*, the past tense and part participle verb endings) belong to the *inflectional* system of the language, a system much reduced in modern English but much in evidence in, say, modern German, where a fairly elaborate case or declensional system is still operative. We call these *inflectional* or *system* morphemes. They are part of the *grammar* of the language, though numerically a small part.

A second type of sub-word morpheme finds its use in modifying the *lexical* meaning (*i.e.*, ordinary dictionary meaning) of a word or a *root* morpheme. Thus we prefix morphemes like *im-*, *un-*, and *a-* (*im*moral, *un*productive, *a*political) or like *pre-*, *trans-*, and *contra-* (*pre*lude, *trans*late, *contra*dictory). The root morphemes of the latter group (*-lude*, *-late*, *dict*ory) seem to be wordlike in a way that the prefixes are not, yet they do not occur in English as words. They do, however, derive from Latin words, and it is perhaps fortuitous that they are not words in English. (Note, incidentally, how *-lude* [from Latin *lūdus*, "game"] shifts from a following position in pre-*lude* to a preceding position in *ludi*crous. Of course, *ludicrous* was borrowed from the Latin *ludicrus* and no morphemic manipulation occurred in English.) These prefixed "meaning-changers" serve mainly to negate or to "adverbialize" the root meaning: *pre*lude, "play *before*."

The third type of sub-word morpheme modifies both lexical and grammatical meaning. In general usage, *possible* functions as an adjective (*a possible cause*). By adding *-bility* to the root morpheme, we produce a noun: *possible-possibility*. (Compare: *probable-probability; capable–capability.*) We must therefore consider *-bility* a morpheme meaning something like "noun-forming suffix." By adding *-ly*, we get *possibly*, an adverb; hence, *-ly* is an "adverb-forming suffix" (and sometimes an "adjective-forming suffix": *the lowly worm*). This type of morphological change is called *derivation*, for it enables us to derive various grammatical functions from a single root morpheme. Try experimenting with *-y, -al, -ity, -ence, -ness, -ize, -ation,* etc.

We should be aware that these various morphological manipulations often bring sound changes with them (changes that are generally masked by our conventional spelling "system"). The so-called *s*-plural is, as we have noted, not always an *s* sound. (Compare "goat*s*" and "pig*s*," "goat" taking an /s/, "pig" a /z/.) A third plural sound is heard in *roses*, where the plural is formed with two sounds, an unstressed vowel (called a *barred i*, /ɨ/, and commonly heard in words like "rested") and a /z/. Even though the singular form, "rose," is *spelled* with a final *e*, the final *sound* is /z/, to which /ɨz/ is added to make the plural. If you make a list of nouns, any will do, and pluralize them, you will discover a regular phonemic pattern. As a little exercise in the inductive method, attempt to state the principle underlying the pattern.

Stress shifts and pronunciation changes in the root morpheme frequently result from the addition of morphemes like *im-, un-, -bility,* etc. Thus: *píous–ímpious; respónsible–responsibílity; mýs-tery–mystérious; convéne–convéntion* (no stress shift, but note the pronunciation of the root *e*); *precise–precision* (note the second-syllable vowel), and so on.

The making of words through *compounding* or combining two (occasionally more) free morphemes (*i.e.,* independent words) is one of the commonest routes to new vocabulary available to English, and at the same time it raises some very interesting linguistic questions, which should be examined in the classroom but are not. Consider the following sets:

(1) stone wall   Stonewall (name)
(2) red neck   redneck
(3) leather jacket   leatherjacket (species of fish)
(4) blue grass   bluegrass
(5) hot dog   hotdog
(6) build up (verb)   buildup (noun)

The phrases in the left-hand column are tied together with the stress pattern /ˆ ʹ/ secondary or medium loud /ˆ/ + primary or loud /ʹ/, whereas the compounds in the right-hand column are structured with the stress pattern /ʹ ˋ/ (primary + tertiary or medium soft /ˋ/). Were it not for the spelling convention of separating the free morphemes in phrases of the first type and attaching them in the compounds, we could not tell the two apart on the printed page (and we don't even follow that convention consistently; consider: *blûe jéans*—jeans colored blue—and *blúe jèans*—the name for a type of pants), but of course in speech the problem doesn't arise because of the contrasting *phrase superfixes* that are used to mark each type of construction, namely, /ˆ ʹ/ as over against /ʹ ˋ/. With the exception of *build up*, the examples are all of the type, modifier + noun. *Build up* demonstrates stress contrast used not only to distinguish meaning but also to shift a construction grammatically (in this case, from separable verb to noun). The morphemic nature of the stress patterns here is evident, for they not only signal differences, but they signal differences in meaning in a consistent way, a fact which allows us to associate each of the phrase superfixes with a specific structural meaning, namely, (1) modifier + noun, or verb + separable particle and (2) compound.

Any segment of speech carries with it intonational elements that are part of its structure and its meaning. From the standpoint of grammatical analysis (in the broad sense), the largest intonational unit is the *intonational clause*, the *intonation contour* that bounds, for example, a one-clause sentence. As a general rule, the intonation clause (an articulation of pitches, stresses, open transitions, and a terminal juncture) contains one primary stress and one /3/ (or /4/) pitch. This "peaking" is an important device in signaling coherence. And the fact that different languages operate according to different intonational "rules" causes a certain amount of cross-language grief. In any event, the contrastive function of intonation in larger structures than the phrases and compounds examined above can easily be seen:

(1) Desmond was sick tóday   (Unemotional report)
(2) Desmond was síck today   (Sarcasm)
(3) Désmond was sick today   (That's right, *Desmond*)
(4) Desmond wás sick today   (You said he wasn't,
                               but I know better)

The morphological value of the intonation contour can further be noted in the not-quite-overheard conversation in which the articulations are blurred but the "tone of voice" (intonational values) comes through sufficiently that we can tell at least whether the speakers are friendly toward each other or angry. We can, therefore, conclude that, say, anger, is a meaning carried by intonation. Any innocuously worded utterance can be freighted with anger simply by manipulations of the intonation contour of the utterance.

The morphological system is one of two linguistic systems commonly subsumed under the term *grammar*, the other being the *syntactic system*. But before examining the complexities of syntax, we should look briefly at the term *grammar*. In common parlance, *grammar* crops up in such contexts as, "Doesn't she have awful grammar!" "*Ain't* isn't grammatical," etc. Here, the word is being used in allusion to certain features of *usage* that the speaker has been taught are "wrong." *Grammaticality* from the linguist's point of view is rarely if ever the issue in these cases, though *acceptability* (a social concept) may be. Usage may be likened to deportment, table manners, and dress. (For convention's sake one wears formal dress to a formal dance, even though overalls will do nicely to cover one's nakedness; in other words, the underlying principles of dress are in both cases the same, but superficial adjustment to the social situation must be made in order that all involved feel comfortable, socially speaking.) From the linguistic point of view, no normal native speaker of a language has "bad" or "incorrect" grammar, though from the standpoint of another person, he may speak in ways that are socially unacceptable. Hence, *no* native speaker will utter a "sentence" like *Last film evening fine very a saw I.* Indeed, it takes a considerable effort even to concoct such an "utterance" because no such utterance model exists in English. Obviously, then, if one is a native speaker, one speaks as natives do. Many native speakers of English use *ain't* regardless of its proscription by other native speakers. One thing is clear, we are dealing with conflicts in usage not in the issue of *grammaticality* vs. *ungrammaticality.*

The non-sentence I cited above (which can be reshuffled to form the properly grammatical string, *I saw a very fine film last evening* or *Last evening I saw a very fine film*) is truly ungrammatical, that is, ungrammatical from a linguistic point of view, for the simple reason that it follows no known structural pattern in English; it is outside our grammatical system. I would have been just as "grammatical" had I said, *I don't want to go to no more movies* or *I ain't got time to waste going to the movies.* At the same time, my double negation and *ain't* would be ruled out of bounds by certain speakers of the language on the basis of purely extra-linguistic principles.

Thus far we have seen that *grammar* is a term for certain aspects of language structure and a term more or less synonymous with *usage.* A third meaning for *grammar* is the formalized *description* of the structural elements that the grammarian identifies, that is, a description of the "certain aspects of language structure" themselves. Or as one grammarian more specifically puts it, "A grammar of a language is eventually a description of its devices for forming predications or combining them into larger predications." (Baxter Hathaway, *A Transformational Syntax,* p. 7.) In summary, then, we may say that the grammar of a language *is* its structure (*i.e.,* aspects of its structure; patterns of linguistic behavior); that grammar is the description and formularization of that structure; and that grammar is another word for *usage.* The linguist feels comfortable with the first two grammars and fairly uncomfortable with the third, for, among other things, it is imprecise, *usage* covering a range of ill-assorted items over which non-linguistic considerations hold sway. If a linguist, to illustrate, identifies a certain syntactic pattern, he can demonstrate its existence with some degree of objectivity. If a speaker of a language says that one mustn't split infinitives (or whatever), he is merely admonishing or proscribing or prescribing on the basis of personal values. Indeed, the "rule" contra split infinitives is about as sound linguistically speaking as the "rule" against sentence-final prepositions. It is not a *descriptive* or even a *predictive* statement, for split infinitives are common in English and always have been. Hence, usage falls properly in the meta-linguistic area of taste and social form. For our purposes here, *grammar* will always be taken to refer to the actual grammatical structure of any given language (unless of course I identify a particular use of the word as meaning something else).

One's ability to produce an infinite number of well-formed utterances (in one's own language) never before heard is one of the miracles of the human mind. This ability is rooted in the mind's abstracting and symbol-using functions, but represents at the same time a specific kind of "programming." Although the precise mechanisms are not understood, it is clear that the child (probably from birth) programs himself for his language by a process of abstraction from actual utterances, though obviously in a far more complex way than Skinnerian behaviorism would suggest. (There is an interesting lesson here for the teacher: the child manages to acquire phonetics, phonology, morphology, grammar, and semantics prior to any formal instruction, and when he enters school he is already fully "languaged." He learns little in school in the way of language *competence* [approximately equal to de Saussure's *la langue*] beyond what he already knows, though unquestionably his *performance* [approximately equal to *la parole*] can be improved. Whether it would be improved without benefit of school is a question worth some thought when one comes to consider what we should be doing in school and if what we are doing is making the best use of the student's considerable resources.)

At all events, lying beneath any particular utterance we make or hear is a grammatical sub-program, a part of the whole grammatical system that underlies the ideal universal speaker of the language. What proportion of the total grammar of a language (*la langue*) any individual speaker (*i.e.*, at the level of *la parole*) commands it is impossible to say, but the likelihood is that it is considerable. This assumption is warranted by the fact that randomly chosen speakers can interact linguistically with relatively little difficulty. Of course, at dialect extremes the difficulties increase, but phonological differences are probably a key factor here.

Grammatical theory is an area of lively controversy among linguists, and it will probably be a considerable time before the issues are resolved. Nevertheless, the three systems of grammatical analysis currently in wide application afford a number of illuminating insights and raise a number of stimulating questions. One may say that no science can be asked to do more. From a pedagogical point of view, this indeterminacy (coupled with demonstrable and usable discoveries) is close to being ideal, for both student and teacher are forced to *engage* the material instead of (as is the usual situation) the teacher's merely setting out the day's fare (courtesy of the textbook) and the student's merely swallowing it (often whole, rarely digestible!). An open-ended subject (as is any genuine science) has intellectual dimensions for exploration. It therefore has the potential for involving the intellect of the student.

My impression is that grammar is generally taught as an essentially closed and finished system, and in a rather mechanical way. What is taught is a system of terminology, a set of techniques for diagramming sentences, and so on. I do not doubt that this has its function, that the student must have a way of talking about language and its properties. But it seems to me that a great opportunity is lost when the teaching of grammar is limited in this way. I think it is important for students to realize how little we know about the rules that determine the relation of sound and meaning in English, about the general properties of human language, about the matter of how the incredibly complex system of rules that constitutes a grammar is acquired or put to use. Few students are aware of the fact that in their normal, everyday life they are constantly creating new linguistic structures that are immediately understood, despite their novelty, by those to whom they speak or write. They are never brought to the realization of how amazing an accomplishment this is, and of how limited is our comprehension of what makes it possible. Nor do they acquire any insight into the remarkable intricacy of the grammar that they use unconsciously, even insofar as this system is understood and can be explicitly presented. Consequently, they miss both the challenge and the accomplishments of the study of language. This seems to me a pity, because both are very real. Perhaps as the study of language returns gradually to the full scope and scale of its rich tradition, some way will be found to introduce students to the tantalizing problems that language has always posed for those who are puzzled and intrigued by the mysteries of human intelligence. (Noam Chomsky, "The Current Scene in Linguistics," *College English*, Vol. 27, May, 1966, p. 295.)

Until quite recently, *structuralism* has been the dominant "school" of linguistic analysis (at least in the United States). Structuralists approach the analysis of the sentence via the concept of *immediate constituency*, wherein any identifiable grammatical *construct* is divisible into its immediate constituents or constructional units. Thus a sentence is conceived of as a *predication structure*, which is in turn divisible syntactically into (as an example) a *modification structure* ("noun cluster") on the subject side and a *complementation structure* ("verb cluster") on the predicate side. The term *modification structure* describes the unit's construction; the term *subject* describes its function in the syntax of the whole predication structure. Consider this sentence:

(1) The tired old man gave his grandson a piggyback ride

The immediate constituents (IC's) of the sentence are

(2) The tired old man (Subject; noun cluster; modification structure)
(3) gave his grandson a piggyback ride. (Predicate; verb cluster; complementation structure)

Moving down one level, we see that the IC's of the subject are

(4) the
(5) tired old man

Why? Since there is no structural unit in English grammar like *the tired old* or *the tired* (where *tired* is an adjective not a noun on the model of the *bad* in *the bad and the beautiful*), we are left with (4) and (5) as the only reasonable analysis. As *the* can not be split into IC's at the grammatical level, it is left alone and we turn our attention to the residuum of the modification structure, *tired old man*, which easily splits into

(6) tired
(7) old man

Finally, *old man* yields

(8) old
(9) man

And we have reached the *ultimate constituents* of the whole modification structure. A similar procedure will reduce the predication half of the sentence to its ultimate constituents, the two sets being the ultimate constituents of the entire sentence. Graphically

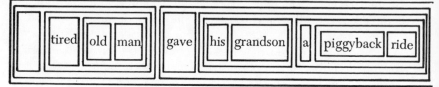

This box diagram, incidentally, has the advantage of maintaining the integrity of the sentence and at the same time clearly revealing the "nesting" habits of English grammatical structure.

In addition to the predication, modification, and comp¹ ᵉentation structures shown in the specimen sentence, the structura...st recognizes the coordination structure (a "matched" pair of constructions coordinated with *and*, etc. (*pencils and books; a loud shout and a faint echo; war or peace*, etc.) and the subordination structure (*e.g., across the river*, where the modification structure *the river* is subordinated to the preposition *across*). Further, these structures can occur at various levels (that is, they can "nest"). A predication structure can, for example, serve as the subject side of a predication and may contain a modification structure and a complementation structure—in traditional terms, we are speaking of a *noun clause* ("*The troops must give us all they have*" *was all he said*). At the sentence level, the structuralist identifies a small number of distinct predication types or *sentence patterns, e.g.,* N Lv (Linking Verb) N (which can take the form *My father is an accountant,* N being the general name of a construct consisting of a noun or a noun plus one or more modifiers, the latter then being a modification structure, the former being a potential modification structure), N V (*Children play*), etc.

Structuralists recognize four *form classes:* noun, verb, adjective and adverb. Nouns, for example, are identified as words that form plurals (by the addition of an inflectional morpheme), perform certain functions (they are commonly subjects and objects), occur in characteristic positions syntactically, and, in some cases, are marked by distinctive derivational endings (*e.g., -ness, -th, -age, -ance*, etc. *cleverness; truth, length; breakage; impertinence*, etc.), and are marked in speech by the stress pattern /ˊ ˋ/: *pérmìt* (as opposed to *permít*, a verb). The *frame sentence* is a useful pedagogical device for identifying members of each of the form classes. Thus, one can say that any word which fits into the following frame is by virtue of that fact a noun:

(1) The —— is/are good.

A refinement of the technique will distinguish a variety of sub-groups of nouns (mass, count, and so on). Note, however, that the traditional definition of nouns as words that "name" has been avoided. At best the definition is unworkable. Is *red* a noun or an adjective? It both "names" a color and "indicates" a quality. In a sentence like *A red truck careened around the corner*, the position of *red* tells us all we need to know insofar as classification is concerned. Likewise: *Red is a color*.

In addition to the four open classes (open because we freely add to our stock of nouns, verbs, adjectives, and adverbs), the structuralist recognizes a variety of *structure* (or *function*) words, words that have little isolatable meaning but which are of great importance in structuring English sentences. While there is, practically speaking, an infinitude of form-class words, the number of structure words is very small and virtually fixed. These are the *determiners* (a/an, the, some, all, my, etc.), *conjunctions* (and, or, nor, for, etc.), *prepositions* (at, in, of, to, etc.), *intensifiers* (somewhat, very, too, etc.), *interrogators* (who, what, where, when, etc.), *subordinators* (that, which, who, etc.), *negators* (no, not), and so on.

In essence, the structuralist is a taxonomist. He examines "frozen" segments of language and attempts to classify them. One of the principal canons of American structuralism (following the direction of Leonard Bloomfield) is that any given segment of speech is an analyzable and classifiable "artifact." The actual utterance is the linguistic absolute. This means, for example, that an English imperative sentence is considered to be just what it appears to be, a subjectless sentence, not an ellipsis (indicating *you* "understood"), for to accept the notion of ellipsis is to engage in an unsalutary "mentalism." The presumption here is that the workings of the mind are beyond the reach of the linguist, whose proper concern is only with what can be unequivocally demonstrated. This mechanistic approach to language was a useful antidote to the whimsicality and impressionism that for so long had pervaded grammar study (excepting the few academicians of the Jespersen stripe). And for a time it seemed as though we had found *the* key to language. But this was not to be so. Consider the following sentences, which the structuralist would accord the same description:

(1) He carried a load of heavy books
(2) He married a woman of impressive wealth

In each sentence there is a prepositional phrase in *of*. Yet, as we think about these prepositional phrases, we feel that somehow they are not *really* alike, or, at least, they are alike only superficially. Structuralism is a system of grammatical analysis based upon *surface structures*. To the *transformationalist* surface grammar is only a manifestation of something beneath, where the "real" grammar is. (Around this point a good deal of controversy has arisen, but if we set aside philosophical issues and are simply pragmatic we can find considerable use in the idea of deep and surface grammar.) *A load of heavy books,* transformationally speaking, is the result of sub-surface structures like

(1) the load is books (N Lv PredN)
(2) the books are heavy (N Lv PredAdj)

to which transformational rules have been applied. The principle here is that sentences (surface level) are rooted in sub-surface *kernels* (*i.e.*, simple predications incapable of being reduced to simpler predications. They can, of course, be reduced to basic sentence parts or phrases, a procedure covered by a set of *phrase-structure* rules). At the sub-surface level, *a woman of impressive wealth* may be resolved into

(1)   the woman is wealthy
(1a) (the woman *has* wealth)
(2)   the wealth is impressive

Thus we see a clear contrast with the apparently similar structure, *a load of heavy books.* Of interest too is the fact that neither of the prepositional phrases in *of* is a manifestation of the inflected genitive (compare: *the wings of the dove* and *the dove's wings*), for neither can be rendered into a possessive noun + noun pattern:

(1) *books' load
(2) *wealth's woman

Because transformationalism looks at language as *process*, it can reveal grammatical strategies in a way that structuralism cannot because of the narrow limits of structuralist theory. Structural ambiguities, for example, are easily understood if we probe for the sub-surface patterns. The sentence

(1) The player left the field a total wreck

though ambiguous is simply a double complement sentence: N V N N from the standpoint of static structural analysis and thus no different from

(2) The player left the coach some mouthwash

Transformationally, the picture is quite different, for one cannot say with certainty whether the sentence is a transform of *the player left the field + he was a total wreck* (which can be further reduced to *he was a wreck + the wreck was total*, a fact irrelevant to the point being examined here) or *the player left the field + it was a total wreck*. Some thought about the relationship between the surface and sub-surface grammar will resolve the ambiguity, the writer or speaker then providing us with either

(1) The player was a total wreck when he left the field

or

(2) The field was a total wreck when the player left it

The latter utterance would probably need some additional context to clarify the issue of whether it was the player himself who wrecked the field. We should, incidentally, appreciate the fact that such an utterance in speech as *the player left the field a total wreck* would probably be saved from ambiguity by the intonation contour. This means that the speaker of the structurally ambiguous utterance is himself not confused about the meaning he intends, but if he *writes* his sentence as he might *say* it, the reader may very well be confused. This is why puns like "Did you ever see a horse fly?" work better on the page than on the tongue, for when speaking we must choose between available intonations and the punny ambiguity is thereby generally lost. From the page, we can "hear" both intonations simultaneously (in, as it were, the mind's ear).

Unfortunately, transformational-generative theory is not without its flaws, nor without its detractors on the one hand and its dogmatists on the other. Professor Bernard Saint-Jacques raises some troublesome questions about deep structure. "How," he asks, "is the Phrase-marker assigned to a given sentence?"

> Is it through the intuitive knowledge of the native speaker? This does not seem to be the answer, because Chomsky tells us that "any interesting grammar will be dealing, for the most part, with mental processes that are far beyond the level of actual or even potential consciousness; furthermore, it is quite apparent that a speaker's reports and viewpoints about his behavior and his competence may be in error." [*Aspects of the Theory of Syntax*, p. 8.] Is it then the linguist's intuition? It is often a source of wonder to me how "naturally" and without any discussion Phrase-markers and embedded sentences are assigned—by transformationalists—to surface structure sentences. But it is even more surprising when two different Phrase-markers are assigned to the same sentence. It might be argued that the choice of one rather than the other is justified by the better transformations yielded by one. This seems to be a very circular argumentation. The result of a similar operation might give a formulation which will be very logical in itself, but one could wonder about the relation of the "formulation" with the language under study, and consequently with language in general. ("The Quest for a Scientific Study of Language," *Word*, 23, Nos. 1, 2, 3, April, August, December, 1967, pp. 489–90.)

But the existence, after all, of various flaws in theory and practice does not render transformationalism useless. No current grammatical theory is theoretically and practically sound in every particular and none, likewise, seems to offer the potential for discovery that transformationalism does. Of course, in this brief look at language, I have room only to provide the reader with the merest hint of the transformational method. But before we move on, allow me by way of summary to quote Professor Baxter Hathaway:

A transformational grammar depends fundamentally upon our ability to track identities in sets of relations among changes of structure. This is not easy to do, or perhaps impossible to do, if we pay too much attention to "meaning" equivalents. The transformational grammarian must keep his eye on structural devices that function more or less identically in the handling of "sames" of meaning and not on meaning alone. But to do this he is crippled unless he realizes that he is dealing with more than one system of structures, often overlapping and often with a vague, ill-defined no-man's-land between them. Modern English is polysystemic, not monosystemic. (*A Transformational Syntax*, p. 32.)

A third type of grammatical study is called *tagmemics*, which since the advent of transformationalism has incorporated certain transformation concepts into its structuralist framework. In tagmemics, any syntactic structure is a *syntagmeme* or *structured string* (*e.g.*, phrase, clause, sentence), in which are *slots* that when combined with an appropriate *filler* correlate to form a *tagmeme* or *slot/filler class*. In plainer terms, the place in the string where a noun can go is the slot, the noun is the filler, and the tagmeme is the correlation of the noun and the place where it goes.

In tagmemic string-type analysis, the construction is viewed as a set of multiple relations. The tagmeme units are points in the pattern, and are related to each other within that pattern. The functional points are not rigidly defined. They are largely intuitive, and correspond to traditional notion of subject and predicate, head and modifier [*e.g.*, *tall* (modifier) *building* (head)]. But this laxness in the early stages of analysis helps to provide flexibility in separating functions within the construction string. Further refinements of this analysis permit a pinpointing of more exact grammatical meanings attached to each functional slot, such as subject-as-actor in active sentences, and subject-as-goal in passive sentences. (Walter A. Cook, *Introduction to Tagmemic Analysis*, p. 8.)

As Father Cook reminds us, the tagmemic approach to linguistic analysis is but one of many. It is, however, an eminently practical model and has proved itself in both classroom and field. Tagmemics seems, of the analytical systems in currency, to be the most aggressively descriptive. Its high degree of explicitness is of value in trying to discover the nature and operations of language, though, by the same token, all but the most highly motivated of students are likely to be intimidated by such explicitness.

In the next three chapters I will discuss the rôle that formal linguistic analysis ("grammar study," etc.) should play in the school curriculum. Suffice it to say here that (1) most teachers are not equipped to teach "modern grammar" or "New English" of whatever stripe, (2) current language arts texts do not adequately equip teachers to do so (despite the claims of the publishers), (3) a workbook type of grammar-centered approach to language study is counter-productive to the development of language skills. On the last point, it has been demonstrated that not only is there no carryover from grammar study to, say, writing, but there is a positive inhibition of writing as a result of formal grammar study. I am, nevertheless, convinced that grammar can be studied productively and will make specific suggestions for so doing.

MEANING

The purpose of an utterance, an actualized segment of language, is to transmit meaning. Except in very special circumstances (such as that of examining language features), linguistic structures are not produced for their own sake. But the term *meaning* subsumes a wide range of concepts, and if we are to deal successfully with language in the classroom, we must have some appreciation of these concepts. Furthermore, we must be able to *convey* meaning with reasonable accuracy; that is, we must be able to transfer all the meanings we intend to transfer and none that we intend not to transfer. This goal is probably not wholly realizable, but it is at least a desideratum.

Any sentence is a congeries of meanings, though the speaker may have only one meaning (or one kind of meaning) in mind when he utters it. In somewhat abstract terms, the intended or *ideational* meaning of a sentence can be (1) informative (declarative), (2) interrogative, (3) directive (imperative), (4) emotive (exclamatory, admonitory), or (5) incantatory (ritualistic). Any discourse may contain all of these meanings, though the character of a discourse is determined by its being more of one kind than another. A presidential inaugural address, for example, is typically more emotive and incantatory than anything else, although it may carry an underlying directive intent. Each of these meanings predicts or requires certain linguistic formulas. We would not, for example, expect to find a largely informational essay on some prosaic subject to abound in the rhetoric of the *Gettysburg Address,* nor, conversely, would Lincoln's speech have been so memorable had he attempted to inform us instead of touch us. As a piece of information, the speech is virtually empty, as an "incantation" it is superb.

This ideational meaning is presumably what traditional definitions of the sentence allude to when they speak of a "complete thought." The silliness of the "complete thought" notion is apparent when we realize that nobody knows what a thought is (in any way that can be satisfactorily demonstrated) let alone a "complete" one, and when we consider that one can persuasively argue that in the context of, say, an entire book, it is the entire book that is the "complete thought" (and so on down through chapter, paragraph, and sentence). In what way, one might further argue, is the "thought" of the following perfectly proper (and complete!) English sentence "complete"?

(1) After thinking about it for a while, I decided not to do it.

How many thoughts? Complete? Incomplete? To what extent? Etc., etc. The real issue is not so much *thought* as *shape.* A sentence is a complete (by convention) *structure,* a structure which embodies, or better, transmits "thought" (meaning). (Like *word, sentence* is a term that linguists have some difficulty with. Perhaps the clearest short definition is that of Leonard Bloomfield: "It is evident that the sentences in any utterance are marked off by the mere fact that each sentence is an independent form, not included by virtue of any grammatical construction in any larger form," *Language,* Henry Holt & Co., 1933, p. 170. W. Nelson Francis offers a definition based exclusively on speech: "A sentence is as much of the uninterrupted utterance of a single speaker as is included either between the beginning of the utterance and the pause which ends a sentence-final contour [terminal juncture] or between two such pauses," *The Structure of American English,* p. 372. In transformational theory, a simple formula like S [Sentence] = NP [Noun Phrase] + VP [Verb Phrase] suffices, though it doesn't convey much of the *sense,* i.e., *feeling,* of a sentence. At any rate, the "complete-thought" nondefinition has died its deserved death.)

Which brings us to another meaning of *meaning*, namely, *structural* (grammatical) meaning. A sentence has the meaning, "sentence" (S). This meaning is the result of relationships that become apparent when certain linguistic elements are brought into jointure; that is, when they become a syntactic arrangement. Thus, an appropriate rearrangement of the following words produces the meaning, *sentence*, a meaning quite different from the dictionary meanings of each word:

an, hour, late, morning, my, this, train, was;

(1) my train was an hour late this morning

or

(2) this morning, my train was an hour late

or

(3) my train this morning was an hour late

or

(4) an hour late was my train this morning

(Despite the fact that English is largely an *analytic* language—i.e., predominantly dependent upon *word order* to signal meaning, as opposed, for example, to Latin, which is largely a *synthetic* language, i.e., heavily dependent upon inflections to signal meaning and not tightly bound to fixed word orders—the user of English does have a certain amount of syntactic freedom, as is clearly demonstrated by the four alternative patterns shown above of the "same" sentence. Transformationally, we would say that the four surface structures are derivable from the same set of sub-surface kernels. This flexibility is of profound importance in developing and understanding *style*.) At the same time, another meaning arises, the ideational meaning, which is also different from the meanings of the individual words. The structural meaning interlocks with the word meanings to produce the ideational meaning of the utterance, the meaning that we are presumably trying to communicate. We have called the structural meaning simply, "sentence"; but it is clear that within the sentence are other syntactic components, each with its own structural meaning; e.g., *my* + *train* = *my train*, a modification structure consisting of a noun marker or determiner (*my*) and a noun and adding *up* to a noun, which in this set of sentences is functioning as the *subject*. (Incidentally, a structure which equals one of its components, as is the case in the example just cited, is called an *endocentric* structure; a structure that does not equal any one of its components is an *exocentric* structure, thus, *Hippopotamuses swim*, a predication, is different from either of its parts, a noun and a verb.) The structural meaning of the syntactic unit is, therefore, *modification structure* (D [Determiner] + N, with its associated intonational phrase) or, more broadly, *noun*; the structural meaning of the syntactic unit within the sentence is subject. Thus it is through grammatical meaning (the result of the structural habits of the language) that ideational (semantic) meaning is actualized. No matter what we *intend* to convey, if the structural preconditions are not met, the meaning will never cross to the receiver, or it will be so damaged as to effectively skew or nullify our intention. This is the situation that obtains in, for example, *Walking down the stairs, the bannister broke*, where the image of a bannister's walking down the stairs "jams" the intended meaning of the sentence.

The intonational component of an utterance (as we have seen) conveys a type of semantic meaning that might be called *tonal, psychological,* or *emotive*. We can contrast two utterances the structure and diction of which are precisely alike simply by modifying the intonation (that is, by redistributing the intonational components):

(1) What a day!   (happy, affirmative)
(2) What a day.   (sad, negative)

Indeed, it is possible to carry on an "intonational conversation." Consider those moments in the dental chair when, with your mouth packed full of cotton wads and apparatus, the dentist asks how you've been or how the kids are. You cannot *articulate* but you can *intone*, and you do, and the dentist seems to get the drift. At least he can judge whether you are generally pleased or generally miserable. On the other hand, try conversing in a dead monotone: Though every articulation be precise, meaning seems almost entirely absent.

In broad terms, there are two kinds of meaning; namely, meaning with regard to the phenomenal (*i.e.,* non-linguistic) world, and meaning with regard to language itself. In the case of individual words, this distinction can be seen between what are called *lexical* ("full") words and *structural* or *function* ("empty") words. Of the former, words like *giraffe, animal, basilisk, think, love, tintinnabulate, weirdly,* and *wild* are examples. Of the latter, *the, and, of, is, very,* and *that.* With words of the first group, one can associate something in the world of non-language, with words of the second, only other words or linguistic phenomena.

Lexical words can be defined *denotatively* and *connotatively.* The denotative meaning is the usual dictionary definition and, except in the case of highly technical terms, is generally of little use to a native speaker. In the main, we know words connotatively. One need only to compare the cool, finally uninformative dictionary "definition" of, say, *Negro,* with what the word "really" means to the people who use it or hear it. In all likelihood, virtually no one means the dictionary definition when the word arises in conversation. It is a word which, like many others, lies at the center of a large, emotionally charged field. Hence, its dictionary meaning is of little practical significance. The words of everyday life are rich in connotation, and many of our problems in verbal communication stem from this fact. The old jesuitical practice of defining one's key terms at the outset of a colloquy is a good idea in principle but, except in the most intellectual of contexts, will not work. The best solution to the problem is simply to tune the child in to these facts of linguistic life and trust that the next generation will be more sensitive to the connotational element in communication.

Giraffe, animal, and *love* illustrate yet another dimension of meaning. The first two nouns we would ordinarily classify as *concrete,* the third as *abstract.* But *animal* is surely more abstract than *giraffe,* though *giraffe,* as we shall see, is also abstract. And can a person in love be convinced that *love* is abstract? The point is that these like all words are simply conventions, and all conventions are abstractions. Further, they are conventionalized representations not of particular things, but of *classes* of things. The word *giraffe* is our linguistic recognition that we have classified a number of "items" under a single heading, that is, all varieties and all individuals in the species are identified by the term *giraffe.* Or, if the word is *dog,* then Mexican Hairless to Irish Wolfhound, dog_1 to dog_n are called *dog.* With *animal,* the range is even broader, and with *love,* we are talking of the idea of love, whatever its particular manifestation.

Indeed, *dog* stands for the *idea* of any member of the canine species, not necessarily this or that particular Fido. Incidentally, not all languages slice up reality in quite the same way, though in the Linnaean system of taxonomy, the agreement is close to universal (though local language names will, of course, differ: *dog, Hund, chien, inu,* etc.). With a concept like *love,* the differences become apparent. In English, *love* covers the field. In Greek, three words are necessary: *eros* (sexual love), *agapê* (spiritual love), and *philia* ("brotherly love"); nor can one say that *agapê,* for example, is a kind of *eros,* and so on, for each term has a clear associational range, each one being thought of as quite different from the other. Perhaps the major implication of these facts of meaning is that we should try to avoid the common tendency to respond to *words* as if they were the things (or events, or situations) for which they are merely the arbitrary linguistic signs. Saying "My kid's the smartest kid in school," says something about the speaker but nothing about the person whom the speaker thinks he is describing. The prime manifestation of prejudice is the labeling that typically goes with it. Expressions like *nigger, wop, pig,* etc., are examples of what might be called reflexive language, which reveals the speaker but says little or nothing about the external (non-linguistic) world. Because language is so intimately related to thought, we can easily fall into the habit of living in a world of language almost wholly divorced from the world "outside." There is no denying that prejudicial, intensional thinking can have its effects on the extensional world, but these effects are commonly destructive ones.

Though function words have no referential meaning in isolation (that is, that cannot be identified with non-linguistic realities), they come to life, so to speak, within a linguistic context. A particularly interesting example is the preposition *of.* In a construction like *the fender of the car, of* marks a phrase that is the syntactic equivalent of the so-called *inflected genitive* (*the car's fender,* wherein *car* is inflected to convey the genitive meaning). Its meaning can thus be read as "possessive particle." Indeed, the usual function of English prepositions is to provide a way of showing meanings syntactically that have been largely lost inflectionally (the inflected genitive being the only marked case that is left to our nouns, though the system persists somewhat more strongly in the pronouns, which mark both genitive and *accusative, i.e., objective*). The contrast between an inflectional (synthetic) and a syntactic (analytic) system can be clearly seen in the following Latin case paradigm (note the English translations):

Nom.	*puella*	the girl	(subject)
Voc.	*puella*	O girl!	
Acc.	*puellam*	the girl	(object)
Gen.	*puellae*	*of* the girl	(possessive)
Dat.	*puellae*	*to* the girl	(indirect object)
Abl.	*puellā*	*from* (or *by*) the girl	

But *of* "hides" other meanings than genitive. Consider such constructions as *dozens of examples, a pile of bricks, a case of perjury, his degree of competence*, etc. Other function words are equally chameleon-like, some even crossing back and forth between the realms of lexical and function words. In isolation, *up* can be "defined" by pointing upward, and it can fill many adverb slots, but its adverbial function is lost or greatly attenuated in *The plane blew up* (it went down), *speak up, give up, put up or shut up, jumbled up, The traffic was held up, Look it up in the dictionary*, etc. One would be hard put to assign a "meaning" to *up* in these examples. And note too the adverbial ambiguity of these:

(1) He walked up the street
(2) He walked down the street

(The street is level; he is simply walking on the street.) If the utterance is changed slightly, however, *up* (and *down*) regains its full adverbial force:

(3) He walked up the hill
(4) He walked down the hill

The foregoing example illustrates a point in language at which form and meaning interpenetrate. This particular interpenetration is called *context-sensitivity* and can provide a great deal of language-study material. Words occur in contexts. Each word has a distributional range. Each word will occur more frequently in certain contexts, less frequently in others, and not at all in still others. Our sense of idiom (our *Sprachgefühl*) is developed through our self-programming for these distributions. The novice writer who relies on a thesaurus is likely to find himself producing some strange utterances, which though "correct" from the standpoint of gross grammatical structure are "un-English" from the standpoint of idiom. Of course, if a writer is really skillful at idiom violation he can get away with it and even expand the range of distributional possibilities (the poet's stock in trade). It has been argued (by the transformationalists in particular) that *grammaticalness* is dependent on context-sensitivity as well as structural convention. Chomsky's famous *Colorless green ideas sleep furiously* makes the case. The sentence is structurally normal but semantically at odds with itself. A construction with *ideas* as the headword rejects modifiers like *colorless* and *green;* further, *colorless* is clearly nonsense when joined to *green.* The meanings are wrong together, though were we to start using such combinations with some regularity, they would begin to "make sense," for the use would mean that the pattern was saying something useful to us. There is no doubt that a macro-context could be fabricated in which the sentence would make instant sense, but, again, this type of special context building is more within the province of the poet than of the ordinary speaker of the language. (Part of any artistic use of language is some degree of violation of the ordinary; note, for example, how dependent Dylan Thomas's poetry is upon contrasts with normal idiom, thus: "When all my five and country senses . . .".). This fact affords the teacher a way into the study of poetry that will reveal far more about poems than is usually the case in classroom poetry-analyzing sessions.

When the poet says, "Heard melodies are sweet, but those unheard/ Are sweeter," we can, if we choose to take him literally, put him down for a madman or a fool. But the meanings of the poet are *metaphorical;* that is, they aren't precisely what they seem to be (*metaphor:* literally, "transference"). Nor is the poet the only user of metaphor. Consider: "Harry made a perfect ass of himself," "It's raining cats and dogs," "When old Sandy flipped his lid, I busted my gut," "She's a real tiger," etc. This bringing together of semantically incompatible words produces new and sometimes shrewd and apposite meaning. Metaphorical language not only extends the range of meaning of any particular context but provides one of the key indices of style. Literal language is the mark of reportage; metaphorical language tends toward poetry (*i.e.,* imaginative writing).

Meaning seems largely a function of context, whichever meaning we are speaking of. Context can be both linguistic (from phrase to discourse) and situational. Meaning can be formal (structural) and semantic (ideational), and all types and levels of meaning are interdependent on one another. Meaning is both the impetus to utterance and the end product. Yet communication frequently fails of its purpose because we are insufficiently sensitive to the kinds of meaning we are producing or responding to. One of the great tasks of the English teacher is to thoroughly explore the ways in which we mean and the ways in which we fail to mean. How much more fruitful would time spent on such explorations be as over against the endless nit-picking that marks classroom language study with its unrewarding formalism, its "definitions," its "rules," and other inapposite busywork.

> Meanings are in persons' minds, not in words, and when we say that a word has or possesses such and such meanings, we are really saying that it has evoked, or caused, those meanings. Until it gets into a mind, a word is only puffs of air or streaks of ink. What a word, sentence, or other expression means to hearers or readers is mainly what it makes him think or feel or do as a direct consequence of hearing or seeing it. (Edward L. Thorndike, "The Psychology of Semantics," *The American Journal of Psychology*, 59, Oct. 1947, 613.)

Here is a set of contexts in which some form of the word *mean* occurs. Try to explicate the meaning of meaning in each:

1. Ten o'clock means bedtime.
2. No turning in the driveway. This means you!
3. What in heaven's name do you mean by that?
4. Do you mean to stay for the whole weekend?
5. Without love, life would have no meaning.
6. What's the meaning of this uproar?
7. Democracy means freedom.
8. Raquel Welch means sex.
9. Mad means insane.
10. The defeat of this bill means disaster.
11. C_2H_5OH means ethyl alcohol.
12. What is the meaning of life?
13. Oversimplification means attempting to explain an event or solve a problem without taking into full account the complexities of the event or problem.

14. *Schwer* is a German word that means "heavy, hard, grave, difficult, or severe."
15. *Je ne sais quoi* is a French phrase that means *I know not what.*
16. *Je ne sais quoi* is a French phrase that means something that cannot adequately be described or expressed.
17. Mozart means genius.
18. Rockwell means illustration, Picasso means art.
19. He never says what he means.
20. The next three hours mean work.
21. He means what he says.
22. I defy you to explain the meaning of this poem.
23. A poem should not mean/ But be.
24. Just what is the meaning of meaning?

With so complex a meaning system (or congeries of systems) as we have, it is not surprising that we have problems in communication. Some failure or ineptitude in thinking, some fault in linguistic feature selection, some mechanical breakdown (as static on a telephone line) can degrade or even nullify communication. Further, there is the question of whether sender and receiver are, so to speak, on the same wavelength. I can speak to you in English and you can speak to me in English. At the phonological, morphological, and syntactic levels we may be operating quite normally. Yet it is entirely possible that we don't understand each other at all. I may be relying heavily on a lexicon that you have only an imperfect grasp of. That is, your range of experience doesn't include the events, situations, and ideas that are called forth by certain of the words I choose. If you have gone no farther in the study of mathematics than high-school algebra, for example, then an un-popularized, un-simplified discourse on matrices will, at the level of thought, have no meaning for you. At the level of utterance, it will, of course, display the usual types of structural meanings that mark it as "normal English." If I popularize my discourse (that is, adapt it to the audience), I can by various means (*e.g.*, using non-technical language, drawing analogies, etc.) bring my ideas into your field of reception and at least some degree of substantive communication can take place.

The squaring of experiential fields between sender and receiver is, therefore, a necessary precondition to genuine ("meaningful") communication. If in front of a child I place two napkins, one whole, one torn into several pieces, and ask the child which napkin is larger,

I know that the child is not going to tell me that they are both really the same size; for the child's cognitive faculty regarding quantity and dimension has not yet sufficiently developed to reach that conclusion. On the contrary, the child will say that either one or the other is "larger." The catch is that whichever choice the child makes regarding "largeness" is perfectly correct, for "large" is not a particular size or dimension. If the pieces of the torn napkin are spread over a larger area than the whole napkin occupies, the child might with good logic select that reality as "large." If the child notes that the whole napkin is just one piece and that the torn napkin is many pieces, the fact of number can reasonably be considered "largeness." And so on. Without *first* reaching an accord with the child about the possible meanings of "largeness," the child and the questioner will be at semantic cross-purposes and communication will be short-circuited.

Communication is controlled not only by local language events, but by the whole world of language that any one language imposes on its users. Edward Sapir, a pioneer in anthropological linguistics, writes

> Human beings do not live in the objective world alone, nor in the world of social activity as ordinarily understood, but are very much at the mercy of the particular language which has become the medium of expression for their society. It is quite an illusion to imagine that one adjusts to reality essentially without the use of language and that language is merely an incidental means of solving specific problems of communication or reflection. The fact of the matter is that the "real world" is to a large extent unconsciously built up on the language habits of the group. . . . We see and hear and otherwise experience very largely as we do because the language habits of our community predispose certain choices of interpretation. (Quoted by Benjamin Lee Whorf, *Language, Thought, and Reality,* p. 134.)

In the European language community, which includes English, French, German, Russian, etc., we have a well defined sense of time. Despite the fact that nobody has ever seen "time" and that we are not even certain what time "is," we speak glibly of the "past," "present," and "future" as though they were locatable entities. We have even developed a spatial orientation for time, the past being "back there," the present being "right here," and the future being "up ahead." If I draw an arrow with the head at the right, I am aiming it toward the "future." The other way round aims it to the past. (This particular imagery is the result of our reading and writing conventions; the future to a Chinese would doubtless require a downward-pointing arrow.) A dot, circle, or X marks the present. In our verbal system we have a grammatical concept called *tense* (*i.e., time*). We grow up using this concept through the formal structure of the language and are quite convinced that we are talking about the real world when we talk about the "past" and the "future." In the Hopi language, by contrast, the verbal system reveals or programs a different kind of reality, one of intensity, duration, sequence, rate, etc. In other words, the Hopi system deals with present reality (which is to say, degrees of reality or *validity*) not with "past" and "future" make-believe.

But even within our own language family there are significant differences in the way each language-culture "sees" the world and classifies experience. English, for example, has only imperfect translations for expressions like *savoir-faire, sang-froid, Weltschmerz, virtú, machismo,* etc., because the terms represent cultural experiences and values more or less alien to the English-speaking world. (Hence, we usually don't translate the terms but use them as they come to us.) And when a child misbehaves, if I may offer a homely and oft-cited example, the English-speaking mother scolds him for being *bad,* whereas the French-speaking mother tells her misbehaving youngster, *soi sage,* "be sensible," "be reasonable." (The root meaning of *sage* is "wise," and is the source of our word *sage,* which we, of course, borrowed from French.)

Even our way of talking about our language is at odds with "reality." We have been taught that in a sentence of the type, *Harry carried the ball,* which is one of the most frequently occurring sentence types in English, *Harry* is the *actor* (subject), *carried* the *action* (predicator), and *ball* the *thing acted upon* (object). If we substitute *day* for *ball,* in what way is the object being "acted upon"? And if we substitute *looked* for *carried* and insert *at* before *ball,* the ball is now in fact doing something to Harry: in the "act" of "seeing," "action" moves *toward* the "actor" not *from* him. The passive voice has some interesting quirks too; for example, in the construction, *A fish was swallowed by me,* the "subject" is really the "object," that is, the "receiver of the action."

The study of meaning in all of its fascinating complexity should be a major undertaking in the English classroom; but, sad to say, questions of meaning are trivialized into "vocabulary study" (sterile exercises in the *Reader's Digest* manner). Or into "What does this poem mean?" (The hoped-for reply being the student's one-sentence "interpretation," which, incidentally, the student comes to believe *is* the "meaning" of the poem and, indeed, the purpose of literary study. His private question, of course, is "Why didn't the poet just say what he meant in the first place?") The observations presented here only just hint at the range and depth of the vexing (and challenging) issues of *meaning*. Suggestions (largely via questions) for explorations in meaning will be found at the end of this chapter and in the following chapters.

The blab-filled quotation that begins this chapter is a way of reminding us that much of what we say is bereft of attachment to the extensional world. The passage happens to be from a political speech (blabs substituted for words that Chase calls "semantic blanks," the stock in trade of the Fourth-of-July orator), but a good deal of what we say in the course of our daily lives is equally blab-filled. This is not necessarily bad outside the classroom, but in the classroom it is deadly. The teacher, therefore, has a special responsibility to rid himself of the blabs, so to speak.

CORRECTNESS

There are not many issues in education which so inflame the passions of so many as that of "correctness." (Even sex-education is not so pervasive an issue, yet.) While "correctness" in the sciences has to do with methodology, in language it traditionally has had to do with the substance of the study itself. One might reasonably argue, of course, that chemical reactions are not a prime means of socialization, whereas language is. But one might argue with equal force that our responsibility as teachers is to open doors not to shut them, and that by imposing—in the name of grammar study (or whatever name it parades under)—a set of prohibitions on the student (who, remember, is already a fully "languaged" person), we succeed only in shutting doors, only in antagonizing and intimidating. This is retrograde to the purposes of education regardless of how "pure" or well-sanctioned the motives. This is in fact a species of institutional insanity that has succeeded in producing a nation of linguistic cripples. Who writes with ease and pleasure? (Precious few English teachers, may I say.) Who recalls his English classroom as a place of intellectual excitement? Why do so many Americans (of *all* generations and backgrounds) assert that "English was my worst subject," "I hated English," "Grammar—ugh!" and so on. Why do otherwise sensible people say to me when they find out that I am an English teacher, "Ooops! I'd better not talk to *you!*"? Why are native speakers of English (at all educational levels) forever stumbling over "who" and "whom," forever saying such things as "They went with Jack and myself" and "between you and I," and so on? In short, why are Americans such flops when it comes to the handling of their own language?

With all of our concern for "correctness" in school, few graduates (at any level) can define "correctness," can say anything useful or informative about English as a language, can write fluently and gracefully (or even accurately enough to say what they "mean"). I fail to see what our received attitudes and values in language arts education have accomplished other than a record of poor performance and neurotic behavior (as evidenced, for example, in the case of a lady of my acquaintance who claimed to get sick to her stomach when she heard a sentence-final preposition and shuddered at the "horrible sound" of *ain't*—though the sound of *saint* she found quite pleasant).

These may be extreme manifestations of our "national mania for correctness," but they are surely symptomatic. It must indeed be a curious philosophy of education which can generate such uneducated responses, for I should think that an educated response would be reasonably free of the irrational. That is, were our students learning to *think* about language instead of learning to perform like trained seals, we could expect intellectually and emotionally healthier responses.

"Correctness" in the traditional school grammar-book sense has mainly to do with the usages of "prestige" dialects. These usages were (for the most part) "officially" formulated during the great age of the prescriptive grammarians and have become the shibboleths of the "educated" person; and since the classroom has over the generations been the place where one learned the "rules," it has in some sense become more of a social arbiter than a place for genuine learning. Likewise, the English teacher has taken on the rôle of a priest or priestess of the mysteries and is quite content with stuffing the student with the doctrines of the faith, which of course brook no questions and offer no explanations. A further problem, as we have pointed out, is that we have come to think of the written word as being in some sense anterior to and more authoritative, linguistically speaking, than speech. Hence, we are inclined to base our study of the language on its written forms, failing to realize that the written forms are as much dialectal as the more obvious dialects of speech. The obvious lesson is that English both spoken and written comes in a variety of forms, that there is no "perfect" English, a master language toward which we all aspire or from which we have all fallen. Even the Queen's English (to say nothing of schoolteacher English) is a dialect. Nevertheless, all the diverse manifestations of English are "English" and we are all, so to speak, in its employ.

The social force of language is easily seen in our responses to the verbal behavior of others. We order the world hierarchically ("democracy" is a theory of government not a mode of living), looking up to some people and down on others, according, in consequence, certain dialects respect, others scorn. As we are educated to believe that certain types of people and certain modes of behavior are "good," we learn (or attempt to learn) those behaviors in order to emulate those types of people. This acculturation is so "normal" that we scarcely think about it, yet at the interfaces of identifiable groups within the society its manifestations can be a source of difficulty, pain, and hostility. When, for example, we meet a dialect that is associated with negative-status speakers, we are both antagonized by and antipathetic to it. An interesting view of the problem can be had by observing the reactions of a prejudiced white to the speech of an Oxford-educated black. "High-caste" British English is the most prestigious of dialects for most Americans (a socio-cultural curiosity that warrants some attention), but from the lips of a representative of a traditionally low-caste group it produces disconcerting effects.

If it is true (and I see no evidence to refute it) that a language or dialect is approximately adequate to the linguistic needs of the speech community that normally uses it, then we cannot reasonably say that one language or dialect is objectively "better" or "worse" than another. Our ideas about "better" and "worse" are based on social issues: the in-group/out-group, the "Pygmalion principle," for did not Henry Higgins prove that a Cockney flower girl will pass for a duchess so long as she *sounds* like a duchess? (On the other hand, Eliza could always make herself linguistically at home within the sound of Bow Bells, which put her one up on high society!) Having at one's command a range of dialects can be useful in many ways. To realize to what extent we all command several dialects, we need only imagine the language of the country-club locker room in the context of the post-sermon coffee hour at church.

Actually, dialects are of several kinds: regional (*e.g.*, Eastern New England, Middle Atlantic, Charleston, etc.), educational (level), caste or class (the "400," etc.), sexual ("man talk" and "woman talk"), occupational (trade jargon), rhetorical (formal, informal), and personal (one's idiosyncratic dialect or *idiolect*). The language features associated with these dialects (which are by no means mutually exclusive) represent the whole range of language features from pronunciation and structure to diction (*i.e.*, word choice: what New York calls *soda*, Boston calls *tonic*). If we examine without prejudice all of these forms of American English (we haven't mentioned the *world* regions of English, which include India, South Africa, New Zealand, and so on), we will discover a great deal about the language but we will have a difficult (to the point of being impossible) time in deciding whether one is "better" or "worse" than another. In the *appropriate context* each does its job. If we wish to assert that Churchillian English is *really* more expressive (taking this as a criterion of "goodness") than ghetto English, we shall have to remind ourselves that Churchillian English would be well nigh incomprehensible in the ghetto and would not, therefore, be expressive in that context at all. (If one says to this, "more's the pity," one is really making an extra-linguistic judgment.) The teacher's responsibility, it seems to me, is to *broaden* the child's linguistic awareness and experience, not to make value judgments which are bound to have damaging psychological effects on those whose backgrounds are not rooted in the "established" segments of society. Besides, as John M. Brewer writes, the private speech of the children of America's ghettos is for many "more meaningful, more facile and more developed than the language of standard English." He says further that during his tenure as principal of a large ghetto school he "found this idiom to be as dazzling as a diamond, invested with the bitter-sweet soulfulness bred by the struggle against poverty's dehumanizing forces." It is just possible that white suburban America is linguistically "disadvantaged" in its own way. Of course, the exigencies of the society require that the ghetto child be linguistically prepared for the establishment world, but this preparation does not require either ridicule of the home dialect or eradication of it; it requires the *addition* of the generally accepted societal standards.

> The social acceptability, and hence "correctness," of any form or word is determined, not by reason or logic or merit, but solely by the hearer's emotional attitude towards it—and emotional attitudes differ from person to person, from group to group, from social class to social class. (Robert A. Hall, Jr., *Linguistics and Your Language*, p. 13.)

As was pointed out in the discussion of the term *grammar*, all native speakers are "grammatical" (according to the structural patterns or grammar of their dialects). What we commonly mean by *grammar*, however, is *usage* or, for example, the preference for *whom* over *who* in a construction like *Who(m) are you going with?* despite the fact that *Who are you going with?* is widely used and sounds "normal" to most speakers of the language. For an utterance to be adjudged truly "incorrect," it would have to emerge like *You with going whom are*, which would strike any native speaker (regardless of his dialect) as being "wrong," "un-English," etc. The preference of *whom* over *who* in the object position is what we might term a matter of local correctness-incorrectness. This feature would be a dialect boundary marker. That is, one who fails to use it in the speech situation where it normally occurs would be marked as being, in some sense, an outsider. A more obvious marker is an utterance like *I ain't got none*, though from the standpoint of the history of the language, the frequency of occurrence of this and similarly constructed utterances, and the inherent grammatical patterns of English, this is "correct" English. From the standpoint of the verbal behavior (a form of social behavior) of that segment of the English-speaking world that has ruled as unacceptable, "wrong," this and similar utterances, *I ain't got none* and its congeners are *verboten*.

It is the teacher's prerogative to prescribe usage—indeed, we have made it his duty—but such prescription should be done in the spirit of enlarging the student's language capabilities. If the teacher makes questions of usage the prime focus of his attention and invests these questions with an emotionally charged system of rewards and punishments (the latter always having the profounder psychological impact), the student stands in danger of being "turned off" and becoming passively if not actively hostile. The plain truth is that fussing over usage and mechanics trivializes language study and inhibits rather than encourages verbal performance. Furthermore, many of the "rules" have little or no relationship to the ways in which the language is actually used by even the most prestigious speakers and writers. It would be well for student and teacher alike to closely examine, say, the speeches of Adlai Stevenson (on record), the transcripts of presidential and other news conferences, the editorial columns of *The New York Times,* and so on, and upon such evidence derive linguistic profiles that truly represent what we are doing with our language right now.

When one brings history to bear on "correctness," the matter is quickly complicated, for if the principle of correctness is strictly adhered to, it becomes its own *reductio ad absurdum.* If it is not strictly adhered to, then what is its rational basis and how is it to be applied? To be strictly correct, we should be speaking Old English (Anglo-Saxon) as that is the language which comes closest to "pure" English. (The historical linguist will here remind us that (1) Old English is a hybrid language and can be thought of as an "impure" form of its continental Germanic—not German but Germanic—ancestors, and so on back to the beginnings, whenever and wherever they were.) Then too there were several regional dialects of Old English, and one would be hard put to choose from among them the most nearly "correct." The "good-English" buff will protest that this is really not what he means by correctness. After all, this *is* the twentieth century not the tenth century and things do change. He will then have to be reminded that the common notion of correctness is rooted in some sort of "good-old-days" view of the world. The rhetoric of "correctness" does, after all, abound in terms like *decay* and *corruption.* But when were the "good old days," linguistically speaking? At what point in time do we stop to choose our models of correctness? In the eighteenth century, a time much admired by those with linguistic purism on their minds, constructions like *he don't, he eat* [*i.e.,* "ate"], and *you was* were common-place and used by all the "best people." (See, for example, the works of Jonathan Swift.) Likewise, *tea* was pronounced to rhyme with *day* and *boil* to rhyme with *smile*. (Try the works of Alexander Pope for these.) At one time, so "correct" a word as *children* was "in-correct," in that it is really a redundant plural (as *irregardless* is a double negation), the "correct" plural being *childer* (still heard in some British dialects and considered "provincial" by the educated public). When the plural force of *-er* was lost, the then fairly com-mon plural in *-en* was superadded to the existing plural that no longer "felt" plural, thus: *child + er + en = children*. And now that *-en* has lost its plural feel (it is used regularly only with *ox* and *child,* occasionally with *brother,* and *ox/oxen* don't occur very often these days), one can hear (as yet rarely) *childrens* (as a plural not a possessive). Who can say that this "incorrect" form will not es-tablish itself exactly as the earlier "incorrect" form did? Of course, in a society such as ours heavily committed to the written word, the likelihood is small, though among non-literate speakers the form has at least the possibility of flourishing; and for the literate, if it does flourish, it will become acceptable, that is, "standard."

A usage much harder to deal with is *bad/badly*. The forms are in competition in such locutions as *I feel bad/ I feel badly*. So com-mon has become the latter usage, even among the highly educated, that the former is beginning to sound "incorrect." Yet to the ultra-precisionist, the former alludes to one's physical and/or emotional state, the latter to one's sense of feel. The former is the "correct" us-age in most of the contexts where *I feel badly* is now regularly used (even by bank presidents, college presidents, heads of state, and English teachers). Nobody who thus regularly uses *I feel badly* is thinking of the state of his tactile sense. I, because of my own lin-guistic conditioning, regularly use *I feel bad* and have more than once got a fishy look for what was thought to be a "grammatical er-ror" on my part. The *good/well* competition is similar.

The really serious problems in verbal expression are not ones of usage, for this is an area of great disagreement even among pro-fessionals in the field (and examination of the comments of the "Usage Panel" of the new and first-rate *American Heritage Dic-tionary of the English Language* regarding a number of key usage items is revealing on this point). The problems are far more profound: rhetorical ineptitude (a broad term covering lack of logical developement; lexical imprecision; lack of vitality, grace, and fluency) and lack, it would seem, of something to say. The teacher who spends his time carping about niggling matters of usage and who forces his students to fool around with diagrams and formulae will do nothing to solve the problems of expression:

> In view of the widespread agreement of research studies based upon many types of students and teachers, the conclusion can be stated in strong and unqualified terms: the teaching of formal grammar has a negligible or, because it usually displaces some instruction and practice in actual composition, even a harmful effect on the improvement of writing. (Richard Braddock, Richard Lloyd-Jones, and Lowell Schoer, *Research in Written Composition*, pp. 37–38, quoted in James Moffett, *Teaching the Universe of Discourse*, p. 164.)

Style is the real issue, and style is what teacher and student know least about. Matters of style will occupy an important part of the new program.

In closing these brief remarks on correctness, I wish to underscore the point that "linguistics" is not to be equated with something like the "new morality." The linguist is primarily an observer and a theoretician. As a scientist he is no different from the physicist or the biologist. It remains for each group in a society to determine its behavior patterns. Correctness, then, is what the group wants it to be. The linguist will dutifully record what he finds. To say that the linguist offers a doctrine of "anything goes" is to misunderstand the rôle the linguist plays. As a pedagogical linguist, however, I feel that it is far more useful for the student to explore language and to draw conclusions according to the best scientific practice than to simply have his head stuffed full of what often are arbitrary "rules" by a teacher who himself is unaware of the nature and operations of language.

A BIT OF HISTORY

I have alluded here and there to earlier stages of our language. Let me now quickly sketch its history. English is one of a group of languages to which scholars give the name *West Germanic* and to which belong (in addition to English) Dutch, Flemish, Frisian, Plattdeutsch ("Low German"), and German. All of these languages except German are members of the *Low* branch of the group. Standard German and the south German dialects (Bavarian, Austrian, Swiss German, etc.) comprise the *High* branch. (It should be understood that *High* and *Low* here are geographical designations and have reference to the northern lowlands and the southern highlands of the Germanic region. The fact that a form of High German—*Hochdeutsch*—became Standard [i.e., School] German should not confuse the issue; Bavarian German is High German but definitely not Standard German.) High German is thus a very close cousin language and Low German a sister language to English. *English did not come from German.* English and German descended from a common ancestor, something we can call *Common West Germanic* or *Early West Germanic.* The other two Germanic groups are *North Germanic* (the *Scandinavian* languages) and *East Germanic* (which gave us only *Gothic*, a language that disappeared about A.D. 1000, but which we have fairly full evidence of through a translation of the Bible made about A.D. 350).

All of the Germanic languages find their place in the family tree of the *Indo-European* family of languages as co-equal members with the *Celtic* languages, *Italic* languages (including Latin and its descendants, the *Romance* languages), *Hellenic* languages (including modern *Greek*), *Balto-Slavic* languages (including *Russian, Polish,* and *Lithuanian*), and the *Indo-Iranian* languages (including *Persian* on the Iranian side and *Sanskrit* and its descendants on the Indian side). *Armenian, Albanian, Tocharian* and *Hittite* (these latter two long since vanished) complete this scandalously compressed survey of our language family. One point is plain: The family is an extraordinarily diverse one. It is indeed a wonder that such diversity could have sprung from a single source (*viz., Indo-European,* a scholar's term, for we have no direct evidence from Indo-European times, estimated to be about 3000 B.C. and earlier, and have therefore no records of these people as a people. What we know of the language has been reconstructed from actual languages). It is indeed a wonder that English and, say, *Gujarati* (a modern Indian language spoken in the western Indian state of Gujarat; a language descended from Sanskrit, surely as exotic a language as a speaker of English might think of) are cousins. And at the same time, Hungarian, spoken in the heart of Europe, is truly the exotic language, for it is wholly unrelated to the Indo-European family.

Prior to the settlement of Germanic tribes (Angles, Saxons, Jutes, and some Frisians) in the British Isles (*British* is a hybrid word with a Celtic root, *bryt-*, which emerges in *Bryth*onic—the Celts of Wales, Cornwall, and *Brit*anny—as opposed to the Goidelic Celts—the Celts of Ireland and Scotland; the *-ish* ending is strictly Germanic), there was no England (*i.e. Engla-land,* "land of the Angles") and no English (*Angl-isc,* English). But once the invasions were substantially completed, during the sixth century (A.D.), these closely related tribes largely from the southern part of Jutland and Schleswig-Holstein formed a fairly coherent culture which we can properly call "English." Linguistically, the span from the first Germanic settlements to 1100 is called the Old English period. During this half-millennium much happened both linguistically and culturally in England which is not even hinted at in the vague term *Old English*. Suffice it to say, however, that the foundations of the language were laid and the long history of English literature begun.

The English of this early period was in many ways like modern German (which has not been subject to a disruption of the sort that came with the Norman Conquest of England), that is, it was a language of relatively full inflections (*e.g.*, nouns were marked for a number of cases) and rather freer syntax than modern English. The sound of the language (so far we can accurately judge this) was clearly Germanic (tense pronunciation in the modern German manner and a strong accentual beat in the Scandinavian manner). To the modern speaker of English, Old English looks distinctly foreign, yet a close examination will reveal much that is familiar:

Ða wæs æfter manigum dagum, ðæt sē cyning cōm tō ðām ēalande. . . .

Ða	Then	*sē*	the
wæs	(it) was	*cyning*	king
æfter	after	*cōm*	came
manigum	many	*tō*	to
dagum	days	*ðām*	the
ðæt	that	*ēalande*	island

Aside from three unfamiliar alphabetic symbols and the inflectional endings, the passage is not very different from its "translation." Of course, this is deceptive, for there are many passages of Old English which require a good deal of specialized study in order to render them accurately. Nonetheless, about 75% of our everyday ordinary vocabulary is Old English in origin and our word order is often not appreciably different from that of Old English.

Somewhat prior to the Norman Conquest (1066), one can detect the beginnings of changes which were to be hastened by the advent of Norman French in England. The elaborate case system was already decaying (a purely linguistic term, no value judgment intended or implied), a process which would continue through the *Middle English* period (1100–1500). For a time after the Conquest, English was a kind of "underground" language, spoken by a few provincial Anglo-Saxon aristocrats and, of course, the major part of the English people, yet all but unknown at court. Nevertheless, by the middle of the fourteenth century, English had reestablished itself as *the* language of England and the Norman hegemony (culturally speaking) was for all practical purposes at an end, for it was now an indissoluble part of the *English* cultural world. (An interesting footnote on the Conquest is the fact that the *Nor*mans were themselves ethnically *Norse*men, that is, they were a Germanic people who much earlier invaded what was to become Norman France, but were culturally and linguistically absorbed by the Romanized people they conquered. Thus we have the irony in the Conquest of a Germanic people conquering a Germanic people (who had earlier themselves conquered a Romanized people), but bringing with them a Roman culture instead of a Germanic one. And a further irony is the fact that there were Norse invasions of England prior to the Norman Conquest which resulted in Danish kings sitting on the English throne but being culturally absorbed into the English world. A tangled web indeed. In any case, the Normans didn't bring any vastly different blood to England, but they did bring a vastly different culture.

The wholesale introduction into English of Norman French words (most of which came to the Normans from Latin) has misled many people into assuming that English comes from Latin. Not only does English not come from Latin, but much of the "latinate" vocabulary considered from the standpoint of linguistic history is only "from" Latin indirectly. The seventeenth- and eighteenth-century scholars who respelled words like *doute* and *aventure* as *doubt* and *adventure* on the grounds that they were "really" Latin, overlooked the fact that we got them in their French forms in the first place and even in Old French the Latin forms were modified. This type of "little learning" has added to the already onerous burden of those who would learn English spelling, and for no other reason than pedantic meddlesomeness. If, of course, we are speaking of the *original* provenience of the present-day English vocabulary we note that perhaps 75% of our learned, technical, and artistic (*i.e.*, concerning the arts) vocabulary is Latin (like the word *vocabulary* itself, as opposed to the Old English *wordhord*, "word-hoard"). In all, we have borrowed from dozens of languages from every continent. Our easy acceptance of imported vocabulary has provided us with perhaps the richest and most diverse word stock of any language in the world, indeed, an embarrassment of riches for the would-be writer, for such a choice can be as much of a despair as a joy.

Middle English as exemplified in the work of Geoffrey Chaucer (1340–1400), whose London dialect was a blend of several of the Middle English dialects, is easily recognizable as English. It has a quaint look about it and would sound very strange to modern ears but there is no doubt what it is:

> In th'olde dayes of the king Arthour,
> Of which that Britons speken greet honour,
> Al was this land fulfild of fayerye.   [with fairies]
> The elf-queen, with hir joly companye,
> Daunced ful ofte in many a grene mede. . . .   [very often]

By this time, most of the case endings had disappeared and the syntax had generally settled into the patterns characteristic of modern English. (There are some notable exceptions but we need not be overly precise in a brief sketch.) Certain changes in pronunciation were of course taking place, though Chaucer's English maintained the continental vowel system in great measure and the velar consonants that we think of as typically Germanic. (These would be the misnamed "guttural" sounds as represented in Middle English by, for example, the *gh* in *light*.)

By the year 1500, the language had moved sufficiently out of its earlier phonological, morphological, and grammatical habits to warrant a new label, namely, Modern English (or, more particularly, Early Modern English, the language of Shakespeare). Between the time of Chaucer and roughly 1500, English vowels had undergone a radical change away from the continental values to the quite peculiarly English values they have now. (Again, I have oversimplified in the interest of brevity.) Hence, for example, *bite* in Chaucer's time was pronounced *beetê*. (The final *e* was pronuonced approximately like the vowel of *but*.) As nearly as we can judge, Early Modern English should be spoken rather like a Dublin brogue, which, incidentally, is a reflex of Elizabethan English; that is, the "brogue" takes its character far more from Early Modern English than from any Celtic features. As the vowels changed, so final *e*'s vanished into silence, though not from the printed page (the first press in England was operating in the last quarter of the fifteenth century, which is to say, before the end of the Middle English period. Not, of course, that Englishmen of that day had any such view of themselves that they could conceive of "Old English," "Middle English," and "Modern English"), as did *gh* (except when it pops up as an /f/ or even a /p/). A passage from Shakespeare looks and sounds *old-fashioned* rightly enough but that we are close to home is plainly evident. From his time to the present the changes in English are really quite insignificant when we contrast Modern English with its two preceding periods.

An important consequence of the dual ancestry of English is our double vocabulary, a Germanic vocabulary matched by a French one: *answer/response; behind/derriere; body/corpse; cooking/cuisine; deep/profound; dream/reverie; give/donate; help/aid; house/mansion; shirt/chemise; sing/chant; world/universe*, etc. Immediately apparent is the difference in "tone" between the two sets. The native words are plain and unpretentious, the borrowed words are learned or pretentious or "precious" or "high class." (Though generally the case, this is not *always* the case. Try to find some examples in which the native word acts more like the borrowed word and *vice versa*.) And an important consequence of our linguistic acquisitiveness is our three-leveled vocabulary of Germanic-French-Latin (sometimes Greek): *end/finish/conclude* (also *terminate, finalize*); *kingly/royal/regal; rise/mount/ascend; time/age/epoch*, etc. If we therefore choose *ambulate*, we are choosing at a very literal level a synonym for *walk*. But we are at the same time bringing into the context the special values of *ambulate* (while avoiding the values of *walk*), the learned overtones, the psychological sets associated with such words, a sound distinctively different from *walk* and, ultimately, a meaning different from *walk*. As I said, an embarrassment of riches (or *embarras de richesse*).

There is little point in attempting to make predictions about the future of English. But there is no doubt that the English we presently have at our command is an expressive tool of surpassing subtlety and flexibility. It is surely the most cosmopolitan of languages and the closest thing we have to a world language. Such losses as the language may sustain through, as it were, rough usage (a small example: the blurring of distinction between *uninterested* and *disinterested*), it more than compensates for in the resourcefulness that so well characterizes the language. We stand in no danger of being at a loss for words.

IN CLOSING

Language can be looked at in so many ways from so many points of view that framing a satisfactory definition is a formidable if not impossible task. Here are four definitions all of which are useful (but like all definitions of language, requiring volumes of commentary):

(1) . . . I will consider a *language* to be a set (finite or infinite) of sentences, each finite in length and constructed out of a finite set of elements. All natural languages in their spoken or written form are languages in this sense, since each natural language has a finite number of phonemes (or letters in its alphabet) and each sentence is representable as a finite sequence of these phonemes (or letters), though there are infinitely many sentences. (Noam Chomsky, *Syntactic Structures*, p. 13.)

(2) Natural languages are vehicles for communication in which syntactically structured and acoustically realized objects transmit meaningful messages from one speaker to another.

Roughly, linguistic communication consists in the production of some external, publicly observable, acoustic phenomenon whose phonetic and syntactic structure encodes a speaker's inner, private thoughts or ideas and the decoding of the phonetic and syntactic structure exhibited in such a physical phenomenon by other speakers in the form of an inner, private experience of the same thoughts or ideas. (Jerrold J. Katz, *The Philosophy of Language,* p. 98.)

(3) Language is a type of patterned human behavior. It is a way, perhaps the most important way, in which human beings interact in social situations. Language behavior is externalized or manifested in some kind of bodily activity on the part of a *performer,* and presupposes the existence of at least one other human participant in the situation, an *addressee.* (J. C. Catford, *A Linguistic Theory of Translation,* p. 1.)

(4) Language is a structured system of overt, learned and therefore non-instinctive, sequentially produced, voluntary, human, symbol-carrying vocal sounds by which communication is carried on between two or more persons. (Harry R. Warfel, *Language: A Science of Human Behavior,* p. 29.)

And to this short list of definitions can be added many more, all of which, like these, cast some light and all of which, like these, raise a host of knotty questions. It is as true of language as it is of many other subjects of investigation that the more we discover the more we realize there is to discover.

Using language is the most human thing we do (despite the fact that we often use it *inhumanely*). Language is the major track we have into the workings of the human mind, a fact which has generated the science of *psycholinguistics* and is having a profound effect on psychological theorizing. And language should be the most exciting subject one can study in school. With more and more English teachers entering the profession with at least some background in linguistics, perhaps it will prove to be something other than the boring study it usually is. However, the danger looms large that "linguistics" will turn out to be just a new word for the same old baloney, that is, for the same old formularized busywork.

Use of elaborate formulas, replete with detailed glossaries or abbreviations and distinctive symbols, has made the usual transformational grammar look like a mathematical treatise or a procedural manual in industry. In Paul Roberts' *English Syntax,* for instance, the transformational rule that would generate a sentence such as *We found John studying* appears as:

T–Vt$_{ing}$: insert: NP$_1$(1)—Aux(2)—X(3)
         matrix: NP + Aux + Vt$_{ing}$(4)—Comp(5)—NP$_1$(6)
         result: 4 + ing + 3 + 6

Whether or not this apparatus is fruitful in computer study and will ultimately lead to the desired end is somewhat beside the point. It does put a surtax on the student of grammar, since it asks him to learn an extensive code in which to record his understandings *after* he has arrived at them. (Baxter Hathaway, *A Transformational Syntax*, p. 19.)

Unfortunately, the competitive need to keep up with educational fashions (and to make current textbooks obsolete) prompts the textbook publishers to rush into print an assortment of "linguistics" textbooks that (as usual) promise much and deliver little. Six weeks (or whatever) spent drawing transformational tree diagrams is little improvement over six weeks drawing Reed-Kellog diagrams (the "old-fashioned" ones), for from the standpoint of the student, patterned nonsense is patterned nonsense. To fasten on formal grammatical analysis as the heart of the matter is the central error of the textbook, and this error in turn engenders the errors that predictably follow. Since, of course, there is something hard-edged and clean about grammatical analysis (at least as it is presented in the textbook), the teacher is attracted to it as something to do that has easily correctable answers, the old comfortable "right/wrong" system of "education." (The fact that even the most advanced linguistic theorists present their findings only tentatively is conveniently overlooked. Much, for example, in the Paul Roberts textbook series is already discredited by advances in grammatical theory since the series has been published. But my complaint here is not that knowledge and understanding grow and that all books of this sort become obsolete to one degree or another in due course but that Roberts and others have presented as authoritative linguistic concepts that do not have a sound theoretical basis and have subsequently been rejected by the theoreticians.) Or, for the more literary-minded teachers, it is something to ignore altogether, often in favor of a good deal of gushing about literary truth and beauty. A sad state of affairs.

By way of warming up to a useful approach to the study of language (which includes not only grammar but language as a cultural phenomenon, with all that this implies), consider the following questions:

1. How is a dog's barking to be let out of the house both similar to and different from a child's asking to go out? How do you know?

2. When we talk, language is manifested as a more-or-less continuous stream of sound. When we write, language is manifested as a linear series of separate little marks. How do you account for these two quite different manifestations of the "same" thing (*viz.*, language)? When we write down what someone says, how do we know how to segment the speech stream graphically? Do the graphic representations "match" actual speech in all particulars? Explain.

3. All humans have and use language, but only a relatively few are literate (*i.e.*, use writing systems). What does this suggest to you?

4. There are from two thousand to four thousand languages currently in use around the world. Each of these languages is approximately adequate to the needs of the people who regularly use it. Each language is different—often radically so—from the other. Hence, for example, there are thousands of speech representations for the object we call *tree*. What do these facts suggest to you?

5. Why do we have "dirty words"? Who decides which words are "dirty"? On what basis do these decisions seem to be made? Why are medical terms for bodily functions relatively inoffensive whereas the "plain English" terms are (for most people) offensive to very offensive? Do you ever use "dirty words"? Under what circumstances? Why do you think young people today (both sexes) are so free about using taboo language? How could you go about getting an unemotional ("objective") answer to this question?

6. Why and how are people moved to violence, even murder and war, by words? Have you ever been so moved? What were the circumstances? Would similar circumstances have the same effects on you now? Discuss.

7. Even though it isn't easy to define *word,* we do have diction-aries that consist primarily of lists of words. Are there *sentence* dictionaries as well? If you were to compile a sentence dic-tionary, how would you go about it? What problems might you expect to run into?

8. When you read or hear a new word—one that isn't in any dictionary yet—how do you find out what it "means"? How do you suppose that dictionary-makers (lexicographers) (a) determine its meaning and (b) decide on whether to put it into the next edition of their dictionary? How would you solve these problems?

9. Are there bits and pieces of experience for which to your knowledge there are no words? Why aren't there any? Can you invent some appropriate words for those realities? (Think of sounds and check your dictionary for useful roots.) *Inter-robang* is a recently coined word for a punctuation mark combining the question and exclamation marks.

10. Do advertisements try to "use" you with language? Can you characterize the various kinds of verbal trickery that adver-tisers engage in? What does an expression like "The *now* taste of Pepsi" refer to in the real world? What is *"now* taste"? What reality is conveyed by "Flavors that never came through a filter before"? Examine other advertising slogans for their "reality content."

11. How much "reality content" was in the last political speech you heard? What are the real-world referents of such phrases as "the communist conspiracy" and "fascist pig"? Don't answer according to your emotional responses. Simply try to find the actual extensional referents of the phrases.

12. What do the expressions "scientific truth," "religious truth," and "psychological truth" mean to you? How is "truth" deter-mined? When a clergyman speaks of "truth" is he speaking of the same "thing" as a scientist when he speaks of "truth"? What do you mean by "truth"?

13. In the past, grammarians labored to make English "logical." They argued, for example, that a sentence like *I don't want none* is "illogical" because one negative cancels out the other and that the person is "really" saying *I want some.* Were the grammarians logical in their assumptions? *Is* the person who

says *I don't want none* "really" saying *I want some?* Consider the curious case of *That is not impossible,* which really does mean *That is possible* but which was not proscribed. Or, *He didn't intend not to do it,* which clearly contains two negatives yet is nonetheless a perfectly "proper" sentence. Can you think of some other "illogical" but acceptable utterances (not necessarily involving negation)? What rôle does "logic" play in the structuring of utterances?

14. In what ways does language make possible the life you lead? Can you write a description of a society in which there is no *linguistic* communication? Try to touch on all the important activities of life.

15. How would you go about discovering the nature and operations of the English verb system? Make believe that there isn't a word written on the subject. Would such a study be of any value? To whom? Why? For two quite different approaches to the English verb system, see Martin Joos, *The English Verb* and F. R. Palmer, *A Linguistic Study of the English Verb.*

16. Grammarians talk about "parts of speech." What does the concept "parts of speech" mean to you? Don't simply name the "parts of speech"—your list in any case would reflect the particular grammar book you or your English teachers were brought up on. (The various books disagree with each other on this and many other points of grammar.) Does the "parts of speech" concept have some rational basis? If so, what is it? Do you use the concept for anything? What?

17. Traditional justifications for the study of "grammar" include claims that grammar (1) disciplines the mind, (b) aids in the study of foreign languages, (c) helps one to read, write, and speak better, and (d) aids in the interpretation of literature. What scientifically respectable evidence can you offer (it is legitimate to draw on your own experience) in support of these claims? You will first have to define "grammar." Then you will have to cite specific examples of "improvement" through formal grammar study. And, of course, you will have to demonstrate that this "improvement" (how measured?) is causally (not casually) related to that study.

18. What constitutes "good writing"? Ideally, form and content

cannot be separated. Yet we generally find ourselves responding to "story" and "message" (at least at the conscious level) and overlooking language (*i.e.*, rhetoric). Pick out a paragraph or two that you think is particularly well written and try to convey a sense of its rhetorical quality. If you assert, for example, that the writing "flows," try to pinpoint precisely what seems to make it "flow."

19. Make a list of useful language information that you learned in your English classes. If you studied sentence diagramming, discuss the ways in which you used what you presumably learned. Can you still diagram sentences? If so, what do you do with this skill? If you teach diagramming, what do you expect that your students will learn by doing it?

20. A new theory of grammatical analysis called *case grammar* is currently under development. The central concept of case grammar is that the sentence is built around case-distinguished nouns. And since we mark English nouns only for the genitive case (*girl–girl's*), case distinctions are realized through prepositions. Thus, *The house was alive with children* can be transformed into *Children enlivened the house,* with *children* considered *causative* or *agentive* or *instrumental* (signaled by *with,* meaning *by means of*). Or note that when active-voice sentences are passivized, the *relationships* among the nouns remain the same, even though the "subject" and "object" labels are swapped. Can you carry case grammar any further? Does this approach to grammatical analysis seem to offer any special advantages to the student of the language?

21. From time to time, a new "artificial" language such as Esperanto appears, its creator claiming that we need an international means of communication free from nationalistic claims and associations. This seems like a good idea in principle. Why hasn't it worked? If you were to attempt to create a new language, how would you go about it? What elements would you include? Would it be basically English or do you think that there are better possible linguistic systems? What features of English might you wish to reject? What would you substitute? Don't confuse the writing system with the language itself. (English and all other natural languages are *phonetic;* on the other hand, the English *spelling* system has a number

of obvious flaws.) Remember, too, that a language is a lot more than a list of words.

22. Make a list of your communication failures for one week. Do you understand in each case *why* communication broke down? *How* it broke down? Can you categorize communication problems? What seems to be the basis of the "communication gap" between generations? What part does language play? Can the gap be bridged with language? How?

23. Can you think of ways of discussing *meaning* additional to the ways presented in the chapter? Why is discovering the meaning of meaning so difficult? C. K. Ogden and I. A. Richards in their book, *The Meaning of Meaning*, assert that "all definitions are essentially *ad hoc*." What are the implications of this assertion? Ludwig Wittgenstein writes: "If we scrutinize the usages we make of such words as 'thinking,' 'meaning,' 'wishing,' etc., going through this process rids us of the temptation to look for a peculiar act of thinking, independent of the act of expressing our thoughts, and stowed away in some peculiar medium." (*The Blue Book*, p. 43) What are the implications of this assertion?

24. What conscious adjustments do you make in your speech habits in varying social and professional contexts? Why? Have failures to make these adjustments ever caused you embarrassment? Discuss. Have you ever noticed other people "shifting linguistic gears," as it were? What did they do? Were there any describable results?

25. Make a list of words that give you a "minus" feeling. Make a list of words that give you a "plus" feeling. Make a list of "neutral" words. What conclusions can you draw from your lists? Are there degrees of "minus" and "plus"? If so, arrange each list in order of increasing emotional content. Can you draw any conclusions from these listings?

26. What are the differences between the speech of three-year-olds and six-year-olds? Between six-year-olds and ten-year-olds? Between ten-year-olds and adults? Don't guess and assume; observe and record. What do these comparisons tell you? The most sophisticated grammatical maneuver we have in English is the inclusion of one clause in another (subordination). How much more sophisticated, grammatically speak-

ing, are the older subjects than the younger? Don't worry about vocabulary.

27. *Nouns* are traditionally "defined" as "names" and *verbs* as "words expressing action or state of being." Choose some words at random from your dictionary and see if the definitions of *noun* and *verb* will serve to adequately categorize them. To get you started, consider *action* (a *noun*) and *see* (a *verb*).

28. *The* has been called the *definite article* and *a* the *indefinite article*, but it can be shown that *the* is frequently far more "indefinite" than *a*. Can you cite some examples that will show it? And while we are on the subject of articles, can you suggest why it is pointless to consider them *adjectives* (even though they are traditionally classified as such)?

29. Choose any paragraph at random and explain what meanings are suggested by the prepositions used therein. Consider: *He walked to his truck/ He saw to his truck* [to]; *He stood on the floor/ He stood on his dignity/ He composed on the typewriter* [on].

30. How do you recognize *slang* when you hear it? How could you determine what slang is without looking the word up in the dictionary? You will find, incidentally, that dictionaries are notable for what they omit. Indeed, just what is a dictionary useful for? Why do dictionaries go out of date? Why are they, in fact, out of date the moment they come off the press?

THE EARLY YEARS

No one knows very much yet about how children can best learn to produce and receive language or what the exact stages of an optimal learning sequence would be.

[James Moffett, *A Student-Centered Language Arts Curriculum, Grades K–13*]

Teaching is a behavior, and as behavior is subject to analysis, change, and improvement.

[Judson T. Shaplin, "Practice in Teaching"]

The basic habit of maintaining a skeptical, actively critical point of view toward all knowledge and opinion must be ingrained. Such habits will minimize the development of unconscious inhibitions against consideration of the widest possible spectrum of possibilities in approaching a problem of interest.

[Jerome B. Wiesner, "Education for Creativity in the Sciences"]

The highly creative child will likely continue to feel estranged and inhibited in the school, unless he has adventurous-spirited teachers who are willing to listen to some of his wild ideas, help him to test and develop these ideas, and enjoy with him the development of his creative faculties.

[E. Paul Torrance, "Developing Creative Thinking through School Experiences"]

The establishment in lower and secondary education is probably the most encrusted in the entire world. They are still teaching children as they were taught 30 years ago. A child today who comes into kindergarten has had from 3,000 to 4,000 hours sitting in front of the television tube, absorbing unstructured data that takes him way past Dick and Jane. And the system just doesn't respond to that.

[Robert Finch, Former Secretary of Health, Education and Welfare]

For more than 100 years, despite the swings in educational philosophy, our method of teaching has been to give our children "courses" in biology, or geography, or social studies. The student reads a textbook containing all of the facts about such-and-such a course. The teacher repeats and elaborates on these facts in the classroom; then, if the student is lucky he remembers the facts at exam time. Our system has rarely attempted to develop a student's imagination, to stretch his flexible mind in new directions, to make him think about what he has learned. He learns one body of knowledge called "history," another called "math," a third called "botany." That these isolated disciplines may be related is seldom stressed in our classrooms.

[Viktor Lowenfeld, "Creativity: Education's Stepchild"]

It is unlikely that curriculum projects can make a difference in [the United States] until they find a way to involve ordinary teachers in creating materials.

[Joseph Featherstone, *The Primary School Revolution in Britain*]

A fixed curriculum for the elementary school is a matter of some necessity and more impossibility. A rigid stratification of grade norms is a near absurdity; organizational dictates force some arbitrary standards and groups, but good teaching presses always for flexibility and the individualized standard.

[Ryland W. Crary, *Humanizing the School*]

EDUCATION, as we all know, goes on continuously. But the school is designed explicitly for education. This isolation of a specific place for education implies a selection of activities specifically identified with "education." Because the idea of the school is an old one in our civilization (N.B.: the etymon of *school* is the Greek *skholē*, "leisure"), the constituents of our educational schema are likewise well established and represent for most of us a "given." From time to time, it is true, we have added a little and taken away a little and changed emphasis a little, but the famous "three R's" are still considered the primary ground of our education. And if we no longer call them by that quaint term (at least not in public), our educational programs (regardless of how fancied up they are with super-textbooks, "teaching materials," audio-visual aids, and the like) are centrally concerned with getting kids to go through the motions of reading, writing, and doing arithmetic. This is not necessarily bad. We do need in our society to read, write, and do a bit of arithmetic from time to time. Unfortunately, the results of our educational efforts in this direction have been less than spectacular. It is probably true that every high-school graduate can do a little reading, writing, and arithmetic, but on the average he does each rather poorly and with little enthusiasm. Yes, he can read and write sufficiently to hold some kind of job, but that is a meager return for twelve or more years of schooling. And I strongly suspect that the ones who finish their pre-college education doing well at these tasks would have done as well without benefit of that elaborate and expensive piece of equipment called the school. This is another way of saying that significant learning takes place outside the locus officially designated for learning. Our schools, then, provide some kind of *training*, the manifestation of which in the child is a minimal level of competence in largely mechanical skills. This is not an idle or churlish charge. Except at the colleges and universities that skim the cream of high-school graduating classes, the charge is easily supported even in the college population, which in any year is, after all, only a relatively small percentage of the national high-school graduating class. And I have overheard Ivy League English professors complaining about the linguistic ineptitude of their students.

The fault, of course, lies neither in the stars nor in the children. If we hope to accomplish something in this educational enterprise, we shall have to stop the eternal (and infernal) buck-passing. The plain truth is that we are doing the wrong things in school. We tinker with curricula that are misconceived in the first place. Teaching the wrong things better is not going to solve the problems besetting education. There is nothing sacred about the received curriculum. It is not a matter of making a few minor repairs on a fundamentally sound structure. The received curriculum is rotten and needs to be swept clean away before we can hope to make anything worthwhile of the school years. With precious few exceptions, "curriculum study" and "curriculum revision" are exercises in futility. What do they result in? A scissors and paste job. A new textbook (of all things). (Mortimer J. Adler: "Textbooks and popularizations of all sorts are written for people who do not know how to read or can read only for information," *How to Read a Book*, p. 57.) Greater use of the overhead projector. And so on. Nothing really changes (or, *plus ça change, plus c'est la même chose*). And in a year or two, once the blush has faded, we're back at it again. The new book somehow failed us. Well, maybe a newer book is the answer. Maybe another gadget or two (not that I'm against gadgets—if they are part of a program that is pedagogically sound in the first place).

I note in my local paper that a school in New Jersey observes twice a year a "Rest the Textbook Week." The superintendent of the borough schools says of his program, "Without textbooks, teaching and learning depend on the creativity, ingenuity, initiative, interest, and effort of both students and teachers." The program is, apparently, a great success (marred only by the fact that for the rest of the year textbook is king). What a pity that the stated dependencies of teaching and learning cannot continue through the year. Let me hasten to remind the reader that while I am very much anti-textbook, I am very much pro-book. There is a difference.

What then should education be if it shouldn't be the "three R's"? Reading, writing, and arithmetic will not of course be banished, but they will be treated as the tools they are. Nobody reads, writes, or figures just to read, write, and figure (except, perhaps, in school). Yes, yes, you will say, he's headed right for the old motivation stuff. Indeed, motivation is paramount, but "old stuff" it is not. The sad truth is that when kids *first* come to school they are highly motivated. But, ironically, the longer they spend in the classroom, the less motivated they become, many even becoming "negatively motivated" or actively hostile toward school and everything officially connected with it.

We destroy disinterested (I do *not* mean *un*interested) love of learning in children, which is so strong when they are small, by encouraging and compelling them to work for petty and contemptible rewards—gold stars, or papers marked 100 and tacked to the wall, or A's on report cards, or honor rolls, or dean's lists, or Phi Beta Kappa keys—in short, for the ignoble satisfaction of feeling that they are better than someone else. We encourage them to feel that the end and aim of all they do in school is nothing more than to get a good mark on a test, or to impress someone with what they seem to know. We kill, not only their curiosity, but their feeling that it is a good and admirable thing to be curious, so that by the age of ten most of them will not ask questions, and will show a good deal of scorn for the few who do. (John Holt, *How Children Fail,* p. 168.)

My college students fit this dismal picture precisely, though there is one question I can count on: What do I need to do to pass (or get an A, B, or C, depending on the success orientation of the student)? When I assign a paper (the subject of the student's own choosing, within the general framework of the course), I can also expect to be asked how many pages I want, how many footnotes, how much of a bibliography. When I tell the class that the paper length depends upon what sort of problem they define and what they do with it, and that I'd rather have them do primary research instead of footnote grubbing, I am received with moans and groans. (Linguistics, my academic field, is a subject eminently suited to "field work" as opposed to the usual kind of "term-paper" tailoring done in the carrels.) Once the ones who haven't been entirely destroyed by their prior "education" force themselves within boundaries they themselves set, they discover that learning can indeed be an exciting experience and that a classroom without traditional restraints "makes sense." (I give no exams and require that the students evaluate their own papers. I reserve the right to dispute their estimates—though I find that I rarely have to avail myself of this right—but the experience for them is nonetheless a good one and one that opens at least a small breach in the system.)

The modern equivalent of Thoreau's "quiet desperation" would be, I suppose, "conflicted." Why are we so conflicted? And at so early an age? I have no doubt but that the school plays a major role in the "conflicting" process. My college students, the children that Holt speaks of—all seem to be similarly afflicted. A teacher reports to me that when he tried experimenting with inductive learning in an eighth-grade English class, the students rejected his language projects in favor of "grammar." When asked why they preferred "grammar" to a variety of interesting and free-wheeling language problems, they answered that "grammar" was what they were "supposed" to be studying now. When asked whether they liked "grammar," they said they hated it. When pressed further, they said that if they didn't "get" it now, they would be behind next year, when they would be using the next book in the language arts series. When asked what they "got" when they "got" grammar, they answered with a few standard definitions which they neither understood nor were able to apply. When it was pointed out how useless all of this was, they laughed and said that they knew that, but that this was the time for studying "grammar" and they'd better study it. This is a species of insanity.

MODEL-BUILDING, GAME-PLAYING, AND PROBLEM-SOLVING

Formal education is education for intellectual maturity and for emotional maturity. These can be got without formal education (perhaps that's where most of us get them if we have them), but the fact of school provides us with an opportunity to do a superlative job. Captives from as early as their third year, our children should leave high school fully capable of coping successfully with the problems they will face from then on, whether they be the problems of the "outside" world or the academic world.

What our children need, then, is something beyond the mere acquisition of mechanical skills. They need to learn, in short, how to *think*. *Thinking* in the sense intended here is conscious, volitional, and orderly. The child should be able to identify problems, delimit them, develop techniques for solving them, and, finally, solve them or at least recognize the extent of their insolubility. The fact is that everyone does these things (rather haphazardly) in the course of daily life, but there are important and obvious differences between informal, subliminal problem-solving and formal, conscious problem-solving. A school built upon the problem-solving concept will look quite different from the school built on any of the various versions of the received curriculum currently in force. The student will develop skills and acquire facts, but these will come as part of a larger purpose. The educational experience to be engaging must be at once coherent, continuous, and challenging. If the right kinds of problems are posed, the child will learn what he must learn in order to solve the problems, and he will remember what he learns because it has sprung from his own "need to know." Writing, for example, makes sense only as a means of communicating. Once the child discovers a need to write, he will write. Telling him to write because writing is what one does every day for twenty minutes is less than likely to convince him that writing is worth bothering oneself about. He may do what he is told, but this is hardly a technique for genuine learning. The teacher who tells the child to write and then shows him how to do it is certainly not *teaching* though he may be *ruling*.

Since our aim is (or should be) to increase the capacity of the child to "handle" his environment, we must bring him to an awareness of the nature of the environment, to the constructs within the environment that can be identified and in some way or another manipulated. A handy way to grasp reality, so to speak, is through the technique of model-building. The theoretical model is one of science's most powerful tools for discovery and there is no reason why the same tool cannot be put to work in the classroom. Of course, when a teacher sets up a "supermarket" in the classroom, he is building a model. Only those features of the market that are significant for the particular concepts to be learned are abstracted and the non-functional features of a real supermarket are ignored. A "total model" would be an actual supermarket. (The weakness of teacher-built models is, of course, the fact that the teacher and not the student builds them.) Likewise, when one person interacts with another, each has some kind of a model of the other in mind.

> When I deal with another person, I want to know what model he is currently working with. We often ask questions of one another with that in mind. If someone is using an inappropriate model of us, we can become quite emotional about it. We feel that it is un-

fair, unjust, or inappropriate. (John C. Lilly, *The Mind of the Dolphin*, p. 94.)

Dr. Lilly goes on to say that if we are to communicate with dolphins (which has been a large part of Lilly's research work), we must interact with dolphins on the basis of an increasingly precise model. It is not our purpose in the classroom to communicate with dolphins (though figuring out how one might do it would be a fascinating project). But it is our purpose to learn to communicate with the world, with each other, with ourselves. "Our problem," writes Lilly, "is achieving a basic communication with our fellow men and fellow women so deep that each of us and them can be satisfied in very basic ways." (P. 20.) In a rather different vein, Loren Eiseley directs us to the same vital center of the human experience:

> Yet whenever I see a frog's eye low in the water warily ogling the shoreward landscape, I always think inconsequentially of those twiddling mechanical eyes that mankind manipulates nightly from a thousand observatories. Someday, with a telescopic lens an acre in extent, we are going to see something not to our liking, some looming shape outside there across the great pond of space.
>
> Whenever I catch a frog's eye I am aware of this, but I do not find it depressing. I stand quite still and try hard not to move or lift a hand since it would only frighten him. And standing thus it finally comes to me that this is the most enormous extension of vision of which life is capable: the projection of itself into other lives. This is the lonely, magnificent power of humanity. It is, far more than any spatial adventure, the supreme epitome of reaching out. (*The Immense Journey*, pp. 45–46.)

Where man truly fails, it is the failure to reach out that is at the heart of the matter. Technological failure is easily overcome, but the failure of the "lonely, magnificent power of humanity" is inevitably catastrophic. The classroom is surely a place where we can work to develop that power and perhaps to insure against its failure.

But little of substance is accomplished by admonition and "inspiration." We cannot tell our students that mankind will be better off for their behaving this way or that. The mind must be challenged, capacities built. Model-building is a technique for capacity-building. The whole range of logical and communicative processes is used. The model becomes for the child a handle on reality. He brings reality under his control, discovers its components and interrelationships and processes. He becomes himself an architect, a shaper of reality, and thereby learns how reality can be shaped, re-shaped, and manipulated. "Models," of course, are words or actual entities. For the very young child, literal models (planes, cars, houses, etc.) are best, though transference to more abstract models can soon be made.

Man's propensities for game-playing are well known. He is called "knowing" (*sapiens*) and "talking" (*loquens*) and "building" (*faber*) and can as well be called "playing" (*ludens*). On this point, Jan Huizinga, in *Homo Ludens,* has written: "It has not been difficult to show that a certain play-factor was extremely active all through the cultural process and that it produces many of the fundamental forms of social life." He continues:

> The spirit of playful competition is, as a social impulse, older than culture itself and pervades all life like a veritable ferment. Ritual grew up in sacred play; poetry was born in play and nourished on play; music and dancing were pure play. Wisdom and philosophy found expression in words and forms derived from religious contests. The rules of warfare, the conventions of noble living were built up on play-patterns. We have to conclude, therefore, that civilization is, in its earliest phases, played. It does not come *from* play like a babe detaching itself from the womb: it arises *in* and *as* play, and never leaves it. (P. 173.)

Game-playing is in essence no more than problem-solving. But because we have come to associate *games* with idle amusement and *problems* with matters of some seriousness and significance, we generally think of games and problems as quite unrelated. Yet in a typical game, we set up one or more obstacles which we then try to overcome. Any problem that requires a solution is precisely the same: one or more obstacles to overcome. Our pleasure in reading detective stories is based on the game elements or the problem elements, whichever way we prefer to think of it. We can and should take advantage of our instinct (if that is what it is) for games by thinking of the classroom as a kind of game room and encouraging students not only to play games but to invent them. If it seems indecorous to think of the classroom as a game room, then it can more austerely be a laboratory, a problem-and-discovery environment, or any other label that is properly pretentious. Indeed, the activities of the classroom will determine its *real* character in the minds of the students irrespective of what we may choose to call it. After all, just because we call a particular building a school doesn't mean that it will not be thought of as a jail by its inmates.

If game-playing in the classroom seems frivolous, it is only our own attitudes that make it so. Besides, there are other games than hide-and-seek and musical chairs. These are essentially physical recreations and not games in the sense we are speaking of here.

> Games are effective teaching and training devices for students of all ages and in many situations because they are highly motivating, and because they communicate very efficiently the concepts and facts of many subjects. They create dramatic representations of the real problem being studied. The players assume realistic roles, face problems, formulate strategies, make decisions, and get fast feedback on the consequences of their action. Also, with games one can evaluate the students' performances without risking the costs of having errors made in "real world" tryouts and without some of the distortions inherent in direct examination.
>
> In short, serious games offer us a rich field for risk-free, active exploration of serious intellectual and social problems. In games man can once again play the exciting and dynamic roles he always enjoyed before society became so compartmentalized. The role-playing that students undertake in games that simulate life is excellent preparation for the real roles they will play in society in later life. (Clark C. Abt, *Serious Games,* pp. 13–14.)

Although virtually any game has its educational uses, the best games are those which combine a high degree of challenge and a low degree of chance. Thus, the most elegant of games—and ones that have for centuries engaged the subtlest of minds—are chess and *Go* (a Japanese chess-like game). These and many other inexpensive and readily available games should be part of the standard equipment of the classroom and play a regular part in the daily educational program. In some schools the WFF'N'PROOF games of logic and mathematics have been introduced with great success. In a later section of this chapter, I shall deal more specifically with the use of games in the classroom, and in the Appendix I have catalogued a number of representative games and puzzles. Suffice it to say here that game-playing and model-building are by far the best means we have of enhancing in the child the motivations for learning and developing in the child the techniques for problem-solving.

THE CURRICULUM

Our curriculum mistakes have been twofold: we have underestimated the child and we have busied him at the wrong activities. (And we have done whatever we have done in a rigid and coercive environment.) Why we should have to think of *a* curriculum at all is beyond me. That it may be administratively convenient to do so isn't of the slightest consequence. We seem to have lost sight of the fact that administrators exist to serve the needs of the central function of the school. Their views and directives are valid only insofar as they contribute to the *educational* well being of the institution. It is their job to clear the way for student and teacher, like the player who sweeps a path in front of the curling stone. The administrator's clerkly compulsion for neatness can be accorded no favor in a school where education is the real, as well as the avowed, business. Hence, the traditional orderly, tightly sequenced curriculum can be dispensed with, being as it is a device useful only to administrators (and lazy teachers, of whom there are, alas, far too many). This means (if the system is to be coherent) abandonment of grade levels as well. But, as we noted earlier, there are certain realities that we must accept (at least for the present). A school that casts off the traditional type of curriculum will in due course cast off the grade-level notion.

In place of the curriculum as we commonly think of it we shall substitute a set of flexible guidelines, based not upon conventional wisdom and received ideas but upon the same principles that work so effectively in the adult world of science and scholarship. (The type of education propounded here is rigorous and demanding, but not in the traditional school sense. It can be thought of as "fun," but fun as the serious researcher has fun. "Fun" has accumulated an odium that colors our thinking. We should remember that we work only for reward or pleasure. Grades are stupid and ultimately empty rewards and there is little pleasure in the typical classroom.)

The ideal school would be a campus school embracing all grades from kindergarten (or even nursery) through at least the first year of college. An egregious example of administrative foolishness is the creation of the isolated "junior" or "intermediate" school. The only possible value of this breaking up of the elementary school is an administrative or bookkeeping one. The isolation of children during those middle childhood years is a mistake from any point of view. The mingling of the pre-adolescent with children both younger and older than he is of great value in his psychological "leavening." At any rate, it flies in the face of social reality to compartmentalize our children as we do. The "outside" world is a mélange, and there is no sensible reason why the school world should not reflect the structure of society itself. Children help each other. They teach each other. Older children assume responsibility, younger children look up to them as models. This is no utopian dream. This type of educational "mix" has proved eminently successful in, for example, Philadelphia's Parkway Program.

Our curriculum, then, will be built on certain broad *principles,* the *practices* to be left to the teacher and based upon his professional assessment of each class situation. This will likewise mean that such notions as "grade-level performance" will have either to be got rid of or radically revised. Considering the wealth of confused and confusing ideas we have about how reading should be taught, what can "reading at grade ——" really mean? It is well known, for example, that the linguistic sophistication of the child entering school (even at the kindergarten level) is far above the books that he is given to read. The reading "expert" has convinced us all that *reading is comprehension* and at the same time has provided us with books that are significantly beneath the child's level of comprehension. Reading and comprehension are, of course, two quite different and not even necessarily related matters, and after the child learns to *decode* (which is all that *reading* is—Milton's daughters could *read* Latin, Greek, and Hebrew very well; Milton, who was blind, was no longer able to read, though he could *comprehend* what his uncomprehending daughters read *to* him), he should be directed to reading materials that are at least on his level if not slightly above it.

Thus, curriculum development should be left to the teacher— perhaps in consultation with other teachers—and the teacher should be free of the "lesson-plan" nonsense that turns many teachers into liars and many others into automatons. Why an administrator should concern himself (even if only "officially") with what a particular teacher is teaching on a particular day, escapes me. Why the teacher should have to lock himself into a pattern that may prove to be all wrong for that day in that class also escapes me. But, I suppose, administrators must administer (or "administrate," as some like to say). I must say that I can think of no other *profession* the members of which allow themselves to be so trammeled (and for such trivial reasons).

READING

Reading has long been the "nuclear" subject of the early school years and has become the obsession of armies of teachers, parents, and publishers. At the same time, there has been a considerable resistance to early reading programs, some of which, like that of O. K. Moore, have been spectacularly successful. (His "talking typewriter" has produced readers at ages 2–3.) The objections to early reading are once again rooted in the nature of the system. The argument runs that since only a part of the school population (an infinitesimal part, as things now stand) will have this advantage, it will be disadvantageous to all. This is a fancied up version of "don't rock the boat" (rather like the teacher who told the parents of a child in one of the schools in my neighborhood that the child should be kept from doing outside reading because it was putting her ahead of the class!). Then there is the line which says that parents, being "non-professionals" (in teaching), will "damage" their children by "forcing" them to read early. Perhaps there is a grain of truth in this argument, but it supposes that by one's waiting and letting the teacher do it, things will work out in good order, which we know is not the case. There's damage all the way round, after all. In the absence of the highly technological and very expensive system of Professor Moore's, the parent would have to become something of an "expert" in order to achieve any appreciable success as a teacher of reading to a young child. Of course, the teacher should be something of an expert too, but rarely is, or at least his "expertise" is based upon whatever reading program the school has been talked into adopting. The "reading specialist" is not much better off, though he does have in many schools a "reading laboratory" to which the purportedly poor readers are remanded for "remedial work" with a variety of impressive-looking contraptions, the value of which has yet to be proven. He likewise commands a vocabulary of double-talk that hides a paucity of content. The sham of the school reading enterprise is clearly displayed in Jeanne Chall's *Learning to Read* (though it was not, I expect, her intention to "blow the whistle").

If we grant that reading is a top-priority item (in the current education *cum* business jargon)—I am not convinced that it is—then there is not a single reason why it should not be taught in kindergarten (or in nursery school for that matter). We have made too much of the supposed difficulty of reading and have got it mixed up with other matters that are fundamentally unrelated to it. *Reading*, as we said, is *decoding*, that is, it is the translation of a graphic symbol into a phonetic value (whether spoken aloud or merely "understood"). Put another way, it is the return of an utterance to its linguistic prime (*viz.*, speech). As soon as someone can say what he sees, he can read. Whether or not he "understands" what he reads is irrelevant at the *decoding* level. The layman faced with a page or two of Kant or Carnap will have no trouble *reading*, though he will have considerable trouble comprehending. Indeed, without special study, he will comprehend virtually nothing. (Remember Milton's daughters. We can be grateful for their ability to read.)

Our aim, then, should be to teach the code as quickly and efficiently as possible and not worry with the notion of comprehension at all. Indeed, the first "words" should be of the child's own contriving (and his pleasure at neology should be encouraged all the way through school). Children love funny and grotesque words and the matching of symbol and sound can be an exciting activity in its own right. At any event, the meaning level of the typical primer is so vapid as to convince most children that "reading isn't so much" (to quote a six-year-old first-grader).

LEARNING THE CODE

Despite the fact that English spelling fits the spoken word rather badly, it is teachable and need not be preceded by the I.T.A. (Initial Teaching Alphabet), though the I.T.A. system does have its partisans and its advantages. George Riemer, a vigorous proponent of the I.T.A. and a vigorous critic of all the currently fashionable reading/writing programs, writes

> There is evidence that the basal-reader system means the basal rot of communication development, yet when school starts this September three and a half million first graders will once again be greeted at the door by Dick & Jane and Jimmy & Sue and all their dogs. Year after year these tint-faced baby-word frauds continue to cheat the United States out of several million writers—your own children among them.
>
> If i.t.a. can give us our first clean chance to teach communication properly, why don't the schools dump Dick & Jane and adopt i.t.a. as the start of a writing oriented curriculum? Or, forgetting i.t.a., why don't schools make an honest move to teach the basal habits of clear, articulate communication?
>
> It's not easy and may well be impossible. Dick & Jane are backed by a rich, squat, and slothful Reading Establishment that's had half a century to settle down tight. The Reading Establishment consists of reading experts, curriculum developers, school principals and superintendents, teachers, school psychologists, librarians, school-board members, education-research organizations, education writers, publishers, and education foundations who collectively believe that the three R's of education are reading, reading, and reading: E = R.
>
> The Reading Establishment has treated *reading* to lush expense account lunches but let *writing* eat out of brown paper bags. It has piddled away the meaning of writing instruction until it now means little more than "correct spelling" or "handwriting." (*How They Murdered the Second "R"*, p. 313.)

For those who may be interested in the I.T.A. system, Riemer's book is a lively introduction. And if I don't agree with Riemer on the necessity of the I.T.A. approach, I do assuredly agree with him in every particular of his denunciation of the "Reading Establishment."

We should appreciate that there is nothing intrinsically difficult or mysterious about a coding system. Children very early in their lives have learned to associate arbitrary markers with various aspects of the experiential world. Any English-speaking child knows that the word *chair* (arbitrary marker) "stands for" something in the nonlinguistic world, namely, any actual chair. Further, it is a rare child indeed who has not learned to associate the printed name of any one of a number of popular products (as advertised on TV) with the sound of that name. It is not at all unusual for a child of eighteen months to call off the names of a dozen or more products in the market, names that he has read from the labels. There is nothing very new or surprising in this. To be sure, it is this ability that led to the "see-and-say" approach to reading that was the prevailing orthodoxy for a number of years prior to Rudolf Flesch's attacks in the fifties. (*Why Johnny Can't Read*, etc.). There is of course nothing wrong with learning words on a "see-and-say" basis. What would be the point of learning to read *the, and,* and most of the rest of the small function words orthographically, when they are, so to speak, morphographs, that is, two- and three-grapheme ("letter") units that are never analyzed. *The* is *the* and is not "part" of, say, *breathe*. On the other hand, the bulk of our reading vocabulary is of a different order, and nothing prepares a child so well for reading as mastery of the sound-symbol coding system.

To familiarize the child with the names of the letters of the alphabet, the teacher should devise a game that tells something about the name and sounds of each letter. If allowed, the class will quickly devise its own letter games. In lieu of formal text materials, magazines and newspapers will provide all that the class will need. One homework assignment can be to ask each child to bring in as many different kinds of one or more letters as he can find and to draw a few new letter designs of his own. The phonotactical-graphotactical habits of English can be established by first asking the class to identify the sounds that are heard in various words and then assigning each student a letter-sound and seeing how many words (actual or "English sounding," *e.g.,* S-N-E-R-G) they can make by forming a kind of living crossword puzzle. Each child can take a turn at being "director." Each word formed should be written on the board and examined later for sound, spelling, and possibility of expansion. The children who wish can try to make up a story with the words, or make more words that sound similar, or scramble the words to make new ones. The principle here is discovery through play; the goal, so far as the children are concerned, is simply to have fun with sounds and letters. A tape recorder and a typewriter can be useful here. Children should not be directed to use them but encouraged to figure out what uses they might make of them in connection with the sound-and-letter play.

Since reading is more passive than active (*i.e.*, productive in the sense of producing something tangible), the child should be writing immediately, and he should be encouraged to "play" with the letters visually. Reproductions of medieval illuminated alphabets as well as printers' type-face samples should be on display and the children should try their hands at both illumination and type-face design. (But no literal copying.) Low, freestanding chalkboards should be available for letter and word experimentation. The classroom will be relatively noisy, a fact which the teacher should accept as evidence that something worthwhile is happening.

The idea of sound-symbol relationship can be easily conveyed by the following "equations":

is a picture of?
(an object: chair)

"chair"
(spoken word)

is a "picture" of?
(an object: chair)

c h a i r
(written word)

is a picture of?
(a word: "chair")

(picture)   "chair" (spoken word)

(actual object)   c h a i r (written word)

K (written symbol) is a picture of? ("k" sound)

The teacher may want to work from a table of sound-symbol correlations, but the child should be urged to discover the correspondences on his own. One thing that will be discovered is that English has far more than the five vowels that the child is often misled into believing comprise the English vowel system. The "five vowels" are simply alphabetic symbols which by themselves and in combination with the two semi-vowels (w and y) are made to represent a considerable number of vowel sounds. The question, incidentally, of why and how we distinguish "vowels" and "consonants" is an interesting one. A good deal can be learned about how we make speech sounds if the teacher opens this line of discussion. The (tentative) answers can be easily derived from close examination of speech. No child is really satisfied to be told, "That's just the way it is."

In the typical "phonics" workbook, the child is asked to distinguish between "long" and "short" vowels. In English phonology this is a meaningless distinction, for we do not make phonemic contrasts on the basis of "length" (*i.e.*, duration), though, for example, Latin does. Thus: *mēto*, to measure; *meto*, to mow or reap. In the first instance, the pronunciation of the medial vowel (marked with a macron) is twice as long as the pronunciation of the medial vowel in the second. Duration or length, then, is distinctive in Latin. Doubling the time it takes to say a vowel in an English word does not result in "another" word, a word, that is, with a different meaning, but merely in an "odd" pronunciation of the same word. "Length" in English textbook parlance is a confusing term attached to a variety of vowel qualities, though *length* (properly speaking) isn't one of them. Consider, for example, these *sounds* of the *letter a:* father (phoneme /a/), skate (phonemes /ey/), cat (/æ/), sofa (/ə/), hall (/ɔ/). The *a*'s in *father* and *cat* are called "short" and the *a* in *skate* is called "long." Why? The so-called long *a* is, in fact, a diphthong (as shown by the transcription, /ey/) and is, despite its being an amalgam of two vowels, no "longer" than the *a* of *father*. Furthermore, the two "short *a*'s" are quite unlike each other. (Then there are those other *a*'s.) What is a child to make of "long" and "short"? (To compound the confusion, note what happens to the length of the *same* vowel in these pairs: *bat/bad; sack/sag; cap/cab,* etc.)

The textbook, in an effort at some kind of terminological consistency (at the expense of linguistic sense), sets the child to work looking for things like "long" and "short *y*'s." In a typical exercise, the child is given a list of words like *by, shy, happy,* and *maybe* and asked to circle first the "long *y*'s," which means, presumably, the final vowels of *by* and *shy;* and then the "short *y*'s," which means the final vowel of words like *happy.* (Note that in transcription the "short *y*" is /iy/ and the "long *y*" is /ay/, both diphthongs, both of equal.length.) If the child circles the final vowel of *maybe,* he is wrong despite the fact that the final vowel *sound* of *maybe* is precisely the same as the final vowel *sound* of *happy* (*viz.,* /iy/). On the other hand, if *pronunciation* is not at issue, then what can "long" and "short" be meant to apply to? The final *letter* (*y*) of both "long" and "short" vowel words, the "correct" ones, is the same in both cases —there is nothing graphemically to mark the appearance of the "long" as over against the "short" *y.* Yet when the teacher is pursued on the matter (as well he should be), he answers that the two *y*'s are *pronounced* differently. Who can make sense of a "system" that shifts its ground this way? Spelling is spelling and pronunciation is pronunciation. This seems a simple and reasonable enough principle, but only in the I.T.A. and strict linguistics reading programs is it clearly established.

In a matter of a few weeks of intensive (yet pleasant) work, the child will master the essentials of the coding system. After all, there are only a relatively few sounds and symbols, and once the principle is understood, it is no intellectually demanding task to make all the basic connections. But the approach has to be free and easy and the game strategy is essential. As soon as possible, the children should be encouraged to produce their own books, which may be no more than a single page of writing put between construction-paper covers, titled, and added to the class library for others to read. At first, the stories may be dictated to the tape recorder for later transcription or for playback and sharing with the group. (On no account should the teacher meddle in what the children are composing. And if he is asked for guidance or ideas, he should offer the very least that will produce results. Redirecting student questions is usually the most pedagogically successful technique.) Children may wish to illustrate their own and each other's stories and should be encouraged to do so. There is no reason why learning to read, write, and visualize cannot go on simultaneously. I believe that it is much the best way to work. It has been convincingly argued that *writing* should *precede* reading, and it is perfectly feasible to develop a program around this idea. I don't think, however, that priority is all that important. The teacher has merely to appreciate precisely what *reading* is and what motivates people to do things.

While the emphasis should be on the verbal production of the child (whether orally or on paper), good (repeat, good) children's books should be used. These are not the pap of the "basal reading series" but those children's stories that respect the children (*e.g.*, the Pooh books, E. B. White, Robert McCloskey, de St. Exupéry, the Babar books, and so on). A way to enhance the class library is to ask each child to contribute on a term-loan basis one or more of his own books. And a great deal can be done with magazines and newspapers. The children should be asked to hunt up new, interesting (*i.e.*, funny) words for the class dictionary, a class project. Children should also make their own personal dictionaries, and a great deal of fun can be had in trying to define words and phrases.

In short, the teacher can easily "break the code" with the class in the first few weeks of school. Many of the so-called reading problems will never arise in a school which approaches reading this way. For the most part, problem readers are really having problems in *comprehension,* which are problems in *thinking;* that is, in seeing relationships, classifying experience, sequencing, making logical discriminations, and so on. The most common cause (other than genuine intellectual disability) of this kind of failure is, at any given stage, some failure in cognition, which will generally resolve itself in due course. (This is the reason that much of the "improvement" claimed by the reading specialists is falsely claimed— the student would have got there anyway, at about the same time, perhaps even sooner.) To isolate a child as a "reading problem" and pack him off to a "reading laboratory" is a sure way to build in him a sense of failure. He should be left in his own classroom and allowed to work at whatever challenges him. We need to get over the belief that everyone must be doing the same thing at the same time. Each of us develops differently. The "reading problem" may very well be extraordinarily good at, say, art. He will come along in other areas by and by. Let me repeat that if one can produce from the printed text the speech that the printed text is meant to represent, one can read. What one can comprehend is another matter altogether. Learning to *comprehend* is a lifetime task, learning to *read* can be done in a few weeks.

SCHOOL AND SCHOOLROOM

Because the school is so much a part of our culture, we take its existence for granted. For the young child, however, the school is very much of a new thing, and much is to be gained educationally if we spend some time with the child exploring school as both object and idea. Questions like those following should be posed, and the child should be encouraged to ask and answer as many others as he can contrive to do. A good deal of this kind of exploration can be done on the move, as the class swarms about the school in pursuit of "schoolness."

Exploring School and Schoolroom

1. What is a school? How do you know? Where did you find out? Make a list of things that mean "school" to you.
2. What is supposed to happen in school? Does any of this happen outside of school? What?
3. Make a list of things that happen in school that interest you. Why do these interest you?
4. Try to describe the school building, inside and out. What's a good way to describe something? Make believe you are describing it for someone who has never seen it.
5. Is the building similar to where you live? How? Different? How? What special things does the school have that your house doesn't?
6. What is a classroom? What goes on in a classroom? Describe your classroom. What are the important things in your classroom? Why are these important? Does your classroom make you feel good? How does it make you feel? Why do you think it makes you feel that way?
7. How big is your classroom? How can you find out without asking someone? Does it matter how big it is? Why?
8. What do you think should be in your classroom? Why? Is there anything important missing from it? What? Why is this important?
9. What do you do with the various things in the classroom? Which things are alike but not the same? In what ways are they alike? Why are these alike things called by different names? How are they different from each other? Are, for example, windows and doors alike yet different? How?
10. What is a teacher? Describe a teacher. How is a teacher different from a parent? How is a teacher similar to a parent?

How does someone get to be a teacher? If you don't know, how can you find out?

11. What is teaching? How do you know? Give some examples of teaching. Explain how you would teach somebody a game that you know and that he doesn't.

12. What is learning? How do you know? Give some examples of learning. Can you learn without a teacher? What have you learned by yourself? Can you learn without going to school? Why go to school?

13. What is a book? Describe the different kinds of books you can find in the classroom. Would you like to make your own books? How would you do it? What would you write about?

14. What are the names of the other children in your class? Describe each child. What kinds of things would you like to do with the children in your class?

15. If you could change your classroom in any way, what would you change? Why?

Among other things, the child's conjuring with these questions will give him the confidence that comes with the verbal control of a situation that is the consequent of verbal expression. Talking about things humanizes them and reduces them to size, so to speak. The child has not only the right but the need to "lay hands" on this new and strange environment. The questions are designed to help him do it. Furthermore, the implications of the questions will provide the imaginative teacher with a vast amount of material to work with. Question 13, for example, leads into reading, writing, the idea of a library, the riches of the written word, and much more. The questions on teaching and learning will be usefully illuminating for the teacher as well as the student. We teachers are, I think, rather out of touch with the child's view of the world and can stand to learn a great deal by listening to what the child has to say to us. There is, in any case, no reason why the child should not be in on the workings of the educational process as well as being its recipient. Our reliance on textbook programs is a *de facto* assertion that we think all children are pretty much alike and should be responding in pretty much the same way to the same material. Their diverse and often wholly unexpected answers to the questions will disabuse us and, at the same time, give us a sound basis upon which

to plan our educational programs as we go: the curriculum
ess instead of the curriculum in being.

THE LOGIC OF LEARNING
AND LEARNING LOGIC

If the teacher ever has doubts about what he is doing in the classroom, he rarely expresses those doubts publicly, least of all to his
students. I would imagine, too, that such doubts as he does have are
largely concerned with the methodology and gadgetry of teaching
and not with the substance of what is being taught. He pushes
ahead with his program of "language arts," "arithmetic" (maybe
"mathematics"), "science," and so on, according to the gospel of
curriculum and textbook, and is reasonably content with himself,
at least on that score. But subject-matter boundaries are increasingly
hard to find, and the old divisions of knowledge make less and less
sense. Furthermore, to be productive, knowledge must arise from
the ground of systematic thought—logic, in the broadest sense of
the term. The operations of thought make possible any subject matter. The study of mathematics, for example, without a grasp of class,
rank, discreteness and relationship, sequence, and process is gib-
berish. Indeed, any subject is. The true subject matter of education
is, as we have said, thinking.

Properly handled, virtually any activity will yield educational
riches. But any activity which becomes mere routine is retrograde to
the aims of education. I find little to commend the tedium of handwriting (printing or writing, it matters not) practice. It is an intellectually barren activity and can be done only to win the teacher's
approval. Approval for what? At least the practice of dance or musical instrument produces immediate pleasures unrelated to teacher
approval. What possible inner recompense can there be in forcing
oneself to print the alphabet according to the style the teacher dictates? In music there are models of performance that are intrinsic to
an entire civilization. Nothing, on the other hand, is so personal and
idiosyncratic as handwriting. The sterile forms of the textbook
(which become the teacher's models) are related to nothing. If neatness and legibility are the issue, then we can do no better than use
a typewriter. Indeed, far too little use is being made of this fascinat-

ing (for children) machine. The hand-labored page of no first-grader will afford him the pleasure of a page of his own typescript. The writing will come in its time. When the child has developed that aspect of self that concerns itself with such things, he will both improve and individualize his writing as his ambition dictates. But, alas, we sweat over an empty issue; we do not improve the hour, we deaden it.

Learning Logic

Perhaps the prime logical process is *classification:* seeing similarities and differences among the realia that surround us. The realia themselves are largely distinguished for us operationally by the culture into which we are born, the culture being represented in this process by its language. Hence, certain identities are made for us by the labeling process. But at some point early in life, the cognitive mechanism grows sufficiently independent of maternal deixis to do its own identifying and classifying. Of course, the language tends to override the individual, and whatever identifications he may make that are outside the cognizance of the language will quickly fade. I suspect that those "vague yearnings" (or whatever they are) that all of us are prey to from time to time are states of mind and being that are not "officially" recognized by the "language/culture complex" and hence without a "local habitation and a name." (Shakespeare clearly perceived the poet's function in finding those "places.") Be that as it may, the child soon is able to mark off a number of literally different items as all belonging to the class, "toy," or "chair," or "car," and so on. (He may, as all parents painfully know, classify under "toy" something like the stove or the iron and may require a trauma to declassify it so.) Thus classification (with its components, *discrimination* and *integration,* operations in *logic*) is basic and essentially automatic—up to a point. One great contribution of formal education to the intellectual growth of the child should be its direction of the child to greater and greater precision in classification and to an increasing range of applications of the process.

Many of the questions about school and classroom that I suggested as a useful beginning to formal education are at heart classificatory and can serve nicely as jumping off points for a more direct handling of classification. A particularly productive project wholly concerned with classification is that of providing the class, or individual students, with a pile of odds and ends (scraps of paper, cloth, plastic, metal, etc.; bits of string, yarn, etc.; buttons, paper clips, washers, etc.; and whatever additional pieces of junk that can be easily got and safely handled) that must be "organized." If any of the students need any prompting, the teacher need only tell them to put like things together. Of course, a number of bases for classification can and very likely will be discovered. After the first set of classifications is made, the teacher should ask questions like these:

1. Why did you put the items together that you did?
2. Is there another way of doing it?
3. Can you make more piles or fewer piles that would "make sense"?
4. What other things around you are similar to each other? How are they similar? How are they different?
5. Are tables and chairs similar? How? Different? How?
6. Are the floor and ceiling similar? How? Different? How?
7. Are buildings and boxes similar? How? Different? How?
8. Are writing and talking similar? How? Different? How?
9. Are dogs and cats similar? How? Different? How?
10. Are birds and airplanes similar? How? Different? How?
11. Are trees and people similar? How? Different? How?
12. Are eyes and noses similar? How? Different? How?
13. Are the sun and moon similar? How? Different? How?
14. What is television similar to? How?
15. What is a pencil similar to? How?
16. What are clouds similar to? How?
17. What are lamps similar to? How?
18. What is a lollipop similar to? How?
19. How are children and grownups similar? Different?
20. What is a book similar to? How?

And so on. There are no "right" answers, strictly speaking, but there may be answers that are "wrong" because they fail to make a convincing case for similarity (or difference). When the student has a grasp of the conceptual basis of comparison and contrast, similarity and difference, the operations can be made more subtle and the discrimination more precise. The student might be asked to distinguish musical tones, timbres, hues, textures and at the same time classify similar or "closely related" phenomena together or on a continuum. More demanding yet is seeing the "likeness" between a plane figure and its folded three-dimensional transformation. This last is a commonly used item in intelligence tests, but there is no reason why it should not be a part of the basic learning curriculum. If the figures are manipulatable (e.g., construction-paper cutouts) instead of mere drawings, even the kindergarten-level child will find the activity engaging and well within his capability. A way to get into the project is simply to give the unfolded patterns to the student for his experimentation. From this type of learning, it is but a short step to topology and rubber-sheet geometry, not, of course, as self-consciously taught "subjects," but as insights into reality.

By classifying, we establish points of connection between realia. At the interfaces of these connections logic is at work, for it is the mind that does the connecting. Closely related to the principle of jointure is the principle of seriation, whereby we identify the concept of seriation by the making of the series; that is, by becoming aware that certain realia have a series potential. The homely activity of bead-stringing is a good place to begin. If the idea of design is introduced (three red, one yellow, three red, etc.) series becomes sequence. Once the student has caught the principle, he is ready to take on less-well-defined series and sequences. These questions and problems will point the way:

1. Describe this design [e.g., gift-wrapping paper].
2. How does it differ from this picture [e.g., any more-or-less realistic drawing such as might be found in a child's story book]?
3. Make some gift-wrapping paper of your own, using your own design.
4. Here are some blocks [same size, different colors]; arrange them in a design. Make another design and explain the differences between the two.
5. Here are some blocks [each slightly larger than the other]; arrange them in some kind of order. Now arrange them in a different order and explain the difference. Can you explain the idea of "order"? What does your mother mean when she tells you to put your things "in order"?
6. Here are some blocks. Build a house or a tower with them.

Which part of the building will you build first? Why? What happens if you pull a block or two out of the bottom of your building? Why?

7. How are the blocks related to each other? How high can you build a tower of blocks? When do they fall over (even if you don't push them)? Why? Can you prevent them from falling over? Is there a relationship between the size of the base or "foundation" and the height of the tower? Try to figure this out.

8. When you get dressed, why don't you put your snowpants on first?

9. What games do you like to play? Describe how you play one of them. Can you make up a new game? How would you do it?

10. [The teacher should say several sentences backward. "Saying am I what understand you can."] Did you understand what I just said? What caused the trouble? [The teacher should now say some words backward: doog, rood, evol, etc.] Did you understand these words Why not?

11. Try to make up as many sets, series, and sequences as you can just from things that are in the classroom. What kinds of sets, series, and sequences are commonly found in the world around you?

When two or more discrete items are brought together into a set, series, or sequence, the *set, series,* or *sequence* is a new thing, a whole greater than the sum of its parts. When 1 and 1 are added, the result is 2, or $1 + 1$ or $2 + 0$; that is, the addition results in nothing but the sum of its parts. This important difference in thinking about realia should be explored:

1. Here is a puzzle. When the pieces are put together, what do you have that is different from the pieces themselves?

2. What other things can you bring together to make a new thing? Describe the new thing and compare it with the individual things that it's made of. Can you explain what happened? What is it that makes possible putting things together?

3. Here are some words. Can you put them together to "make sense"? What is the difference between the words and the sense you made of them when you put them together?

4. Here are some letters. Can you put them together to "make sense"? What is the difference between the letters and what you made with them? A letter that is in a word is no longer just a letter—can you explain what happens to it?

5. What is a [any object] made of? How is it different from what it is made of?

The idea of "making sense" must of course be examined in detail, and the student should be asked to explain what "making sense" means, how he knows that something "makes sense," and how he "makes sense" of anything he does.

The final awareness in the process of comprehension is that of causality. To grasp the concept of the chain of relationships is to be able to think in the full sense of the word. Many of the preceding questions are only obliquely directed at the discovery of causality. Those which follow meet the issue frontally (though not self-consciously, which is to say, there is no need to tell the student precisely what underlying logical process he is likely to discover):

1. [The teacher should read the fable of the rooster who thought that it was his crowing that caused the sun to rise each morning. But the "punch line," when, that is, the rooster learns the truth, should not be read.] What do you think of the rooster? Does the rooster's crowing make the sun come up? What do *you* think makes the sun come up? [The teacher can now read the end of the story.] What was wrong with the rooster's thinking? How did he ever get the idea that his crowing made the sun come up?

2. Can you make the sun come up? What kinds of things can you make happen? [The teacher will have to carefully distinguish between genuine causality and apparent causality—and lead the student to the same awareness via questioning *only*. Telling outright is, of course, counter to the spirit of this type of education.]

3. [The teacher lights a candle and asks someone to blow it out.] Who made the candle go out? How? Maybe it was just an accident. [Repeats experiment.] Can you make up a rule about what just happened?

4. [The teacher turns on a flashlight and "blows it out."] Did I "blow out" the light? How do you know? Isn't a flashlight the

same as a candle? How are they different? [Passes around flashlight for students to turn on and off.] Can you make up a rule for the flashlight? What about the classroom lights? Can they be blown out? Why not? A candle, a flashlight, and an electric light are all alike in what way? And are all different in what way? Are the candle and flashlight alike in any way that makes them different from the electric light? What about the flashlight and electric light in contrast to the candle?

5. Suppose you drop an egg and it breaks—did *you* break the egg? Suppose you squeeze an egg and it breaks—did *you* break the egg? But aren't dropping an egg and squeezing an egg different, even though the egg gets broken in both cases? What is the difference? [Chain of causality.]

6. If you let a ball go at the top of the hill, it will roll down. But if you let it go at the bottom, it will just sit there. How come? Furthermore, if you roll it up the hill, it will come down all by itself. Who's making what happen?

7. Explain how one of your toys works. What makes what happen, and in what order does it happen? Let's see if we can figure out how these work? [A few pulleys, levers, etc., will do nicely. These simple machines should be made by the students right in the class. I would urge that no equipment that can be made should be bought.]

9. [The "Rube Goldberg Invention" is causality at its most playful and entertaining. The teacher should suggest a simple "Rube Goldberg Invention" and let the class take it from there. The causality of each additional step should be explained by the students.]

10. How can you find out what causes what? Make a list of things that you'd like to find out about. Is it always necessary to ask someone? What if nobody you ask knows the answer anyway?

Whatever particular line of questioning the teacher may wish to pursue at any particular moment, the student should be encouraged to pursue his own lines of questioning continuously. And wherever it is feasible, he should be involved in some kind of manipulative (preferably productive) activity. As was suggested earlier, model-building can start with more-or-less traditional kinds of models (cars, planes, etc.), but the *rationale* of model building must be derived from what is being done. Thus:

1. What are you doing when you build a model?
2. How is the model different from and similar to the thing it is a model of?
3. What *must* be left out of a model? Why? What *may* be left out? Why? What must be included in order to make it a "good" model? Why?
4. What can you do with models that you can't do with the original "real" things? Explain.
5. If you wanted to make a model of your house or of your classroom or of your school, how would you do it?
6. If you wanted to make a model of a friend of yours or of the teacher or of your parents, how would you do it?
7. Suppose you wanted to get an idea of what it is like to be a fish or a bird, how would you do it?
8. What ideas do you have about people like the astronauts or policemen or the President of the United States? How can you figure out what it is like to be any of these people?
9. What do you have to know before you can actually build a model? Suppose that you want to build a model of a car for which there is no kit. How would you do it? What about a car that people from, say, Venus might have (assume that there really are people on Venus, but that they might not be like Earth people, just as Venus is not like Earth). Do you have a kind of model in your head (mind) before you actually build the model? Explain that model in your mind.
10. Make a list of models that you'd like to build. What besides cars, planes, ships, and rockets would make interesting models? Why?

As the student progresses, he can be challenged with problems demanding more complex manipulations of logic. It is here that the various intellectual board games and games of logic can be introduced. And once these games have been introduced, they should be kept in constant use. If the class is so inclined, they can be formed into teams for tournament play, but the focus should be on the games and not on the competition. All the tactics and strategies of the board games should be discussed, and all the implications of the games of logic should be explored. The WFF'N'PROOF games lead neatly into a variety of mathematical concepts, which should of course be examined in conjunction with the games. Among the challenges that can be put to the student are those of making interesting modifications in the rules and contriving new games different from though similar to existing games. Game design itself is a stimulating area of exploration:

1. What makes a game "good"? What do you mean by such terms as "fun" and "interesting"?
2. Can you make up a new game that can be played on a chess board? What do you have to think about to make up a game?
3. What makes a game "difficult" or "easy"? Why is playing an easy game less fun than playing a difficult game?
4. What is "chance"? What games make use of chance? What games make little or no use of chance? Is a game of chance more fun than a game that makes little or no use of chance? Explain.
5. Can you make up a card game that doesn't depend upon chance? Explain your thinking.

(See Appendix for an annotated bibliography of effective and engaging games.)

> The central idea of teaching with games, both in and out of the classroom, is to use the time spent in the classroom or doing homework to create a laboratory environment—an environment in which experiments can be made, hypotheses formulated, and new and better experiments planned. Games help to create this laboratory feeling by providing objectives and procedures. They also encourage imaginative freedom to experiment with alternative solutions, while at the same time offering a realistic set of constraints on less practical responses to problems. The students can learn not only by observing the results of the games, but also by playing and indeed by designing them. (Clark C. Abt, *Serious Games*, p. 28.)

Because the grasp of logical operations is the *sine qua non* of proper education, some part of every school day should be given over to the kind of work suggested here. Thus the teacher will be preparing the student for rational inquiry into any area of study. The student whose education is predicated upon an understanding of class, relationship, sequence, causality, and so on, will be capable of defining problems and developing reasonable methods of solving those problems. He will be privy to the process of learning itself and not merely the receptor of the end products of learning.

NUMBERS

Since mathematics is a form of logic—or since logical and mathematical manipulations require the same intellectual processes—numbers, numbering, and number theory will fit comfortably into the program I have been outlining. Again, no textbooks are necessary or even desirable, but a ditto machine is basic. I would urge, too, that a small electronic calculator be available for student use. (The electronic calculators are silent and jam-proof, but they are more expensive than the mechanical devices.) Happily, educational theorists in mathematics have long since got away from the sterilities of traditional arithmetic, and "modern math" is almost universally taught. Unhappily, the text-workbooks commonly used are for the most part pedagogically traditional and rather dull. There is no need, for example, to introduce the four arithmetical operations sequentially. They are all understood better if they are introduced at once and used to illustrate each other. Indeed, subtraction, multiplication, and division are all forms of addition and can be shown to be such as soon as the student is ready for the concept of addition.

Learning about Numbers

Like the language function, the number function seems to be built in (even crows can count)—Professor Skinner notwithstanding. Hence, long before the child comes to school he has a sense of number and probably no later than age five has learned to count to ten (or more). Since numerals are no different perceptually than letters of the alphabet, it is no great task to teach the child to associate the names ("one," "two," "three," etc.) with the numerals (1, 2, 3, etc.), and at the same time to associate both name and numeral with number concept by actual counting. The pebble board, abacus, or any other simple device can be used to reinforce the principle. It would be especially valuable for the student were he to "invent" his own counting devices. And he should be encouraged to play with the calculator. (In the course of fooling around with the machine, he will probably stumble on something like 7 divided by 33, which produces this dramatic display of numbers: .212121212; there is something "magical" in this, even for an adult, and it will assuredly pique the child's curiosity about numbers.)

It is important to appreciate, however, that mathematics is a tool and that the child will most willingly learn its use when he has a use for it. Hence, the child can be led to discover what he can do with numbers or why he *needs* numbers to do certain things. Since, in fact, the child meets few occasions when he really does need numbers, an artificial need can be stimulated through mathematical games and puzzles, as we have already suggested. And, of course, the fun of just playing with numbers both creates and satisfies a need. If the teacher but multiply the .212121212 by 33 (on the calculator), the unexpected result will open up a great deal of discussion and suddenly a kind of disinterested intellectual activity has been created. Once the student has been "hooked" thus on numbers, he will require no external "motivations." Since a vast quantity of very fine material is readily available, it would be redundant for me to offer any detailed mathematical materials here. In the Appendix on games and in the Bibliography, I have listed and commented on a few items that the teacher should find very helpful in his mathematics program.

Suffice it to say, that through the proper application of set theory (the linch-pin of "modern math"), the student will quickly grasp the four basic operations (these simultaneously), fractions, decimals, and algebraic relationships. Furthermore, he will understand the operations through perception of their inner workings, which would not be the case were he to learn them (as he has in the past) through rote. (The average high-school graduate of, say, a generation ago was unaware that such a concept as "number theory" even existed.) The interrelationship and continuity of learning is effectively demonstrated as the student tries out his insights in the mathematical games he will be playing. Further, as soon as the rudiments of number theory are grasped, the student can be set to discovering probability via the classical experiment of statistics, the casting of dice. Probabilities can be worked out for individuals and for the class as a whole, and they can be used predictively and be refined. Once the student has the idea, he will think of other probabilities to play with (and the uses of these probabilities) and will have learned yet another way of coping with and controlling reality. Just doing workbook exercises in arithmetic ("modern" or otherwise) is meaningless, and to offer grades as the inducement for doing meaningless activities merely underlines the bankruptcy of this type of "education."

LANGUAGE

Language (I have insisted) being the heart of the matter, I devoted an entire chapter to it both as a subject of study and a phenomenon of human existence. That extensive (though in fact limited and superficial) treatment is warranted in such a book as this because the teacher who is ignorant of at least that much of what we know of language is incompetent to teach, certification notwithstanding. The term "language arts," in wide use today, is misleading, for language is pervasive in a way that nothing else is. Mathematics, science, literature, all these and more are rooted in the language function and are realized through language. Hence, *any* use of language is a "language art."' The term, "language arts," is, of course, educational jargon for "English," or reading, writing, and speaking. The teacher who appreciates the real nature of language will avoid making specious distinctions among the so-called language arts themselves and between the "language arts" and the other other areas of education.

Using Language

If the "instant" reading program I offered earlier seems inadequate for what has been made the Big Issue of education in the early years, that is because we have for too long been sold a bill of (shoddy) goods by the "experts" and the publishers. The revenue and prestige (such as it is) that are involved make it highly unlikely furthermore that there will be any great enthusiasm for junking the current elaborate programs in reading.

With regard to the reading specialist, let me say that if a child has a genuine reading (*i.e.,* decoding) problem, either his teacher doesn't know how to teach, or he needs the services of an ophthalmologist and/or a psychologist, neither of which a reading specialist is. (Many of these "specialists" are "language arts" teachers who have been dragooned for the school's "remedial reading" program.) If he has a comprehension problem, then he needs a teacher who can take him through the logic program I have outlined, but then every student needs that. Most of the gadgetry native to the "reading laboratory" is concerned with (despite any contrary claims) some aspect of speed reading. Tachistoscopes, reading machines, and the like are used to increase the efficiency (*i.e.*, rate) of "grapheme grabbing." But slow reading isn't really a *reading* problem, it is a problem in intellectual (in)efficiency and can probably be better handled in the classroom (instead of in a kind of "isolation ward"). Actually, if reading were taught properly in the first place, this type of disability would in all likelihood not arise at all, except perhaps in those children who are genetically or organically incapable of rapid decoding.

Once the decoding (and the concomitant coding) is learned, the stress in languaging should be on production; that is, on speaking and writing. While it is a truism that the avid readers are often the best writers in, say, a college freshman English class, one can persuasively argue that those who write soonest and most will be both the best readers *and* the best writers. I would in fact urge that reading, at least in the early years, should *never* be treated separately from writing. The best books to begin with are the books that the children themselves write, even if the "writing" at the outset is done via the tape recorder (and the teacher's transcription therefrom). We must remember that writing is first of all *composition*—that is, the composing or constructing of something. Writing it down or speaking it into a tape recorder is only secondary to the creative act itself. There is nothing creative about the mechanics of making arbitrary marks with the fist or punching keys on a typewriter. The shaping, constructing, composing goes on inside and is "valid" whether it is memorialized in print or not.

But since literacy is useful, we can help the child to move the created thing from inside to outside, though we need not feel that writing it down is inherently "better" than speaking it. Nevertheless, the child will enjoy making his own "books," and they will be the best primers for the class because they represent what is in fact on the minds of the children. If anyone doubts that children are better writers than the "experts" who write the pap for the class readers, he need only read something like *Children's Letters to God*. Which, of course, reminds us that children can, in the absence of something to say, be prompted to write to and about all kinds of people and things. And if God is too touchy a subject, then the president, the governor, Winnie-the-Pooh, or anybody else who strikes their fancy. This can be made a regular daily activity if it seems to be working particularly well in a given class. Children like routines so long as the routines have some meaning for them.

Le style c'est l'homme. So we are told, but one wonders when one comes up against the sterility of college freshman (or college senior or graduate student or . . .) writing. Are all these people the same? Are they the dull, graceless souls that their writing makes them out to be? Why are they so insensitive to the feel of language? Two quite obvious reasons: they are not made aware of the idea of style, and the models of writing that are provided by their various textbooks, to say nothing of their class readers, are stylistically execrable. Here are some questions that can start the child on the road to the discovery of style in language as early as kindergarten:

1. How many different ways can you describe falling rain? Start with "It is raining" and go on from there. Which ways do you like best? Why? Could you use the different ways of saying "It is raining" for different purposes? Give some examples.

2. Here is a flower. What can you say about it? Here is a different flower. Would you say the same things about both flowers? Explain.

3. Here are two little poems about flowers. [The teacher should use genuine poetry *not* textbook versification.] Which one do you like better? Why? Try making your own poem about flowers. [The children's poems and their own illustrations can be bound into a book. This can, of course, be done on a wide range of subjects, but flowers are a good place to begin.]

4. What are your favorite words? Why do you like them particularly? Here is a poem with lots of funny words. [Teacher reads the "Jabberwocky Song."] What is the poem about? Did you like it? Explain. Try making up your own poem with funny

words. Notice though that not all of the words in the *Jabber-wocky Song* are funny. [Teacher reads it again.] Which ones are not? Let's see what happens when we substitute funny words for the ones that we recognize. Now can you tell what the poem is about? Why not?

5. What kinds of sounds do you enjoy listening to? The wind in the trees, for example—do you like that? Can you describe how that sounds? [If the sound of the wind in the trees is inappropriate for the particular circumstances of the children, substitute something that is appropriate.]

These kinds of questions and a diet of good writing, well read (most teachers I've observed are poor oral readers, usually read-ing in a patronizing sing-song; a small collection of spoken-word recordings of high quality poetry and stories read by skilled ac-tors would be a valuable addition to classroom resources), will go a long way toward developing a finely tuned language sense. Of course, to be of any use the "style program" must be continued, broadened, and intensified. When the teacher deems it useful, he should raise stylistic questions with the class about other matters as well—music, dress, architecture, and even the life-style itself. Our sense of style, our aesthetic sensibilities, our taste should not be allowed to develop haphazardly. (A haphazardly developed taste is almost inevitably a stunted taste.) The classroom is an ideal place for its nurture. Again, this requires teachers who themselves have a reasonably well developed sense of style and taste; but given this as a desideratum, I see no reason why we can't at least look for it in new teachers.

Our academic bias in favor of the printed word has tended to make us vaguely hostile in our schools toward any great use of the normal urge to talk. For a large part of the school day, the child is enjoined to silence or allowed to speak only to ask or answer a question. Yet such suppression of talk runs harshly against the human grain. We, in contra-distinction to other primates, are chatterers. (The fact is that monkeys and apes are *not* chatterers.) But educational folklore has it that talking in class is disruptive. And so it is if the teacher is doing the talking and wants to be listened to. Let us, however, imagine a non-teacher-centered class-room. A kind of forum wherein the student can with official sanction talk out loud and interchange ideas with his peers. Where he can stage impromptu performances, can join committees for some suggested, appointed, or self-generated task, where, in short, he can test his tongue publicly. Noise, after all, is self-limiting. Furthermore, in those classrooms where this kind of "free speech" is allowed and even encouraged, there is remarkable self-constraint. If the student realizes that he is being taken seriously, that people (the teacher in particular) believe that he has something worthwhile to say, he will respond accordingly and allow others their say. The ability to work in groups toward some mutually desired goal is of great value in our society. Were groups of students left to themselves to work up a play or performance of some kind each week, the type of verbal skill it takes not only to do the performance but to manage things so that a diverse group of individuals can function together to produce a performance would be increasingly enhanced each time around. But we would make a mistake to focus on the performance as the measure of what has been accomplished. It is the process along the way to the product that is of prime importance. To get where they wish to go, the group must solve in common a number of problems. In the process, each child must be able to communicate his ideas and wishes to his peers; he must be able to listen to his peers and take such direction as is offered; he must, in short, give and take incrementally, so that the group together will have made something that wasn't there before. Verbal skill, a sense of logical relationships, a sense of form, the ability to think in terms of the group are some of the results of this kind of activity. But if it is merely a once- or twice-a-year thing (Christmas Pageant, etc.) it will be of little value (except perhaps as a type of teacher gratification, for then it is the teacher who presides, gives orders, makes the Big Decisions, and generally rides herd over a bunch of kids who are happy to have a vacation from school work).

A typical set of "language arts" workbooks covers such matters as "phonics" (in quotation marks because the scientific sound of the term is belied by the materials it labels), reading and word study, spelling, and writing. These are all treated as separate subjects and the pedagogical theory that underlies them is "developmental," which is to say that the child is meant to accumulate little bits of learning along several tracks, each little bit learned, presumably, in order to get to the next step: a kind of squirreling-away-nuts-for-the-future approach. This, of course, makes the daily work a lot of tedious nonsense which the child goes along with because he is compelled to by the pressure of grades, ridicule, or whatever else the teacher can pressure him with. The only excitement I've noted on the part of the child working in such books is that which comes at finishing the page and closing the book. "No more pencils, no more books, no more teacher's dirty looks!"—the kids have known for a long time.

If one does indeed throw away the textbooks and rethinks the problems of bringing a child into literacy, one soon realizes that textbooks are a crutch for the teacher and a hindrance for the child. There isn't a thing of value that these books offer that cannot be got from an honest book or magazine or newspaper. A proper classroom should have a stock of *real* books (preferably paperbacks, not those plasticized tomes with titles like *Discovering Your Language*) and periodicals (other, I would hope, than *Reader's Digest*—one of the minor disasters of American education was its acceptance of *Reader's Digest* as a kind of semi-official publication). I shall have more to say on books and periodicals in Chapter 7. Suffice it to say here that the sooner we get the real world into the classroom, the sooner our education can mature into what it should be. With a little imagination and a ditto machine, a teacher can get all the phonics, reading, word study, spelling, and writing he can use right out of the daily newspaper. Of course, it is a bit more demanding of the teacher to do this than simply to tell the class to do page 23 in the phonics workbook. Teacher and class *together* can devise exercises, make rebuses, frame sentences, frame words, and the like. The fact is that the more one thinks about the excitement and genuine learning that can come out of this kind of cooperative venture, the more one must be amazed at how the teacher has allowed himself to be sold into the slavery of the textbook/workbook program.

Any classroom activity offers all the opportunities for writing or any other language work that one might wish for. A class tournament of some kind is the ideal subject for "TV, radio, and newspaper coverage." There can be descriptions of the event itself, interviews, written reportage. The class should have its own newspaper, and everyone should be encouraged to make some kind of contribution to it, the various assignments being swapped about regularly. The point is that the child should be writing about something that interests and concerns him. The vapid little assignments are *ex nihilo* for the child, and, as Lucretius has advised us, *ex nihilo nihil fit*. To guide the student toward accurate and informative reportage, these questions will be useful:

1. What is happening?
2. Who is doing what?
3. Where are they doing it?
4. How are they doing it?
5. Why are they doing it?
6. What are some words that are good for helping people "see" what you are trying to describe?
7. Did you spell everybody's name right? What might happen if you misspell someone's name?
8. What came first? What followed? What came last?
9. What are the most important things about the event? Why are they the most important?
10. Did you include all the important things in your report?

(Incidentally, these reports of actual events can be very well used as the bases of imaginative writing. Turning a news story into a fictional story is an interesting and challenging problem and neatly combines a variety of language activities.) The student's own reportorial work should be supplemented by class discussion of simple news stories from the local newspaper and by, perhaps, a homework assignment to watch a news broadcast on TV and to report it to the class the next day. (This can be a "rotating" assignment—each student will get a chance to be the class reporter.) Other uses of the media are detailed in later sections of the chapter.

It is remarkable that some textbooks in current use present "grammar" exercises and "definitions" as early as the second grade. Not only is the "grammar" study wholly without educational value, it is confusing and misleading because it is based upon notions of language that are to language what astrology is to the night sky. The traditional definitions of the "parts of speech" (a concept, incidentally, that modern theorists have by no means adequately defined) have long since been thoroughly discredited, and it is a wonder that the author of any textbook can still offer them without embarrassment. At any rate, the introduction of grammatical terminology in the early years is without useful purpose. The child already knows what nouns, verbs, and the rest are *functionally* and to be able to attach labels to them at this stage of the game is like being able to write one's name upside down and backwards while standing on one's head. There's something impressive about it, to be sure, but it seems at best rather a hermetic accomplishment.

What the student needs is experience in using language, in synthesizing not in taking apart. He has to discover the capabilities of language, its tones and voices, its ranges and multitudinous uses. He has to develop an ear and a touch and a set of "muscles." Labeling "parts of speech" is guaranteed to militate against the accomplishment of every one of these goals. Still more so is sentence-diagramming, the archetypal busywork. The teacher who wastes his students' time diagramming sentences should be required to pay his students for their time. Every bit of research done to determine the value of "grammar" study (of the sort I have been speaking of) supports the conclusion that not one of the claims made in its behalf is warranted. As early as 1906, a researcher in the field could conclude:

> [The] position seems reasonable that the study of formal grammar as ordinarily pursued below the eighth grade, being ill adapted to immature pupils, will tend to retard the natural development of the child, rather than further "training in thought" and the disciplining of the understanding. (Franklin S. Hoyt, *Teachers College Record,* quoted in Neil Postman and Charles Weingartner, *Linguistics, A Revolution in Teaching,* p. 64.)

All subsequent research has merely supported and amplified that conclusion. Quite simply, anyone who claims any educational benefits for traditional grammar study doesn't know what he is talking about.

The proper aim of schoolroom language activities is the development of skill and ease in using language. A language program which depends upon the memorization of definitions and rules can be of no use to this aim. This is all the more true when the definitions are unworkable and the rules often irrelevant (and imposed rather than discovered). In any case, spelling and punctuation, for example, are arbitrary and not, even among the educated, universally consistent. By focusing so intensely on these matters, we not only trivialize language but we condition the student to think of language activities as potentials for pain far more than for pleasure. Writing should not be thought of as evil-tasting medicine that we must take on the faith that it will do us some good, some time. *Taking* pains can indeed be pleasurable, but investing what should be pleasurable with pain is asinine. Hence, the child should be stimulated to write, copiously, about all manner of things and experiences of concern to him, but he should not have to expect his labors to be trod over with the red chicken tracks of a persnickity teacher who can see no further than punctuation and spelling errors. Standards can be arrived at in due course through the student's own discovery of them. Questions like these can start the student thinking about the conventions of writing:

1. Here is a page from a magazine. Describe everything you see on the page. Have you described *everything*? Look again and see if you can find some more things.
2. Why are some letters bigger than others? Where do you find these big letters? [Differences in fonts will complicate the issue, but the whys and wherefores of these differences should as well be explored.]
3. In addition to the letters, what kinds of marks did you find? What are these marks for? Where do you find each kind?
4. Try writing something with no spaces between the words, with no punctuation marks, and with no capital letters. Is it as easy to read as the regular way of doing it? Describe the problems. There was a time when people wrote "as the ox plows," which means that the direction of the writing was reversed in each successive line. Try writing something this way. In Hebrew and Arabic, the writing goes from right to left. Try writing this way. And in Chinese and Japanese the writing goes in columns from the top of the page to the bottom, starting on the right and going to the left. Try writing a letter to a friend that way. Which method of writing is "best"? Why? Do you think that people who write in ways other than ours have any special difficulties? Explain.
5. Some languages (Biblical Hebrew, for example) are written only with consonants. Thus, *Birds are singing* would be

written *Brds r sngng.* Try writing a little story with all the vowel letters missing. Now write the same story with all the consonant letters missing. Thus, *Birds are singing* becomes *i ae ii.* Quite a difference, isn't there? What have you discovered?

6. In ancient Egypt, where writing probably began, one stage in the development of writing was the *rebus,* in which pictures were used simply for the sounds of the objects for which they stood. Thus, s + = sigh. Can you tell a story in rebus form? Tr + !

7. A *palindrome* is a group of words that says the same thing whether you read it forwards or backwards: *Madam, I'm Adam* when read from right to left, says, *Madam, I'm Adam* (of course, the capitalization and punctuation have to be changed, but both ways of reading produce the same *sounds*). Try making up some palindromes.

8. It's fun to do crossword puzzles. It's even more fun to make them up. Try it. Then explain how you went about making up a crossword puzzle.

9. An *anagram* is a word or phrase made from the letters of a word: from *punishment* we can make the anagram, *nine thumps* (an anagram that certainly fits the original word nicely!). Pick a few promising-looking words and see how many words and phrases you can make with each one. But you must not use any letter more times than it is used in the original word. (For some words, all you have to do is read them backwards: *evil–live.*)

10. The spelling of many English words is odd, which is because a letter or a group of letters doesn't always stand for the same pronunciation. What are some examples? Can you make up any funny spellings for simple words? Consider, for example, that *sh* as in *show* can be written *ti* as in *nation; f* as in *fine* can be written as *gh* in *cough; i* as in *hill* can be written as *o* in *women,* and so forth.

These questions and problems lead the student *into* the whole issue of writing mechanics and provide him with the materials for discovery. A project for the class at large would be for them to try to create a consistent spelling system for English, wherein there will be, without exception, one symbol for each distinctive sound. What they will arrive at will be a *phonemic* alphabet (see Chapter 3), which is in fact what the Initial Teaching Alphabet is. This type of language play will prove far more useful both in terms of substantive learning and in terms of attitude development than all the rote memory and disjointed drill in the world. An excellent source-book for orthographical games and puzzles is Dmitri A. Borgmann's *Language on Vacation* (Scribners).

In respect of "ain't," double negation, and the like, one might say that never have so many labored so much for so little. Such deviations from linguistic norms (I should say from *classroom* linguistic norms, because "ain't" would certainly be standard otherwise) as the student exhibits will be smoothed away in their own time by virtue of the example the teacher sets and the examples of the reading materials used. (The genuine linguistic problems presented by, for example, ghetto children, are outside the scope of this book. A great many experimental projects are underway aimed at linguistically acculturating the seriously disadvantaged speaker, and the teacher who is faced with a teaching assignment in a ghetto school or a school with a large number of children who deviate grossly from the linguistic norms of the society should acquaint himself with those projects. See Bibliography.) It is useful to examine differences in usage, not to make invidious comparisons or to assert the "superiority" of classroom English over other dialects, but simply to bring the student to an awareness of the multiplicity of his language (it *is* tricky) and to sensitize him to the ways in which its variety is used. In addition to many of the questions at the end of Chapter 3 (rephrased, of course, to suit the audience), these will open language for exploration:

1. Do you ever have feelings for which you have no words? Can you describe the feelings? Can you make up some good words for them?
2. Words are made up in different ways. For example, *classroom* is made of *class + room*, and *baseball = base + ball*. Can you name some others? Do the two parts of the word tell you something about the meaning of the word? Why is a *greenhouse* (*green + house*) named as it is? After all, a *greenhouse* is usually made of glass and whitewashed. Where can you find out about these mysterious words? Here are some others to figure out: *mincemeat, nightmare, pinwheel,*

railroad. Then there are words like *farmer* (*farm* + *er*), in which one part of the word is a word itself, but the other part isn't (even though it has some kind of meaning—what is the meaning of *er* in *farmer?*). Can you find some other examples? Is *father* an example? Why not? What about *singer?*

3. What words make you sad? Why? What words make you happy? Why?

4. Can you arrange these words to say something besides a list of words? What is the difference between the list and what *you* made of the words in the list? [Any simple sentence with its words rearranged into alphabetical order can be used here. This might be a good place, incidentally, to touch briefly on the *idea* of alphabetical order. After discussing the concept with the class, the teacher should encourage them to think of ways of teaching how to alphabetize. The discussion must reveal the usefulness of the process, otherwise the exercise is merely sterile busywork.]

5. Here is a boxful of broken sentences. How many sentences can you put together from these parts? [The teacher can print one word on each slip of paper—there must be of course be a good variety of nouns, verbs, adjectives, adverbs, and function words—and then ask each student to draw several from the box. Through swapping and mutual "kibitzing" the class can put together a number of sentences. Or, the students themselves can make the slips from sentences they've already written. Other variations are possible and all should be explored. If several sentences fit together to make a larger sentence or even a story, so much the better. The teacher must use some ingenuity and must allow his students to use theirs.]

6. Here are some sentences with pieces missing. What can you put into each empty slot? [Children enjoy playing at slot-and-filler, but they need not be bothered about terminology except perhaps in passing. It is better to *describe*— as opposed to *labeling*—the kinds of words that can go into the various slots. Changing the noun number—*i.e.*, singular to plural and *vice versa*—of verb-deleted sentences and the concord form of the verb in noun-deleted sentences will like-

wise be instructive and will draw attention to the concept of *agreement* without making a big issue of it. The class should be urged to make their own sentences with "holes" for their classmates to fill.

7. Does everybody talk the same way? What kinds of differences have you noticed? Next time you watch TV, try to listen for different ways of talking. Why do you think that some people talk differently from others?

8. A *pun* is a play on words like *Did you ever see a horse fly?*, which is a very old and very tired pun. Sometimes, just to be punny, people say that a bad pun is two-thirds of a pun, P–U!, which is also very old and very tired. Can you make up any puns? How does a pun "work"?

9. When we talk, we also sing a little tune. This tune often tells us something about the feelings of the person speaking. He may, for example, say something as simple as *It is snowing* but say it in a way that tells us whether he is happy about it or sad about it or mad about it. Can you say *It is snowing* in those ways? Say some other simple things in several "tones of voice" to convey various feelings. But the rules of the game require that the *words* and *word order* remain the same.

10. What other kinds of things does the "sing-song" or *intonation* of speech tell us? Try these: *When I eat too much chocolate, I get a rash.* [*Sustained juncture* at the comma marks the dependency of the preceding word group, *When . . . .*] *Harry, the milkman is on vacation; Harry the milkman is on vacation.* [And so on. The students should of course be encouraged to make up their own sentences. Wherever there is a clear relationship between intonation and punctuation, this should be pointed out.]

"Of the making of books there is no end," someone has said. In the classroom, this should be the case *a fortiori*. I have said so before, but it is well worth saying again that the most valuable type of languaging is that which the student *produces*. And there is nothing quite like the pleasure that comes of being able to offer one's creations for public use. Hence the stress I place on the child's production of his own books. In the early stages, a page with one or two sentences on it and folded into a sheet of construction paper, illustrated inside and out, will constitute a "book." With the child's name on the cover and a library card in the back (made by the child himself), the book is placed on the classroom library shelf and becomes something of great value for the child. As the months and years go on, these "books" give way to much more elaborate productions and continue to be a source of both satisfaction and stimulation to their young writers. We give a lot of lip service to the importance of the "peer group" to the child, but we show little respect for its members. The cold oatmeal of the reading series has nowhere nearly the appeal, freshness, and positive psychological feedback of the work that the students do themselves (*if we but give them the chance and the encouragement*). I'd far sooner a child spend his school day at work on his own book than spend the same time doing a hodge-podge of pre-planned and drearily predictable assignments in various workbooks and readers.

Generally, only the child who has been inhibited by fear of failure or rejection seems to lack for something to say. In the type of open classroom situation that is basic to the philosophy of education presented here, such inhibitions simply do not develop. Of course, home has its influence, and there are children who for inexplicable reasons are unable (or unwilling) to express themselves. Nevertheless, even the reticent ones can be drawn out in an environment which offers no threat. These questions can serve both the imaginative extroverts and the (apparently) unimaginative quiet ones:

1. [After the teacher has read a story to the class.] Can you make up a different ending for the story? Supposing . . . [the teacher can modify some aspect of plot or character] . . . what then?

2. Suppose you dreamed you were in a strange country where the people had wings. Can you describe what a day in the life of a family of winged people might be like?

3. Suppose one of the astronauts on the moon fell through the crust of the moon into an underground world—what would he find there?

4. Suppose you meet a boy or girl about your age from a far distant country who cannot speak a word of English. Write a story about how you would make friends with him and what you would do together.

5. Make believe that you are going to be the teacher today. Write a story about what you will do in class.

6. Suppose there were no electricity. Describe what life would be like without electricity. Remember, you'll first have to think about all the things that need electricity to run. No batteries either.

7. Make believe that you are a piece of chalk and tell a story about a day in school.

8. Make believe you are an automobile and tell a story about a day in your life.

9. Make believe you are one inch high. Describe the way your room at home looks from one inch high. What do you have to think about to write the description? [If asking for a description of one's room is inappropriate, any other familiar environment can of course be substituted.]

10. Can you write a story about monsters, vampires, and other spooky things?

11. Write down what you think about or imagine when you hear this music. [The teacher should have an anthology of music on tape, *excluding* the so-called children's music put out by record companies catering to supermarkets and bad taste— children can respond to quality as readily as to trash. See Appendix.] Now this . . . [music in a different mood and style]

12. Write a letter to your favorite TV person. Ask him questions; tell him things.

Play acting, as we have noted, is a languaging activity comparable in importance to reading and writing. Some type of cooperative dramatic performance should be a weekly project. Here are some questions and problems to get things started:

1. What is "make-believe"? What do you do when you make believe?

2. If you want somebody else to make believe or to act the part of another person, what does he need to have? How will he know what to do and what to say?

3. Can you turn one of your stories into a play? What do you need to do in order to make a story into a play?

4. If there is more than one person in your play, what has to be

done to make sure everybody does and says the right thing at the right time. How do all the musicians in an orchestra manage to play together? What would happen to the music if they didn't play together?

5. What things do you need for a play besides the different people to act the different parts? What if the play is supposed to take place in a haunted house or a ship or an airplane or a rocket to the moon?

6. What are some important things to think about if you are going to put on a play for the class?

7. Listen carefully to people talking to each other. Can you write down the way they talk? What are some of the things people say when they first see each other? What are some of the things they say when they are about to leave each other? Do you ever hear people talk about the weather? What do they say? Why do people talk about the weather? What other everyday things have you heard people talking about? What things that people talk about really interest you? Why? Would they be interesting in a play?

8. What would be fun to put on a play about?

9. What makes you laugh? Tell a funny story? Can you make up a funny scene for a play?

10. What makes you sad? Can you make up a sad scene for a play?

MEDIA

By the time an American child has been graduated from high school, he has behind him on the average of ten thousand hours of formal education and fifteen thousand hours of TV time. When he starts his formal education, he has already logged about four thousand hours in front of the tube. Since it boots us nothing to bemoan the fact of this massive TV exposure, we should take advantage of it. (A point to remember here is that youngsters today—whether we like to admit it or not—are much more aware of the world, much more sophisticated culturally and linguistically, than children of past generations. Our children are, in many ways, wise beyond their years and perforce quickly bored by classroom experiences that are below their level of sophistication. Dick, Jane, and the rest of the pre-media dimwits are thin gruel indeed to our children of the seventies. As much as anything, 'twere the media killed the primer and the schoolmarm.) And this means more than an occasional hour of classroom tube watching. Not that this can't be valuable (though the quality of the usual classroom TV fare is not much higher than that of Dick and Jane), but, again, like so much of what happens in the classroom, it is passive experience rather than active.

> Because the medium of television is so interwoven with man's mind, one can be distinguished from the other only when the set is dead—that is, off—and has become an object that has assumed its static features. Indeed a television set alive is no longer a set: the image filling the sensory space of viewers forces them into dialogues that reduce perception of the set as such to a negligible minimum. To talk of the medium of television is in a way to talk of man the perceiver, the responder, the expander, and the processor of images. (Caleb Gattegno, *Towards a Visual Culture, Educating Through Television,* p. 15.)

But we have either scorned TV or used it "educationally" to deliver lectures, a tedious and wasteful use of the medium. But Gattegno's program unfortunately requires specially prepared materials that are not yet generally available and, of course, a closed-circuit television system, thus far a "luxury" in the minds of most taxpayers and hence found in relatively few schools. On the other hand, there are all of those hours of TV experience past or yet to come, and it is here that we can plug into the media at no expense to the taxpayer and at great gain to the education of the child. (The experimental series *Sesame Street* should be required viewing for the whole educational establishment and all parents. The kids, apparently, need no urging. One is entitled to ask why the "educational experts" who run our schools have so consistently fallen short of offering classroom experiences of the quality and impact of this extraordinary TV venture.)

Using Television

The questions and projects which follow not only make productive use of the child's ongoing commitment to television, but, consonant with the synoptic approach to education, require that he draw on all the basic learning skills (as we have defined them).

1. What is your favorite TV program? Why?
2. Describe the program. Include everything you can think of from the very beginning of the program to the very end.
3. Can you make up a TV program? Try it.
4. Are the commercials different from the rest of the program? How? Do you like the commercials? Why?
5. Can you make up a TV commercial? Try to sell something in the classroom with your commercial. What are the things that really make you interested in something that you see advertised on TV?
6. Does your family buy a lot of things that are advertised on TV? What? Why? Are they always happy with these things?
7. Are the toys that are advertised on TV as much fun as you thought they would be when you saw them advertised? What did you expect and what did you get? If you wanted to convince somebody that a toy is bigger and better than it really is, how would you do it?
8. What is a cartoon? Do you like cartoons? Why?
9. Try drawing some cartoon stories. [If a movie camera is available, these stories should be turned into animated films. See Bibliography.]
10. If you wanted to put on a make-believe TV program in the classroom, how would you do it? What are some of the differences between what really happens and what you see on the TV screen? For example, do people really get blurry or bigger and smaller the way they do on TV? How do you suppose that they make that happen on TV? Why do you suppose they make it happen? If you see a friend of yours in a crowd of strangers, do you really *see* the strangers? Think about how you look at things and what precisely you see when you look at them.
11. What are some funny or interesting words you've heard on TV lately? See how many new words you can collect in a week of TV watching. Make a dictionary of your new words and try to find out what they mean.
12. In addition to your favorite TV program, what do you like to watch on TV? Why? Have you ever been scared or upset by what you have seen on TV? What has scared or upset you and why?

13. What new and interesting things have you learned recently as a result of watching TV?
14. If you could decide what to put on TV, what kinds of programs would you like? Why? Can you make up one of these programs?
15. Do you know how TV works? How can you find out?

This is merely a beginning. The teacher and class will undoubtedly think of more questions and projects, which is a clear sign that the classroom is "going creative." Needless to say, *none* of the lists of questions and projects (or problems) I've offered here is exhaustive If they have any merit, they should engender many times their number. This in turn requires the most flexible of schedules and the willingness on the part of the teacher to pursue a project so long as it productively engages the student. Arbitrary time limits are merely administrative conveniences—but schools should not be run for the convenience of administrators (though commonly they are).

Where it is feasible, the class should be taken to a TV studio. All facets of what the class has seen there should be discussed and examined, and when the class puts on its next "TV production" (in the manner of the plays discussed earlier), it should be encouraged to include whatever features of a real TV production that it is capable of managing. The creative potential here is vast, especially with regard to the visuals necessary for TV commercials. Where it is possible to see a TV studio in action, it will be worth the teacher's while to do some research on TV production in order that he can make suggestions for adding authenticity to what the class is doing. The students, likewise, should try to find out what they can. Though the networks will probably cringe at the idea, I would suggest that some or all of the students write to NBC, CBS, and ABC asking specific questions about this or that program. (*E.g.,* how are the "little people" in *Land of the Giants* [ABC] made to seem little?) Another resource to be taken advantage of is the media center at local colleges and universities. Film and TV production programs are entering the curricula of increasing numbers of schools (high schools included), and they should be given the stimulus of community interest (through, in this case, the involvement of the community lower schools). The greater the interrelationship between and among the educational institutions, the more successful the overall educational enterprise.

Exploring Newspapers and Magazines

Of the other mass media, newspapers and periodicals offer the greatest opportunities for exploration and discovery for children in the early years. Radio is either a teen-age medium (music) or an adult medium (news, sports, and late-night talk shows), and the films that children are likely to be taken to are no different from what they see on TV programs like *The Wonderful World of Walt Disney*. As familiar as the newspaper is (I would guess that virtually every child in America has at one time or another seen a newspaper), it is almost *terra incognita* to most children (except for the funny pages). Yet, the newspaper is the richest source of easily accessible materials on life at every level from the local to the world (indeed, universal, what with moon walks, eclipses, and the like) community. Newspapers are an incredible bargain in this expensive, gadget-ridden age and can even be used to make *papier-maché* when they have given up their intellectual content. Periodicals are rather more costly, but nevertheless cheap measured against the resources they afford the classroom. They are cheaper still if the students are asked to bring the family castoffs to class. By this means, the class will be no more than a week or so behind the community in its periodical reading. What the students should probably not be asked to waste their money on are the periodicals aimed specifically at the schools. Most of these have all the disabilities of the textbooks, being tailored to the presumed level of perception of some "ideal" student in each grade. The result is mostly bellywash and cutesy, patronizing writing. The *Reader's Digest* will undoubtedly show up in class, for it is (more's the pity) a very widely read magazine. And while it has for years provided lazy teachers with officially approved busywork, the occasional issue that will turn up will serve the purposes of the creative classroom.

1. Make a list of all the newspapers and magazines you have seen at home or in the store. Do you ever look at these? Which ones do you like the most? Why?
2. How does a newspaper differ from a magazine?
3. What kinds of things can you find in a newspaper? If you don't know, what is the best way to find out? What kinds of things can you find in a magazine?

4. How would you go about starting a class newspaper? Think about the newspapers you have looked at and then think about which things the class can do and which things the class probably can't do. [A variety of newspapers should be available in class for examination.]

5. Here is a newspaper story about something that happened in town yesterday. [Teacher reads story.] What did the story tell us? Why does it have a headline? How does the headline relate to the story? Try writing a story about something that happened in school recently. [The teacher can ditto these in the form of a newspaper and let the class take the idea from there.]

6. Is there a difference between these two statements? [Teacher reads a straightforward descriptive sentence from a news story and then an editorial comment from the editorial page.] Try to explain the difference. Is the second statement sort of like a TV commercial? How? Can you write a descriptive statement and then an editorial comment about something going on at school?

7. Try to describe something that happened in school to somebody who wasn't there to see it. [The teacher should discuss the results, contrasting *facts* with *opinions*. When the class has firmly grasped the sense of this contrast, the range of exploration can be broadened.]

8. What kind of information can you get from various newspaper ads? Is the ad for a supermarket sale pretty much like the ad for an automobile? Can you describe the similarities, if any, and the differences, if any? Do ads have *facts* and *opinions*? Can you find some of each?

9. Write and illustrate some newspaper ads for things you would like to sell—perhaps some toys or clothes that you don't want any more. If you wish, make believe you are a store or a company.

10. Are newspaper ads generally different from magazine ads? What differences can you find? Write a magazine ad for something you would like to sell. What kinds of ads would you not expect to find in, say, a monthly magazine? [The magazines should of course be available in class.]

Though at least some of these questions may seem excessively demanding for younger children, they will not be if the child has been brought along through inquiry/discovery techniques. Our traditional notions about what a child can or cannot do at a certain age are just not supported by the facts. And if those notions had some validity once upon a time, they surely do not now. Children are more informed about and more acutely conscious of their environment than they have ever been. We must accordingly set our sights higher. The intensification of intellectual demands, however, does *not* mean a tightening up of the classroom ambiance. Quite the contrary— the intellect will flourish only in the sunny climate of the free classroom.

WHAT MAKES THE WORLD GO ROUND?

Children have a boundless curiosity that we, alas, very quickly bound. The purpose of the "science corner" of the classroom is, I suppose, to introduce the student to the ways of the phenomenal world. But, like the rest of what we do in school, it is programmatic and "curricular." We assume that if we tell a child something he will be interested in it. What we have on the contrary to do is to (1) be prepared to explore where the child's interests take him and (2) stimulate those interests by the questions we ask. Certainly the "teach-us-what-we-want-to-know" approach is the most exciting. Without question, there is a school-year's work in trying to do just that (and, may I say, there are far less valuable ways of spending the school year—plodding through workbooks, for example). The teacher will need a goodly store of reference books and a great deal of patience and imagination. He will further have to put aside such prejudices as he may have about what a child "should" know or be able to do.

In a world so filled with machinery and gadgets we can expect youngsters to be curious about how things work. Furthermore, we should be happy about that curiosity, not threatened by it. No teacher can know how everything that his students may question him about works, but he can keep a copy of a book like *The Way*

Things Work (Simon & Schuster) on his desk and be willing to explore the diagrams and explanations with his students. And wherever possible the class should examine the actual items—a few dollars spent on light switches and the like will be well repaid. A few hours spent garnering old and broken gadgets for classroom dissection and possibly even repair will likewise be well repaid. And with the almost limitless variety of inexpensive kits on the market, there should be no reason why a class cannot put together a simple radio, telephone, electric motor, etc. (A working radio can be made with copper wire, an old razor blade, and a set of cheap headphones; a working electric motor with copper wire, paper clips, and a battery.) Further, the teacher has to be willing to let the students work away as they will and not require that they break off when the "science period" is over.

Discovering What Makes the World Go Round

The child who is encouraged to ask "Why" and "How" about his world will not have to be prompted, but his urge to discovery can be helped by the following "theoretical" questions (that is, questions that can be applied to virtually any gadget and which provide a technique for exploration):

1. What does it look like? What is it made of?
2. Where is it found?
3. What does it seem to do?
4. Is it a part of something else? How is it related to what it is part of?
5. Is it made of one piece or several pieces?
6. How are the pieces, if any, related to each other? How are they connected to each other?
7. Is it self-powered? If not, how is it powered?
8. Does it have controls? What are they like? What do they seem to do?
9. Does it move when it works? How? Does it change temperature? Which way?
10. Can it be taken apart? If so, how? What is inside?
11. Does it operate all the time (like a clock motor) or intermittently (like a toaster)?

12. If it is a "black box" (that is, a sealed unit) that can be known only by what is on the outside, what can you figure out about it from the outside? (A molded electrical plug is a simple example.)

A similar line of questioning can be taken with respect to biological entities (*e.g.*, the digestive system) and physical events (*e.g.*, the weather), *mutatis mutandis.* Here is a more narrowly focused line of questioning designed to stimulate interest in or to come to grips with a particular topic—in this example, the eye:

1. There are supposed to be a number of similarities between the eye and the camera. Do you know how a camera works? Let's try to build a camera. [The teacher can put together a pinhole camera with a piece of waxed paper at the back or film end of the box—a shoebox is best because cheapest and handiest. As soon as an image appears on the waxed paper, there will be numerous questions. And very quickly the students will learn something of elementary optics. They should be asked to make their own shoebox pinhole cameras. More ambitious students might even want to try taking real photographs, which is perfectly feasible but will require some fairly sophisticated "engineering" on the part of the student.]

2. What part of the eye is like the pinhole of the shoebox camera? Where is the "film" of the eye? [An anatomical model of the eye would be helpful here, but it isn't absolutely necessary, for the shoebox camera will serve. It may, incidentally, interest the students to know that *camera* takes its name from *camera obscura,* Latin for "darkened room," the darkened room being what amounted to a room-sized shoebox camera in which people could sit and look at the outside scenes projected onto a wall of the *camera,* or "room."]

3. Is it possible to control the amount of light that goes through the pinhole? What happens if we make the pinhole larger in order to let more light in? [Enlarge the pinhole to the diameter of a pencil.] No image? Why? How does the eye control the amount of light that gets to the "film"? [The teacher can shine a penlight beam into his eye in a semi-darkened room.] Does the picture blur and disappear when the iris opens the way the picture blurred and disappeared

when we enlarged the pinhole? [A few cheap lenses can be used here to demonstrate the ways in which light can be controlled.] The lens in a pinhole camera is merely the pinhole. The lens in your eye and in more elaborate cameras is more than just a hole. The lens in your eye and the lens of a camera bend light differently from the way the air of a pinhole bends light. Can you make a lens with water? [The experimental and analogical possibilities here are numerous.]

4. Where is the shutter of our shoebox camera? Where is the shutter of our eye?

5. What can the eye do that a camera can't do? Does a camera "think"? What does *thinking* have to do with *seeing*? Do you really see everything in front of you? If, for example, you are looking at TV, what else do you actually notice at the same time? Why? [The phenomenon of selective perception can be further illustrated with a tape recorder *vs.* human hearing.]

Wherever possible, the student should be put in touch with whatever it is he is trying to find out about. And always he should be pressed to develop ways of seeing and solving problems. If, for example, a question arises that involves measurement, the student should be asked to figure out a feasible measuring technique. This may mean that he will have to contrive his own measuring devices. Finding the cubic volume of irregular spaces may require the construction of cubic containers of suitable sizes (for filling with sand or water) or, solving other problems, the fabrication of flexible measures (perhaps strips of construction paper appropriately marked and taped together).

At all events, the teacher can avail himself of virtually unlimited science resources without ever having to put a science textbook into his students' hands. As with reading, the student should make his own science book, which will be a record of his questions, discoveries, experiments, and so on. The student should be encouraged to do some kind of experimentation or "research" at home. If a particular child has a parent whose profession is in science, he can greatly enrich the class's scientific studies by making reports to the class about his parent's work. And parents who are interested should likewise be encouraged to come in (if, naturally, this is feasible) and talk about their work.

The class (as opposed to the teacher) can put together a small science museum, the responsibility for the operation and maintenance of which belongs to the class. Included might be a small terrarium and a fish tank. If there is a choice to be made, I would opt for the former, lizards and toads being rather more hardy than tropical fish and (to my way of thinking) more interesting to children. The museum should be considered an *integral* part of the class activities, and those students who wish to spend their class time tending to it should be allowed to do so. Interests change and no child will get hung up on one thing to the exclusion of everything else, at least not over a long period.

And always the questions. This is the way of the scientist and must be the way of the student. He must learn science, that is, the *scientific way,* not learn *about* science, which is merely the accumulation of odds and ends of information.

SOCIETY

"Social studies" in the early years are all but non-existent, which is probably just as well, for they are sufficiently trivialized and disjointed in the later school years to make one wonder how they could be made more so (though that does seem the way of things in education—what is yet pap as late as the second year of college is watered down to the point of sheer inanity when one finds it in the lower levels of education). If of course we aim at *doing it* rather than *talking about it,* there is no reason why even the very young child cannot be involved in some respectable behavioral and social science. I would far sooner see the child doing some exploring on his own, however halting it may be, than memorizing a lot of foolishness about "The Father of Our Country" and "The Great Emancipator." Why anyone ever thought that having children commit such arrant nonsense to memory was in any way valuable, I cannot tell. I do know that when a child who has done so is asked what all the fine phrases mean, he shrugs.

What is important to the younger child is developing some sense of where he is. His world seems to be bounded by home and school, with the larger local community vaguely felt as being "out there." Likewise the national and international communities, though these are even more vaguely felt. I doubt, for example, that very many children have much of a notion about the relationship of the astronauts to anything else. The Apollo missions represent exciting isolates that are probably associated in the child's mind with the Saturday morning TV space adventures. My judgment is that other than the prematurely wise children of the ghettos, no American child has the foggiest notion of what his community "is," what it is part of, how it differs from other communities, what being a part of any particular community means to the individuals in it, what the values of the community are, how and to what degree the various members of the community interrelate to form a sense of community, and so on. I will go further and assert that most college students don't know, nor do most adults. There can be no justifiable excuse for this degree of ignorance about ourselves. And were we less ignorant, we might have fewer of the societal problems we are now coping so ineptly with. It is not too soon to begin to develop this awareness in the first year of school. But doing it from "social studies" textbooks will not answer. A glut of discrete "facts" will not answer.

Discovering Society

At some point early in life, a child wants to know where he came from. From that moment he carries with him a self-consciousness (that is to say, consciousness of self) and a desire to know about self that is a "natural" concomitant of being human. And if we are inclined to blush at trying to answer the teleological question, we need have no hesitation in posing questions for the child that will help him find himself in his world:

1. Describe your street. Tell about the houses, the cars, the people, the businesses. Are the nearby streets similar? If they are different in any way, what are the differences? If you can't remember, how can you find out?
2. Is your street noisy or quiet? Is there a lot of activity going on in the street? What kinds of things do people do on your street? Is there a lot of traffic? What kind of traffic is it?
3. How far away are the stores from where you live? Can you walk to any of them? What kind are they?
4. Who does the grocery shopping in your house? Do you ever

go along? Do you like to go shopping? What do you like about it (or dislike about it)? Describe the stores that you go to.

5. Where is "downtown" from where you live? What is "downtown"? Can you describe it? Do you go there often? What for? Do you enjoy "downtown"? Why or why not?

6. What kinds of stores do you go to besides the food market? Where do all the things in the stores come from? Where does the food come from? Where does the clothing come from? How does it get to the stores?

7. Have you been to parts of your town other than where you live and where your parents shop? Are those places like your street?

8. Are all the people in your town pretty much alike? What differences, if any, are there? What questions would you like to ask the people who may be different from you, your family, and your friends?

9. What is "crime"? What do you suppose causes it? Have you ever heard about any crime around where you live? For example, have any houses been robbed? What do you think about this?

10. What do policemen do? Do you know any policemen? Why do they carry guns? Why do they wear uniforms? What do you think about policemen? What kinds of questions would you like to ask a policeman?

11. Does your town have a mayor? What does he do? Is the school principal sort of like the mayor? What does the principal do? What kinds of questions would you like to ask the mayor and the principal?

12. Who pays to run your school? Who pays for the policemen, the firemen, the mayor, the school-teachers, and the principal?

13. What are taxes? Do you pay taxes? Who pays taxes? Interview your parents on the subject of taxes and write a report based on what you find out.

14. Where do the streets and sewers and street lights come from? Who pays for them? What about post offices, mail boxes, and mailmen? Try to imagine your town without any of these. Write a description of life in your town without them.

15. Where does electricity come from? Have you ever been without electricity at home? What was it like? Try to find out what causes electrical power failures. How is electricity sold? (Sugar, for example, is sold by the *pound*, gasoline by the *gallon*, oranges by the *dozen*.)

16. Are there any hospitals in your town? What are hospitals for? Have you ever been in a hospital? Describe your experiences as well as the hospital itself. Who works in hospitals? Who pays for hospitals and for the people who work there? Suppose someone is sick and doesn't have enough money to go to a hospital, what does he do? What is a doctor? How does someone get to be a doctor? What kinds of questions would you like to ask your doctor?

17. Why do cars have license plates? Why do drivers have to have driver's licenses?

18. What else do you need to have a license for? Why?

19. What other schools are in your town besides your own school? Have you been to any of them? Are they in any way different from yours? What is a high school like? A college? Who goes to college? Why do people go to college? What do you do in college?

20. Are there any factories in your town? What kind? Do you know anybody who works in a factory? Can you find out what he does there? What other kinds of jobs do people have besides being factory workers, doctors, teachers, policemen, and firemen? How do all these people help the whole community get along? Why do we need factories and stores? Why do we need schools?

21. How do people get around in your town? Do they all have cars? Is there any other kind of transportation besides walking? What happens in a big city when there are too many cars?

22. Have you heard anything about *pollution*, such as *air pollution* or *water pollution*? Is pollution a problem in your community? What are some examples of pollution? What causes pollution? What happens to waste, garbage, broken toys, abandoned automobiles, and so on?

23. Your town is in a *county*. What is a county? Your county is in a *state*. What is a state? Your state is part of a *nation*.

What is a nation? Can you figure out why we have things like towns, counties, states, and nations? When you are out driving you will see some roads called *county* roads, some called *state* roads, and some called *U.S.* (federal) roads, each type of road being marked with its own distinctive number sign. Why do we have these different kinds of roads?

24. Where did nations, states, counties, and towns come from? What do we need them for? Could we get along without them?

25. Here is a map. Describe what you see on the map. What is a map for? What is the relationship between a map and the real world? How could you use this map to find your way around in a strange place?

26. Why does it seem as though the earth is flat even though it is really round?

27. If you want to show a picture of the whole world, which is round, on a flat surface, how can peeling an orange in a certain way help you out? Try it.

28. Try making a map of your classroom. The school. Your street. What do you have to think about to make your maps?

29. Here is a road map of the state. What can you do with a road map? List all the information you can find on this road map. Try to find on the road map where you live.

30. Try making a road map of the school. Distinguish between the "main roads" and the "secondary roads." Show the distances between important places.

31. What would life be like for you in a place where it was winter all year round and where the ground was always covered with snow? What must you think about to answer this question?

32. What would life be like for you where it was summer all year round and the temperature and humidity were always very high? What must you think about to answer?

33. What would it be like to live on the side of a mountain? In a huge desert? What must you think about to answer?

34. How would you describe the kind of place we live in: climate and so on?

35. Does it matter whether it rains a lot or not? What does rain have to do with the way we live?

These are but a few of literally thousands of questions that can be raised around the general topic of "society." Many of the questions given here are difficult and demanding of both teacher and student, but they are pertinent and mind-stretching and will help the child to develop both perspective and insight. The broad aim of the questions is not to produce information as such (and "right" answers) but rather to refine the process of inquiry.

CREATIVITY

No word today is more popular in educational circles than *creativity*. Indeed, I have used its adjectival form in the title of this book. Yet, the word is grossly misused. To *create* is to make, form, shape, produce. I see very little of this going on in the schools. Like so much in our society, the word suffices for the deed.

Copy work, memory work, lockstep work—"the class will now do . . ." (Simon says!)—this is not creative regardless of how mod a box it comes in. The classroom is a place for mutual growth, teacher and students alike growing through doing and discovering. "Our texts continue to deal with cold facts, but students are rarely encouraged to use these facts to serve their own thinking. The cold fact system has outlived its purpose, and we can toughen the system forever without making it serve education in a changing world." (Lowenfeld, p. 11.) It is of course true that in even the most traditional of classrooms there is more going on than sweating over textbooks. But one may properly ask what in the child's mind becomes the quintessence of the school experience. What are the examinations (that the schools place so much value in) about? What are the all-important grades largely based on? At least if the text/ workbooks are thrown out, genuine creativity (for teacher as well as student, a profoundly important point) has a chance of coming in.

As this whole book is taken up with the issue of creativity in the classroom, it perhaps seems redundant to devote a separate section to it here. Without doubt, the teacher who follows the educational principles set down in this chapter would perforce be conducting a creative classroom. But there are matters as yet untouched or touched only tangentially that warrant our special attention.

Though many of the questions offered here can be answered by the simple expedient of looking up the answer in a book, the thrust of all the questions is toward the process of discovery more than it is toward the nailing down of a specific answer—not that answers are to be scorned as unworthy ends, for they can provide the base upon which other discoveries can be made or other questions asked. But *process* is the real issue. One of the most useful problem-solving techniques is the "brainstorming" session, which, incidentally, need *not* be a group activity. Whether brainstorming is done solo or in committee, the principle is the same: the mind has to be allowed to float free, so to speak, to divest itself of the accretions of prejudice (of all kinds) that it is subject to almost from birth. This means that a brainstorming session can take on the aspect of a surrealistic happing. This should not bother us a bit. For once the imagination is "unleashed" marvelous things happen. The whole world takes on a new character as it begins to open up for exploration. Teacher and student cease to worry about conventional rôle playing. Things which are unknown but which have the potential of being known become deliciously mysterious and tempting. Questions abound. New relationships are seen. Meaning emerges from experience.

Though creativity can be defined (as in the dictionary), I think it need not be. Like humor, we have a feeling for what creativity is, and just as definitions of humor are depressing and constricting, so too are definitions of creativity. It is sufficient to appreciate the fact that all humans are creative, but that creativity manifests itself in a variety of ways. I have a colleague who believes that only when one writes poetry, plays, novels, or short stories can one be considered a creative writer. This of course is nonsense. As the critic Northrop Frye points out, such reasoning requires that the genres themselves contain the creativity. A work like Loren Eiseley's *The Immense Journey* is, by my colleague's standard, not an example of creative writing. Read it and judge for yourself whether it is! My point is that we can write creatively or not (regardless of of what we are writing), we can solve problems creatively or not, we can respond to experience creatively or not. The classroom *Gestalt* will have a powerful effect on the creative potential of those within it.

If it is true that it is a normal human thing to be creative, then releasing the child's creativity should be no very difficult task. The problem, I fear, lies with the teacher and the system in which he is forced to function. Being the product of a stultifying education in the first place and being further stultified by the school program (which is more concerned with avoiding controversy than with offering good education), the teacher is not likely to be a very powerful creative force. (My hat is off to the exceptions, "the happy few.") Perhaps the teachers' unions and professional organizations can include freedom from boneheaded administrative domination of the classroom in their demands. And this should be nonnegotiable. If the teacher is a professional (as he professes to be), then he should be left alone to make his professional decisions. On the other hand, the time servers will continue to serve their time, but this can't be our problem here. The questions with which I have closed the final chapter of the book can, if acted upon, smoke out the deadheads and at least embarrass them a bit. I believe in teacher independence, but I don't believe that fools should be suffered (gladly or otherwise).

Being Creative

Since being creative means (among other things) making new patterns instead of following old ones, one can conclude that any kind of activity that settles into mere routine is uncreative. If creativity is "building anew," then any activity which is, so to speak, pre-built is uncreative. The logical concomitant of these views of creativity *vis-à-vis* education is the perhaps overwhelming question, *What's worth knowing?* The implications of this question for student, teacher, and school are profound indeed. The pursuit of the answer has to be *par excellence* an exercise in creativity. Such a question, after all, blanks out the coordinates that have been laid down for us and upon which we are at any moment impaled, and we are thus required to survey suddenly virgin territory (and with, in all probability, new instruments of our own devising). Such a prospect promises a kind of intellectual vertigo, at least until we begin to pull form out of chaos. The media like to toss about phrases like "adventures of the mind," but these "adventures" are generally pretty dull stuff. To launch oneself on the question *What's worth knowing?* is to launch oneself on an adventure of the mind worthy of the name.

It is appropriate to contend with this question at some point or points in every school year. If one begins and ends the year with the question and compares the discussions and conclusions drawn on each occasion, one will have learned much about the thought process and about himself in relationship to the experiential world. A few of the questions that *What's worth knowing?* might breed:

1. What do you know now? How do you know what you know? Make a list of the different kinds of things that you know. Can you explain how you learned these things?
2. What can you do with what you know? What do you need to know to do whatever you do? Consider talking, playing games, eating, getting dressed, going somewhere, asking questions, answering questions, getting along with people, and so on.
3. How do you decide what's important to you? What *is* important to you?

The mining of these questions, their parents, and their offspring can occupy a week, a month, or an entire school year. If a class had spent a year on the question and had arrived at some idea of what *is* worth knowing (which could be done only by testing what seemed to be worth knowing), it would be a year uncommonly well spent.

Painting and related art work are perhaps the most overtly creative activities of the classroom, although even art can be made uncreative and often is. Where the child is asked to color outlined drawings, where the teacher demands of the child that he draw or paint representationally (against the natural urge of the child simply to explore the world of form and color), an activity of high creative potential is reduced to routine busywork. To encourage a child's creative growth, Professor Lowenfeld offers these suggestions:

> [G]ive him a box of good thick crayons and a pad of newsprint. Peel the paper from the crayons and break them in half so he won't feel compelled to keep them new and perfect. Then leave him alone

and he will create. If he says he "can't draw" you can recall with him the smell of the leaves, the feel of the cat, the motions he goes through to throw a ball, the way a tree looks. Or give him a box of scrap materials—paper, string, yarn, toothpicks—which he may want to organize into a collage with the aid of some glue. As he tries to transfer his sense impressions to paper or materials he will gain facility and confidence. You might also give him several pounds of pliable clay to experiment with; or give him a box of water colors or show card paints and a pad of newsprint. Just a few colors will do. He can learn to mix the rest. You'll soon find that there is no surer way to nourish a creative instinct than to provide the means for a child to seek his own kind of expression. Don't worry about the forms such expression takes as long as it flows freely. Don't, for instance, "show" him how to stroke with a brush. Let him discover his own ways. Don't, whatever you do, suggest that his paintings and drawings must "look like" whatever he claims they are. His scribblings and daubings may open the door to a far more creative life than perfectly-copied drawings his little friend makes from a magazine. (P. 16.)

From the beginning of life, the child learns by experiment, and he learns remarkably well. Making things "easier" for the child by giving him shortcuts to his goals can do nothing but demean the goals.

In many schools, "art" is taught by a kind of circuit-riding "art teacher," who manages about half an hour a week in any given class. I marvel at such an operation. What is it supposed to accomplish other than to allow the school to claim an "art program"? Let the school system use its funds more wisely by providing in full measure the materials for art needed by the child and by hanging real art shows under the direction of a real artist. Let the children see lots of good art and produce as much art as they wish to produce. The classroom teacher can pose problems and ask questions that will help the child move from discovery to discovery.

FILM STUDY and filmmaking have quite suddenly become a part of the school curriculum in a number of systems. Some schools boast film production facilities fully capable of turning out work of professional quality. And the work coming out of these schools often comes close to being professional. Since filmmaking is, for the school, a wholly new type of program, its designers are free of the claptrap that surrounds the "traditional" disciplines—they are free, that is, to be creative. Here, then, is a torch from which everyone can take heat and light. But, someone says, we are supposed to be talking about the *early* years—little kids, not high-school kids. Uncreative thinking! As soon as a child can see something through a viewfinder and knows which button to push to make the camera go, he is ready for movie-making. Television has built into our children a "viewfinder image" of the world. The world, that is, with a frame around it. They have an instinct for film technique: zooms, cuts, animation, and the rest. Furthermore, in a few pilot programs (fantastically successful), third-grade children not only made movies, but made good movies, using three-dimensional animation and voice-over-music (yet).

For the teacher who knows nothing about filmmaking and its application in school programs, there are numerous readable and inexpensive books available (see Bibliography). One set of all the equipment needed for making and screening a movie can be got for under a hundred dollars. When the class has its first annual film festival, it will be seen to be money wisely spent. The affinity of children for both the gadgetry and its creative potential is phenomenal. Rather a month spent on making a film than an hour spent filling in blanks in a workbook.

There is little point in taking up space by listing filmmaking projects. As soon as the students are introduced to the idea, they will produce far more ideas than can ever be brought to fruition. The teacher would, however, be wise to try to get the students thinking in terms of fairly detailed treatments of small things rather than in terms of an 8mm. *War and Peace*. Much mileage can be got from a lump of clay (three-dimensional animation), for example, or a small collection of odds and ends: paper clips, erasers, etc. Children's films (*i.e.*, films made by children) and experimental films of all kinds are readily available for screening in the classroom and some time should be spent looking at them and discussing them.

There is little to be gained by measuring creativity, though scholars (as we might expect) are at work trying to do just that. We can, however, so stimulate the child that he makes the most of his creativity. "The nation that neglects creative thought today

will assuredly have its nose ground into the dust of tomorrow."
(Fred Hoyle, quoted by Viktor Lowenfeld, "Creativity: Education's Stepchild" in *A Source Book for Creative Thinking* [Parnes
and Harding].)

IN CLOSING

There is much more that might be included here: music and foreign language study, for example. This chapter could easily become a book in its own right, but this would be counter to my
purposes. The creative teacher in his creative classroom can do
what he wishes. My program is meant to open doors not to set limits.
For the many teachers who have asked me what they should do
in the textbookless classroom, I think I have given an answer. But,
as I tell my own students, I would hope that *my* answer quickly
becomes irrelevant. The truly creative teacher doesn't need *my*
program, he can make his own.

I likewise have made no effort to set up daily lesson plans or
semester syllabi or yearly curricula. These must be merely roughed
in according to what is happening in each class. The goals for a
class should come from the class in the course of its explorations.
I have provided numerous and, I think, rich materials for exploration. Any teacher who has stayed with me this far is surely ready
to fill in such gaps as he feels need filling.

Conspicuously absent too is a rationale for testing and evaluation. Testing is easily taken care of: dispense with it. There is nothing in the educational program that requires *testing* (if we mean
by *testing* periodic performances by the student to prove that he
can do some kind of testable activity according to some established
standard). Growing skills, broadening and deepening perceptions,
increasing sophistication (in the best senses of the term)—these are
the true measures of education. The British system of passing along
to the next teacher the year's work of each student and a detailed
narrative profile of the student seems to me entirely satisfactory.
As a parent, I am mystified by number grades on, for example, a
page of writing (handwriting, that is) my eight-year-old daughter
has done in school. What does 93% mean? And merely getting the
right answers on a page of addition problems seems pretty trivial.
If getting the right answers is the aim, she'd be better off using an

adding machine (which she knows how to do very well). In any case, grades for the early years are an exercise in administrative humbuggery—grades are for parents, though parents should have better sense than to demand them. Of the British approach, Joseph Featherstone writes, "If American parents could ever see some of the detailed histories kept of each child's separate path, including his art work, they would feel, quite rightly, that a report card is a swindle." (P. 6.) British schools, incidentally, normally have upwards of forty students in a class and British schoolteachers make about $35.00 per week, not much even in the somewhat lower British standard of living.

We need to ask ourselves what grades are for and what evaluations mean. Middle-class America is neurotic about getting its children into Harvard or, at the very least, State U. This obsession with college admittance is evident even in advertising, where an insurance company has a good thing going with its picture of the concerned father looking down at his infant son and promising that when Junior is ready for college, Dad will be ready for him (even if Dad's dead). This parental hangup (status, no matter how you want to color it) has no place in the educational program. Besides, the colleges themselves are beginning to rethink the old numbers game. Bowdoin College has just dropped its use of the College Boards. The entire structure of education will be radically different in the future from what it is today, and one of those differences will be the end of grades. Some schools have been getting along successfully without them for a long time (*e.g.*, Reed College, Sarah Lawrence College). More and more courses in less *avant-garde* colleges are being offered on a simple pass/fail basis. Some high schools are going over to the pass/fail system, the halfway house to a gradeless system. This doesn't mean no work, no standards, and no evaluation. It does mean something new and in many ways far more demanding of both student and teacher. The student, in short, who can do college-level work will find a place in college. Dad needn't worry overmuch. Besides, what does an "A" mean? If all schools were comparable, a grade might have some demonstrable meaning, but they aren't and it doesn't. Not even class rank means much. But a folder full of the student's papers and the teachers' commentaries allow one—parent or college admissions officer—to make a reasonable evaluation. It's coming.

THE
MIDDLE
YEARS

The intermediate program is freighted with information which comes out of books. The child with reading troubles therefore picks up less than his intelligence could absorb. And the very bright child picks up such gobs of verbal information that the teacher cannot be sure how much he really understands. At these years the social class problem is particularly severe, because the working-class child senses a widening gap between the apparently ornamental skills and knowledge rewarded by the school and the survival kit of abilities demanded by his home community,

[Martin Mayer, *The Schools*]

Most schools are designed for adults, for the comfort and convenience of faculty and administration. The Beloit-Turner Middle School in Wisconsin, by contrast, was clearly conceived as a place for kids—or, more accurately, it was artfully designed to house a program based on the special nature and needs of early adolescents.

The visitor's first impression of the school is one of openness—of wide-open, visually attractive space. His second impression is one of almost constant movement, relatively quiet, purposeful, and relaxed, but unceasing. Only later in the day does he realize that he has heard no bells ringing to signal the end of class periods, and that classes of various sizes have met for differing lengths of time, and then have dissolved and re-formed with a minimum of disturbance.

[James Cass, "A School Designed for Kids"]

Not long ago I spoke to a PTA meeting at a very good elementary school. As always, I urged that children be given greater freedom to decide what they should learn and how they should learn it. One parent came up to me after the meeting and said, "It seems to me that what we have to do is give children gradually less and less freedom as they grow up, so as to get them ready for what adult life will be like." Many people have said such things to me, at one time or another. It is hard to know how to reply.

[John Holt, *The Underachieving School*]

School deprives the child of opportunities to make meaningful communication with his friends and avoid his adversaries. Talking to schoolmates, even "whispering," is a veritable sin in the classroom. The school does not hesitate to intrude on the child's privacy; it eavesdrops, intercepts and reads his notes, and makes his personal matters its institutional business, to no other effect than to teach him distrust and evasiveness.

[Ryland W. Crary, *Humanizing the School: Curriculum Development and Theory*]

The typical school is organized on the assumption that if one child talks to another he is either out of order or he's cheating. At Beloit-Turner, however, the school building is designed to encourage social activities and relationships. For example, the cafeteria is used by the children for a variety of purposes. Besides eating lunch and socializing here, they may come at any time of the day to work in small groups or merely to take a "Coke break" from their studies.

[Dr. Rolland Callaway, Professor of Education, University of Wisconsin-Milwaukee, quoted in "A School Designed for Kids"]

Should a student or group of students become inspired to engage in role-playing or the construction of a model or set, he is allowed to proceed to the Creative Interests and Abilities area to take advantage of his momentary inspiration. The same holds true if a student feels that he wishes to listen to music, or paint a picture, or work out an experiment in the physical environment area. Although it is absolutely necessary to have some sort of schedule structure, whenever possible, it is ignored.

[Carl Strassburg, in "A School Designed for Kids"]

THE specific grade levels encompassed by the terms "early years," "middle years," and "later years" are indeterminate. The grade-level concept is, as I have urged, specious and should be altogether done away with; yet intellectual, social, and emotional maturity are realities (about which we know less than we pretend) that can be loosely bounded, hence: "early," "middle," and "later." The teacher must be the final judge of what is suitable for any class of students or any single student.

The early years provide the rationale for education itself. But once the student is *thinking*, he is ready to press on, ready to cope with larger and more complex problems and to handle greater quantities of data (N.B., *handle*, not merely *store*). Thus the middle years expand and intensify the materials of the early years. There is no discontinuity (particularly in the "campus school," K through 13), no sense that we've got something "out of the way," but rather an uninterrupted flow. One of the most curious results of our traditional education is the feeling that we study things merely to get done with them and as soon as we're done with them we can forget them. This is not, of course, the "official" view, but it is the practical result of the grade-level, graded-textbook plan of education. One finishes a book, puts it aside and starts a new book with a new number on the cover. The old book is dead, we're "above" it—the number on the new book proves it. This may not be the textbook writer's or teacher's intent, but there it is none the less. Where there are no textbooks to delineate the presumed grade boundaries, there is no sense of simple linearity. What was done before summer vacation is still alive and worthy of attention—it's not the "old stuff." Such a program is enhanced if the grade-level rigidities of classroom and teacher are abandoned in order that the child can easily pick up the thread of his work and not be arbitrarily put into the X-grade class.

My focus in this and the following chapter will narrow to deal primarily with "language arts" materials. I would hope that those whose major teaching responsibility is in the other areas will work at building programs in those areas based on the pattern offered in the preceding chapter. The relinquishing of textbooks in those areas should afford no insurmountable difficulties, and the quality of education possible of achievement without textbooks is worth any difficulties that may arise. Wherever feasible, the teacher should derive teaching materials from current sources (*e.g.*, periodicals, television, student questions; much valuable help can be got from books like

— *The Literary Time Line in American History,* which, as the authors tell us, "is designed to provide teachers and children in grades five through nine with resource materials which should make it possible to proceed with the teaching and learning of American history almost entirely through the use of trade [*i.e.,* as opposed to text-] books.") Paperback books are a boon to education impossible to overestimate. We have only just begun to make proper use of this resource. Administrators have to be weaned away from the idea that schoolbooks must be heavy, washable, expensive, and "permanent." Furthermore, every school should have a bookstore (or stand, at least) well stocked with a rich variety of paperback books. The habit of building one's own library should begin early.

The teaching of history and related subjects can, for example, be based upon the discovered concept of historiography—*i.e., What is history* as opposed to *What are some facts of history.* Before any type of history book is examined, the student should *write* history. Perhaps the history of the preceding year at school. Here he will quickly learn the differences between, say, biography (autobiography) and the broader historical view. He may also learn something about myth, legend, and fiction. He will not be long in seeking out examples of historical writing, samples of which will of course be available in the classroom in the form of a paperback library of history. And he will be able to make comparisons in the same way among history, historical novel, biography, mythology, and so on. Memorizing a few half truths about Columbus, the Puritans, the "Founding Fathers," etc., serves no purpose that I can determine. When the student has been "hooked" on the idea of history, he will be ready for some serious historical reading, and he will then learn something substantive about Classical, European, American, and other history.

Likewise, let the student *be* a scientist, mathematician, geographer, sociologist. He will need tools, reference works, time, and encouragement. He will not need textbooks. *National Geographic, Nature, Scientific American, Sky and Telescope,* and the like will give the student more "textbook" material than he can possibly deal with.

But it is, after all, language which is central. Understanding and expression are linguistic processes regardless of what we are understanding and what we are expressing. The approach to history I have suggested is essentially a set of language activities. The classification of concepts in science is manifested as a classification of words. The logic of science and of thought itself is part of language. Thought is language.

> Actually, thinking is most mysterious, and by far the greatest light upon it we have is thrown by the study of language. This study shows that the forms of a person's thoughts are controlled by inexorable laws the pattern of which he is unconscious. These patterns are the unperceived intricate systematizations of his own language —shown readily enough by a candid comparison and contrast with other languages, especially those of a different linguistic family. His thinking itself is in a language—in English, in Sanskrit, in Chinese. And every language is a vast pattern-system, different from others, in which are culturally ordained the forms and categories by which the personality not only communicates, but also analyzes nature, notices or neglects types of relationship and phenomena, channels his reasoning, and builds the house of consciousness. (Benjamin Lee Whorf, "Language, Mind, and Reality," in *Language, Thought, and Reality*, p. 252.)

USING LANGUAGE

Speaking and writing are manipulative, reading is receptive. This is another way of saying that the former two are active and overtly productive and that the latter is passive and overtly non-productive. (What is covertly produced can be determined only by either speaking or writing.) And if all three are basic, then the former two are "more basic," for it is through actions performed that the most profound learning takes place. Ideally, the three should not be separated from each other. They are all "languaging" and that is sufficient. Reading can be written or spoken about, writing can be read, speech can be written or written about, and so forth.

The language program of the early years like that in other fields should be continued and enlarged. Plays and other performances arising from current experience will be a normal part of the weekly activities. If, for example, a student has got interested in some historical event (or current event), he should be encouraged to write a play about it. Or about a myth, or whatever. At the same time, the teacher can direct the class to the plays in the class paperback library. Some students may want to try acting them out. Some of the problems of dialogue writing can be explored. Comparisons can be made between actual dialogue (via the tape recorder) and dramatic dialogue. The beginnings of an awareness of literary quality can be developed. Questions like these will point the way:

1. What are the differences between a tape-recorded conversation and this conversation [from any play the class may be reading]? What happens if in a play we try to imitate actual conversation exactly?
2. How can you tell two characters in a play apart? (Other than by their names, of course.) Do they have different ways of talking? Describe these differences in this play. What about real people—do they have different ways of talking? Can you describe some of these differences?
3. How do you know what a character in a play is like as a person? Are the characters in this play distinctly different people? Can you describe each character? (Not necessarily his physical appearance but his personality. What do we mean by *personality?*)
4. What makes a play seem believable to you? What does *believable* mean? Are some plays more believable than others? Can something that is make-believe still be believable? How?
5. Are some plays easier to follow than others? Why?

And so on. I would also play records of plays (dozens are available) and discuss ways in which actors give character to their parts. Several students can try reading a passage in a play and the class can discuss the effects of each reading. A dittoed student play would be most useful here, for the author himself can both read his lines and comment on other readings. The atmosphere, of course, must in no way be hostile, negative, or carping. (Though I suppose it is inevitable that feelings may at least be sensitized when one's own work is being manhandled. These feelings, incidentally, can themselves be discussed openly. Everything is grist for the inquiry mill.)

Closely related to dramatic readings and productions is the writing and reciting of poetry. Of all the literary subjects poetry is, among Americans, the most widely and cordially disliked. There is nothing in poetry itself that requires its dislike. It is man's oldest literary mode; and in another context, namely that of song, it is at least accepted. The feelings contra poetry arise from several causes: most of the poetry found in language arts texts is either bad or irrelevant. Banal, patronizing little "poems" in forced rhymes and gallumphing rhythms are not likely to win even the young child over to poetry. Nor are the tortured "analyses" that the student is subjected to later on. Furthermore, there is too much of silent reading and too little of writing and saying and listening. I have seen students listening as though hypnotized to Dylan Thomas reciting his own poetry (on record) without their having the foggiest idea of the intellectual content of the poetry. Poetry is in large measure ritual, and it can be readily responded to at that "primitive" level—if the poetry is well written and well spoken. The insensitivity of many teachers to poetry comes through in the limping, sing-song recitation of students who are asked to read aloud. It is no wonder that so many people think poetry is a lot of "flowery nonsense." It is nonsensically taught by teachers with tin ears.

The special values of poetry can be got at most readily by asking the student to discuss the differences he can detect between poetic and non-poetic writing. (In the middle of this scale, the differences are subtle and require subtlety on the part of the student to detect them.) One obvious difference will be between *recursiveness* (poetry) and *discursiveness* (prose). It is recursion (broadly, *repetition*) that gives poetry its ritual flavor. Popular song lyrics (especially in the work of such exemplars as Arlo Guthrie, Bob Dylan, the Beatles, and so on) can be very effectively used ("relevance"); and contemporary poets (Frost seems to work quite well) can be mined for suitable examples of *good* poetry (as opposed to the typical "kiddie" poetry and *kitsch* like Vachel Lindsay's *The Congo*, which some teachers still unaccountably try to fob off on the worldly-wise youngsters of the seventies). Again, the paperback will come to the rescue. Let the students browse at will and share their own favorites with the class. Or write imitations. Or write poems on similar subjects to the poems they read. As with the reading of lines in plays, students should read and record each other's poetry and the poetry they find that they especially enjoy. They should listen to the great readers of poetry on record, Dylan Thomas and the rest. The study of poetry should be done in the manner of a workshop. And while the teacher can raise all manner of questions, he should never impose "interpretations." *Involvement* is the thing at this point, not scholarly pretension.

It has been said that "poetry is syntax." It will serve the student's ear well to explore the implications of that assertion. This gets to the heart of what makes poetry poetry. Try these questions (and as many more as the class can devise):

1. What happens when you change the word order of this poem? [Any poem can be used.] Try writing the poem over, using the same words but moving the words and phrases around. Is something lost? What? Is something gained? What?
2. Can you substitute synonyms for the key words in the poem? What happens when you do it? Does the *feeling* of the poem change? How?
3. What happens if you change the poem so that there aren't any rhymes left? Is the poem as effective without the rhymes?
4. What happens if you add a word or two to each line—if, for example, the word *tree* occurs in a line, add *big* or *beautiful,* etc. Does this kind of change improve the poem? Discuss.
5. Can you rewrite the poem so that it sounds like a paragraph of prose? What did you do? How does it compare with the original? What is lost? What is gained?

Light verse (*e.g.,* Ogden Nash), parodies (*e.g.,* S. Hoffenstein), and limericks should also be read and written. Once the student understands the structure of a limerick, he will work at producing limericks with the same compulsion as the jigsaw- and crossword-puzzle addict. Don't try to force "official" opinions down his throat. Let him wait for college or graduate school to discover the joys of Wordsworth. On the other hand, don't palm off Edgar Guest and the simpering sentimentality of "inspirational" verse on him, for he will develop not taste but distaste or bad taste.

As a matter of principle, students should not be burdened with notions like "great" and "beautiful." If something is worthy to be called great, then it will be discovered to be so. If it is not, all the exhortation in the world won't convince anybody. Simplistic value judgments are not very useful pedagogically—they may even get in the way of learning. Nobody likes being constantly shoved in front of an altar and made to offer supplication. The student can't help but scratch his head over a teacher who is gurgling and gushing over something that he just cannot see (and very likely isn't ready to respond to). Let's explore poems, not "great poetry" (not much of what the student is normally given to read in the name of poetry is all that "great" anyhow; but the teacher feels obligated, by way, I suppose, of self-justification, to urge its "greatness").

I have found in teaching creative writing to fifth- and sixth-graders that asking them to write their impressions as they listen to various kinds of music is eminently successful in setting up what might be called a poetic trance. Sharing the writing, and discussing it in the workshop format, is important and will lead at least some students to do some rewriting. At this point the student will grasp the significance of, for example, Keats's revisions of *The Eve of St. Agnes*. To present poems and other works of art as jewels magically sprung from the heart of the creator is to deny the process of creation. There is art in making the final work seem the inevitable one, perfectly born, bearing none of the marks of the forceps, so to speak. But it is the rare work that not only looks that way but in fact came into being that way. Art is hard work, and we do well to let the student in on it. It is surely defeating to a student to believe that only a person with that magical "inspiration" can produce anything worthwhile.

Modifying existing stories (rewrite "The Cask of Amontillado" from Fortunato's point of view, for example), writing TV scripts based on series with which the students are familiar, turning newspaper stories into fiction, turning fiction into news stories, writing poems in response to paintings, sculpture, and photographs, and so on are but a few projects to get the writing habit well rooted. One kind of writing that is probably best avoided is the "composition" or "theme." The opportunities for *de facto* "themes" are many, but they must be "organic," that is, they must arise from a context which naturally demands a piece of writing: scientific reports, minutes of meetings, historical and sociological writing (as earlier discussed), but never the set-piece "composition." For the teacher who envisions mountains of papers to grade, put aside your fears. It's not *grades* students need but *encouragement*. I do not think it at all wise to put the student in the bind of having to produce something only to look forward to having it spattered with the teacher's red ink. We are looking for confidence, fluency, and, most of all, the desire to express oneself. Papers can be examined and discussed in workshop, and on occasion the teacher can read a set of papers and make detailed constructive comments on them. Narrow questions of "correctness" should not be bothered with. In time, the mechanical problems will evaporate. They certainly have not been mitigated by all the fussing we do. The obvious reason is that the students write rarely, meagerly, and reluctantly. What can they possibly learn about writing under such a regimen? Even if they would conscientiously memorize every rule that pleases any given teacher (the diversity is quite remarkable), they would have precious little occasion to use the rules. Better to write all the time (for a variety of reasons) and let the mechanics smooth out (as they inevitably will), for the student will at the same time he is writing be comparing and contrasting what he writes with what he reads and with what others write. He will have the leisure to get inside writing to find out what makes it tick. Niggling over commas and spelling as if they were the most important things in the world is no way to get anyone interested in anything. As far as that's concerned, John F. Kennedy, F. Scott Fitzgerald, and lots of other pretty fair writers were pretty bad spellers.

It occurs to me that if a child were to do some writing *every day* (the amount to increase appropriately as the years go by), he would at the very least be an extraordinarily competent writer by the time he was graduated from high school. This, of course, does not mean filling blanks in workbooks but, rather, free discursive writing. And certainly those students who wish to write at length should be left alone to do so. Nothing any teacher would interrupt him for would be worth the work he was doing on his own.

The separation of "English" into literature, composition, and "grammar" is pedagogically indefensible. As we have seen, it is the *language experience* which is the core of English, and literature, composition, and grammar are merely a few manifestations of language. We have talked about drama, poetry, and writing in general, but underlying these is language.

> We have three levels of the mind . . . and a language for each of them, which in English-speaking societies means an English for each of them. There's the level of consciousness and awareness, where the most important thing is the difference between me and everything else. The English of this level is the English of ordinary

conversation, which is mostly monologue, as you'll soon realize if you do a bit of eavesdropping, or listening to yourself. We can call it the language of self-expression. Then there's the level of social participation, the working or technological language of teachers and preachers and politicians and advertisers and lawyers and journalists and scientists. We've already called this the language of practical sense. Then there's the level of imagination, which produces the literary language of poems and plays and novels. They're not really different languages, of course, but three different reasons for using words. (Northrop Frye, *The Educated Imagination*, pp. 22–23.)

In devoting an entire chapter to language, I hoped to provide the reader with an orientation to language that would inform our considerations of the educational program and lead us to an appreciation of the ultimate unity of all that we teach. Within the framework of "English," that unity obtains *a fortiori*.

This means that splitting "grammar" off as a subject to be studied in isolation from other aspects of language is educationally unacceptable. With the appearance of "linguistic" language arts texts, the old grammar folderol has been newly legitimized, and the teacher can go on playing the same old games with a new set of "scientific" terms. Like any new product, "linguistics" is being appealingly packaged and advertised as the answer to a teacher's prayer. Invariably, in teachers' meetings, conventions, workshops, I am asked which "linguistics" series I recommend. I have angered a great many teachers by replying that I recommend no series and that if they intend simply to unplug the old grammar series and plug in the new "linguistics" series they might just as well stick to the old and comfortable; for in the absence of any radical revision of the whole program, "linguistics" will accomplish the same nothing (or the same failures) that their old grammar series accomplished. Reed-Kellog diagrams or transformational trees—for any but the college student of grammatical theory, both are equally unrewarding. To an elementary school or high school student, grammatical diagramming is pointless busywork. This is not to say that any discussion of grammar is taboo. Not by any means. But we have to understand when and how grammatical insights can meet a felt need on the part of the student. This does not come at a predictable class period every week or during the first fifteen minutes of every class period or whatever.

In any event, to fasten onto "grammar" as the issue seems odd. As we have seen, those aspects of language which have to do with the ways in which language daily affects us are what we should focus on; for example, the three reasons for using language that Frye speaks of. And here we are back to writing and literature and speaking and reporting and propaganda and science and everything else with a linguistic component.

But let us look at grammar anyway and see what we can find that might be of use to the student. We are not, remember, looking at rules of usage, but at the grammatical structure of the language. When we spoke earlier of poetry as syntax, we were touching on a grammatical question, and in that context one might spend some fruitful moments trying to discover with the class the syntactical components of language and how they are manipulated. English has but a few basic structures which are in turn combined in a few different ways. Professor Harry Warfel's discussion (*Language: A Science of Human Behavior*, p. 149) of a well-known passage from *Macbeth* is suggestive of what would be illuminating for a class studying poetry or *Macbeth* or the skill of Shakespeare as a writer. The passage:

> Will all great Neptune's ocean wash this blood
> Clean from my hand? No, this my hand will rather
> The multitudinous seas incarnadine,
> Making the green one red.

Warfel makes the point that while, as John Crowe Ransom has said, the interleaving of Latinate with native English vocabulary is "one of Shakespeare's supreme poetic strategies," the brilliance of the passage resides far more in his inversion of the object (*multitudinous seas*) and the double valence he gave to the participial (*Making the green one red*) by putting this adjectival modifier into an adverbial slot and forcing out of it both adjectival and adverbial meaning. "Shakespeare doubtless smiled as he wrote down the big adjective [*multitudinous*], but he patted himself on the back over the successful syntactical deployment." The teacher in making such an explanation or in leading the student to make the discoveries should of course use such technical terminology as is necessary, but he need not feel compelled to stuff the student full of the language of grammatical analysis; the student will be wise enough to recognize the need to name what was formerly unknown to him.

In a suitable context, grammatical and other linguistic insights (*e.g.*, etymologies, etc.) are engaging and informative. Grammar taken as a separate "subject," nouns this week, verbs next, and so on can be nothing but boring. Children want to see connections and interrelationships. What I am suggesting, then, is a gradual burrowing into language through its various manifestations. We noted, for example, that the prepositional phrase covers a multitude of subsurface meanings. It would be most instructive for the class to explain the meaning of all the prepositional phrases in any paragraph of any book or magazine they might be reading. And, further, to try to categorize all the different meanings for any one preposition and to categorize all the different prepositions that seem to have approximately the same meaning. Then the students can try to rewrite the paragraph using the sub-surface equivalents of the prepositional phrases and discuss what they think the author accomplished by using the one syntactic maneuver (the prepositional phrase) in preference to the other (its sub-surface equivalent). Here is a grammatical exercise that illuminates both a feature of singular importance in the language and something of the way a writer manipulates his linguistic resources. The same kind of exercise can be done with, say, the infinitive. Never, however, should this be made a labeling game. The prepositional phrases (and infinitives, etc.) should be identified for the student. It won't take him long to recognize them on his own anyway. Though, to repeat, he should *never* be asked merely to *label* grammatical items. The student with a real bent for close analysis can be encouraged to try to discover if different writers do different kinds of things with infinitives and the like. This is sophisticated work and not for everyone; perhaps in a particular class, not for anyone.

Another useful type of exercise in transformational grammar is to attempt to take a passage of poetry or prose down to its kernels. This kind of exercise not only has the appeal of a puzzle but, again, it is most informative about the broader question of how the language works and the narrower question of how a writer takes advantage of the potential operations of the language. For some real fun and games (linguistically speaking), try this exercise on "The Jabberwocky Song" or one of the more linguistically unorthodox poems of E. E. Cummings. Play with language. Don't make the study of language a deadly (and deadeningly) serious affair.

The creation of an artificial language for general use is a task that has taxed the ingenuity of numerous scholars, but it is a task with great appeal for the student. Most children at one time or another develop some sort of little secret language—on the order, say, of pig Latin—which they use both for fun and for achieving a degree of privacy from outsiders—out-group children and eternally nosy adults. So the concept is not a foreign one. However, the traditional children's "languages" are generally based on grotesque pronunciations not on any serious restructuring of morphology and syntax, nor on the re-sectioning of reality. But these are the areas in which language construction can prove genuinely illuminating. These questions should get things started:

1. In English, we can say *the boy* (meaning *one* boy) and *the boys* (meaning *any* number more than one). In some languages there is a way of saying *two* of something (without using the numerator). This is called *dual number*. Would there be any advantage in having a special ending for the dual number in English? Invent a marker for dual number that can be attached the way the *-s* (for plural) can be attached. (Incidentally, Anglo-Saxon or Old English, the earliest form of the English language, has a dual number form.) Use your new dual number markers in a few sentences.

2. In English, we *shrug* our *shoulders*, we don't use *shrug* for a similar movement elsewhere on the body—we don't, that is, shrug our ears or our stomachs or our chest or whatever. Can you make up an appropriate word for "shrugging," say, your stomach? What guided you in contriving the word as you did?

3. All words have some degree of *context sensitivity*. *Shrug*, for example, has a very high degree of context sensitivity. That is, it can occur only as a transitive verb with *shoulders* as the object (*he shrugged his shoulders*) or as an intransitive verb (*he shrugged*). Can you find any other words like *shrug*, words that can occur only in very limited contexts? Contrast a word like *is*, which can occur with thousands upon thousands of words and phrases. Is context sensitivity a useful or a bothersome feature of language? Discuss.

4. In English, we say *I have been here since yesterday.* In Japa-

nese, this sentence would read *Katakushi wa kinō kara koko ni imasu,* the literal meaning of which is *I* + subject marker (*wa*) *yesterday since here* + place marker (*ni*) *have been.* Strictly speaking, the Japanese sentence means (to a Japanese, as opposed to an American studying Japanese), *I have been here since yesterday, and I continue to be here.* If I am now leaving, the past form of the verb (*imashita*) must be used. The Japanese way of expressing the concept that we express by saying *I have been here since yesterday* must seem strange to you. (And our way seems strange to the Japanese.) Does each way have its advantages and disadvantages? Can you explain them? How does Japanese thinking seem different from ours? Can you make up some sentences built on the Japanese pattern but using English words?

5. Some languages (Japanese, Russian) do not use words equivalent to our articles (*a/an, the*). Try writing a paragraph without using any articles. What problems did you run into? How do you suppose that article-less languages solve the problems you had?

6. Some languages make use of *honorifics* or special linguistic forms that show what kind of social relationship exists between the speakers in a conversation. Thus, simply by listening to the forms of the language each uses (irrespective of what they are speaking about—business, the weather, or anything), one can tell who is considered higher on the social scale. Is this a useful feature of language? Explain. Does English have anything that serves the same function? Create some specific "honorifics" for English and show how they would be used.

7. English (and most other natural languages) has a high degree of *redundancy.* This means that we have "back-up" systems built into the language which help to assure that the message gets through. For example, when we are angry and call someone a bad name, we don't do it in a monotone. There is a definite "tone of voice" that indicates anger co-equally with the words we use. Or, in a sentence like *He plays the piano,* there are three ways of knowing that *he* is the subject of the sentence: (1) it is marked for the subject (contrast *he* with *his* and *him*), it precedes the verb (*plays*), and it is

"tied" to the verb, that is, if we change *he* to *they* we must change *plays* to *play*. Or, *Dad bought himself a new car,* where *himself* is really a repetition of *Dad*. Your problem is first to hunt up some other, different examples of redundancy, second to try to write a paragraph totally free of redundancy, third to discuss the difficulties in doing this, and last to discuss the problems in communication that would arise in a language with no redundancy.

8. Our language abounds in *metaphor* (from Greek, "transfer"): the *mouth* of the river, a *head* of cabbage, the *eye* of the hurricane, *he blew his top, she was floating on air,* and so on. Can you account for the origins of these metaphors? Can you write a paragraph completely free of metaphors? Make a list of the metaphors you find in any randomly chosen paragraph. Are metaphors useful? How? Why do poets use so many metaphors? What metaphors do you often use in everyday conversation?

9. Why do many people prefer to say that a person has *passed away* instead of *died*? Why do *undertakers* prefer to be called *morticians* or *funeral directors*? This kind of substitution of terms is called *euphemism* (from Greek, "good speech"). Can you find any more examples in everyday speech? Try to make up a dialogue in which the "plain" words are used instead of any euphemisms one might ordinarily be tempted to use. Do you feel more comfortable when you use euphemisms or when you use plain speech? Can you explain your feelings?

10. In Latin, all of the following sentences mean the *same* thing, namely, *Paul saw Mary:*

Paulus vidit Mariam	*Mariam Paulus vidit*
Paulus Mariam vidit	*Vidit Paulus Mariam*
Mariam vidit Paulus	*Vidit Mariam Paulus*

Yet if we invert our original English sentence to *Mary saw Paul,* we have changed the meaning. (The other possibilities aren't really English: Mary Paul saw, etc.) Can you explain why (1) all the "different" Latin sentences are in some sense the same and (2) the two English sentences are really very different? How much word-order freedom do we have in English? Can you write some sentences which are substantially the same as each other but in which various words and phrases have been moved about? Here is a simple example (you try more complicated ones!): *Tomorrow, I expect to go to California/ I expect to go to California tomorrow.* Can you classify sentence elements or certain kinds of words according to the degree of freedom they have in a sentence? *Tomorrow* in the above example is quite free. It can be put elsewhere in the sentence, too—where? The integrity of meaning is maintained in the Latin sentences through the use of *inflections* (in this instance, *case endings*). Can you find any examples in English that are similar to the Latin? [Teacher: *him you are to give it to; whom do you wish to see,* etc.]

11. Choose a paragraph from anything you are reading and look up the *etymologies* (word origins) of every word. Some words will, for example, come from Old English (Anglo-Saxon), some from Latin, some from French, and so on. What proportion of the words are "native" (*i.e.*, from Old English)? What proportion from French and Latin? Other? What *kinds* of words fall into each category? (Technical, "everyday," etc.) Can you rewrite the paragraph using only native words? Using only borrowed words? Does each kind of writing sound substantially different from the other? Explain. Check out the word origins of something you have already written. How does your proportion of native, French, Latin, etc., compare with the paragraph you analyzed first? Does it seem reasonable to conclude that different writers use the vocabulary resources of the language in differing proportions? Can you demonstrate this? Does this affect "style"? How?

12. What kinds of words seem to have some readily definable meaning all by themselves? Give some examples. Is the dictionary definition of *the*, for instance, of the same kind as that of *beautiful?* Or *window?* Or *swim?* Discuss the differences? Can *walk,* for example, mean different things? (*It was a long walk; He walked around the corner; He walked in the first inning; He walked away with the contest; He walked right up to the captain and told him where to get off,* etc.) Try some other words, explain the differences in meaning, and try to determine how these meanings came about.

13. Many words have emotional associations for people—some positive ("good") and some negative ("bad"). Make a list of words that have emotional associations for you. Try to explain why. Then try the list on several members of your family and several of your friends (even on some teachers) and see what kinds of emotional associations they have for the words. Don't come right out and ask them what their emotional associations are but just ask them to tell you as quickly as they can what each word makes them think of. Tabulate your results and make them into a report for the class. What did you learn by doing this research project? Can you (1) write a paragraph in which all the key words are negative, (2) write a paragraph in which all the key words are positive, and (3) write a paragraph in which all the key words are neutral (*i.e.*, lacking emotional associations)? Try to describe someone in each of these three ways. Find some examples in books and magazines and newspapers of writing that uses emotionally associative words to achieve an effect.

14. We are told that a verb form like *plays* is in the *present tense* (*i.e.*, present time), yet *He plays tomorrow* (in answer to *When does Joe play?*) is perfectly good English. Does this sentence mean *present* (now)? What about the *past tense* (*played*) in *He will have played six years at the end of this season*. Make up as many verbal groups (*e.g.*, *will have played*, etc.) as you can think of and try to explain the *time* meaning of each. (One of the chief features of the *verb* is its association with time.) Do we also convey time without the verb? When we say *the time is the future* (as in a stage direction for a play), does the verb (*is*) have any time component? Examine the verbs in any paragraph and try to figure out what they reveal about the sense of time within the paragraph. Don't be afraid to ask if you're not certain which are the verbs. We're not concerned with *labeling* but with *meaning*.

The tendency of these questions is clear. The student is brought to a variety of linguistic insights of a very practical kind within the framework of a rather sweeping challenge, namely, to make up his own language. The questions are some of those that would perforce be lurking in the mind of a language inventor, for he would need a fairly profound grasp of the nature of language and its normal human uses before he could hope to create a language that would have even the faintest chance of being used. Or, if the teacher prefers not to try the language creation problem, the questions are intrinsically interesting and will engage the student both in learning about language and in expressing himself about his discoveries. Nowhere are there definitions to be memorized or rules to be learned. Only discoveries to be made which relate to the "real" world of language not to the classroom/textbook/workbook world of language.

Issues of "correctness," propriety, and appropriateness in expression can be handled with questions like these:

1. Within any human society there are various groups of people that are identifiable in some way or another. Do you belong to one or more groups (or "identities")? What are they and how are you aware of their existence? Do these groups have objectively recognizable characteristics? What are these characteristics? Does your group have "standards" of some sort? What are they? Can you recognize other groups by the way they talk, dress, behave, etc.? Explain. Is there only one "right" way to talk, dress, etc.? Explain. Are these groups or identities useful to a society? Explain. Are the "standards" useful? Explain.

2. Do members of your group always talk the same way? Can you define more than one way of using language in your group (formal, informal, etc.)? Can you tabulate the characteristics of each type of usage? What happens when you speak in a way that is not expected in that context? Do you speak the same way with your parents as you do with your friends? What happens if you speak with your parents the way you speak with your friends? (Or the other way around.) Try it.

3. Can you "shock" people with language? How? Have you ever done it? What was "shocking"? Can you explain what there is about certain words that dismay, anger, or discomfort people? Can you be shocked with language? Discuss.

4. Have you ever been told that you mustn't say *ain't?* Were you told *why* you mustn't say *ain't?* Why do you suppose that you aren't supposed to say *ain't?* Have you ever heard people use *ain't?* Who used it and under what circumstances?

Ain't is a contraction of *am not*. Do we have another, "acceptable," contraction of *am not?* Some people in order to avoid saying either *ain't I* (which is presumed to be "wrong") or *am I not* (which is pompous) end up by saying *aren't I* which is the question form of *I are not*). Is *aren't I* any "better" than *ain't I?* What should guide you in your use of "forbidden" forms like *ain't?* What are some other usages that you have been told to avoid? Discuss the whys and wherefores following the reasoning regarding *ain't*.

5. Are there different kinds of writing? What are some of the different kinds? Think about newspapers, magazines, books of all kinds, pamphlets, instruction sheets, advertising, etc. How do all of these differ one from the other? What does the presumed *audience* for a piece of writing have to do with the way the writer expresses himself? Would you write in the same manner for (1) your teacher, (2) your friends, (3) your parents, (4) some public official you wanted to tell something to, (5) children younger than you? Can you demonstrate how you would modify your writing for each audience? Why is it of some importance to think about your audience as you write (or speak, for that matter)?

6. Mechanics (punctuation, spelling, capitalization, etc.) can be troublesome to the writer. Try to figure out some guidelines for mechanics based on the books and magazines you are reading. You may be interested in knowing that once upon a time neither the separation of words in writing nor punctuation existed. Everything was run together. How are the writing conventions of punctuation and word separation helpful? Keep in mind that (for example) *where are you going?* does not come out this way in speech (it is more like, *whereya goin'?*). Can you find some more examples of the differences between the way we speak and the way we render language into writing? Write a paragraph on anything you'd care to and then rewrite it as it would actually sound if you read it aloud speaking normally (conversationally) and not like a fussy English teacher. Now write a paragraph discussing what you discovered.

7. Make a list of words that you would not use in the classroom. Why wouldn't you use these words?

8. Some people make an issue over certain supposed differences in meaning between *shall* and *will*. Do you use these words with different intentions? Explain what meaning you intend with *shall* and what meaning with *will*. Some people say that it is "wrong" ("incorrect") to "split" an *infinitive* (*e.g.*, don't say *to completely finish*; say instead, *to finish completely*; *to finish* is the infinitive). Search around in your reading for some "split" infinitives. Do they sound "bad" or "wrong" to you? Is there a difference in meaning between the "incorrect" sentence, *he failed to completely solve the problem* and the "correct," *he failed completely to solve the problem?* What does this exercise teach you?

9. People are forever running to "The Dictionary" to settle language arguments. What kinds of arguments can a dictionary settle? What kind can't it settle? Is the dictionary really the "final authority" on matters of language? How are dictionaries made? By whom are dictionaries made? Are all dictionaries pretty much alike? (Compare, for example, a "supermarket special" with *The American Heritage Dictionary of the English Language*. Compare all features and write a report for the class on what you discovered.) Can any dictionary include every word in the language and every current meaning of every word? Why not? What kinds of information can be found in a dictionary? What can you do with this information? How does your dictionary *define* its words? What does your dictionary say about, for example, *put on* as in the expression *he's putting me on?* What other common expressions can't you find in your dictionary? Compare your dictionary's entry for *run* with that of the *New English Dictionary on Historical Principles (Oxford English Dictionary)*, unabridged. [Teacher: If your library doesn't have this extremely valuable work, see that it gets it, all thirteen volumes, not the two-volume version, which is all but useless.] What does this comparison tell you about dictionaries and dictionary-making?

10. Find some examples of what you consider to be *good* writing, writing that is fresh, readable, and appropriate to the audience for which it is presumably intended. Try imitating a few paragraphs. Explain what makes this writing appealing to you. Explain what the concept of *appropriateness* means to

you. Write a paragraph in a way that would be *inappropriate* for a specific type of audience (you choose the audience), explain why it is *in*appropriate, and revise it accordingly.

Spelling and vocabulary need not be singled out for special attention. The student who is doing lots of coordinated reading and writing and who has been made genuinely interested in these activities will enlarge his vocabulary as he needs to and will gradually have fewer and fewer spelling problems. At any rate, spelling is such a sterile matter to be concerned about that even so-called problem spellers should be left alone. Some people just don't get the hang of English spelling as quickly as others and the teacher shouldn't worry either himself or others about it. The *Reader's Digest* "increase-your-word-power syndrome" has infected the whole of the educational world and the sooner it is stamped out the better. Vocabulary lists and vocabulary tests are pedagogical hokum. Our three vocabularies (speaking-listening, reading, and writing) develop in functional linguistic contexts. Words are not used and responded to on the basis of presumed synonymy. It is, for example, nonsense to say that *big* "means" *large* (in the manner of a multiple-choice vocabulary test). Consider: *Jack's a big man around here, though Jack's not a very large man.* Here, Jack is *big* but not *large.* So what is our multiple-choice "increase-your-word-power" test going to do with this rather simple problem let alone the complexities and subtleties of the baroque vocabularies featured by the testers?

> I never looked at our dictionary. I don't use one today. In my life I doubt that I have looked up as many as fifty words. Perhaps not even half that.
> . . . I have talked about this with a number of teachers. More than once I have said, "According to tests, educated and literate people like you have a vocabulary of about twenty-five thousand words. How many of these did you learn by looking them up in a dictionary?" They usually are startled. Few claim to have looked up even as many as a thousand. How did they learn the rest?
> They learned them just as they learned to talk; by meeting words over and over again, in different contexts, until they saw how they fitted. (John Holt, *The Underachieving School*, p. 82.)

My experience squares with Holt's. I expect that the reader's does too. But because we feel compelled to "test" (in quotation marks because all we are "testing" is *memory,* not *learning*) and because discrete items of trivia are both easiest to "teach" and easiest to "test," students spend countless hours being forced to swill and regurgitate "spelling" and "vocabulary." And with what result?

THE MEDIA

The new media have busted the linear monopoly of print. Like most revolutions, this one was not led by the establishment. The elite culture, especially the schools, are the vested interest here. Western education is built around the book. Much of our research is patterned on the fragmenting habits of print. Even Freud is culture-bound. Even our movies and TV have not broken the spell of print-oriented man, because they are made by such men. The monopoly of print is over. It's only now a question of ratifying the fact and adapting ourselves and our institutions to the fact. It will not be easy.

Is it worth doing? Is anything else worth doing? Our habits and modes of perception pervade everything we do as men: our interpersonal relationships, our habits of inquiry, our psychological makeup, our work. It's that basic. Our current frantic and almost neurotic concern about literacy is but one example. An *all media literacy* should command the same sense of urgency and commitment. It will if it is understood. Understanding takes time.

What agencies of society should lead the way?

Those two giants who don't speak to each other—the school and the mass media.

Anyone for dialogue? (John Culkin, S.J., in *McLuhan: Hot & Cool,* p. 57.)

Media awareness and impact broaden during the middle years. There is some fall-off in TV-viewing by the brighter student, but radio, movies, and the print media take up at least some of the lost TV time. But whatever the mix, the media world is ever present in the lives of our children and we should take advantage of it.

The child's TV expertise can be called upon for increasingly complex "programming." And the motion-picture camera (better still, the video tape recorder) can be effectively used for mixed-media productions, "commercials," and "location shooting" for a "program."

Here are some questions and projects on the media that should sharpen the student's perceptions of the interplay between the media and the audience:

1. What classes of products make up the bulk of advertising in each of the media (TV, radio, periodicals)? Are the proportions different among the media? Can you explain this? Which products lend themselves best to the nature of each medium? Explain. How does each medium differ from the other?

2. Can you describe the differences between a TV ad for a product adults are most likely to want or to buy and a product a teen-ager is likely to want or buy? Are there any other *market* differences that you can detect between types of products? What TV ads "get to" you most effectively? Why? What ads are you most negative to? Why? Can you make up a commercial that you think would convince your parents to buy something, or at least convince them that they'd like to have that thing? What do you have to think about in order to do a good commercial?

3. Do you pay any attention to ads in newspapers and magazines? Which ads? Why? Can you make up an ad that will convince your teacher to buy or want to buy something? What do you have to think about to do a good job? How is writing a newspaper or magazine ad different from writing a TV commercial? What part does *language* play in each? Does language *written* effect you differently from language *heard*? How are visual effects in a printed ad different from visual effects in a TV ad?

4. Try writing a radio ad that will convince your friends to buy or want to buy something. What are the special problems of writing for a medium that can use only sound (*i.e.*, no visual effects)?

5. Advertising agencies, the companies who create ads and commercials, do a great deal of *market research*, which means that they try to find out what the public wants, likes, needs, and responds to with regard to the various products that the manufacturers and businesses are trying to sell. You have just invented a new gizmo (anything you please—even a new *service* as opposed to a new gadget) and you have hired

yourself as an advertising agency to set up an advertising campaign to sell this great new product (or service). How would you go about it? What kind of market research would pay off? Consider potential need, use, demand, price, size of market, etc. [This can easily be expanded into a class project in which the class becomes the ad agency and actually mounts a program for the product, including market research, ad design, and so on.]

6. Does there seem to be any relationship between the type of product being sold and the type of TV or radio program sponsored? If you were advertising automobiles, for example, what kinds of programs would you favor and what kind would you definitely reject? Why? Answer the same questions for other types of products.

7. What attention-getting devices are widely used in TV commercials? Radio commercials? Newspaper and magazine ads? Which of these really get *your* attention? Why?

8. Analyze a few newspaper ads for *factual* content. In other words, how much of what an ad says can be objectively validated? Do the same for radio and TV commercials. Are there any differences?

9. Write a script for your favorite TV program. Be sure to watch an episode of the program very carefully before you start—note the dialogue, sets, lighting, camera positions and movement, size of cast, music, etc. Then try a radio script for the same story. With all the visual material taken out, what problems do you have and how do you solve them? Can this lack of visuals be advantageous to a writer? How? Will the dialogue have to be changed when you switch over to the radio version? What about a *stage* version? What problems do you face now? Remember that in a stage play, the relationship between the actors and the audience is virtually unchanging—there is nothing like camera movement to, so to speak, move the audience in, out, and around.

10. Try now to turn your play into a story for a magazine. What new problems arise? What can be accomplished on the printed page that can't be accomplished on stage, TV, or radio? What are the advantages and disadvantages for the writer of each medium?

11. What activities in your daily life depend upon the existence of print (*i.e.,* the written word)? What proportion of your school activities depends upon the written word? What kinds of things can be taught and learned without the written word? How, for example, did you learn your language?

12. How does the experience of reading differ from the experience of watching TV? This is a difficult kind of question to deal with. Perhaps thinking about the nature of the static print medium in contrast to the nature of the active visual medium will help you to get started.

If these questions seem pretty sophisticated stuff for youngsters to be working on, that is only because we have been underestimating the youngsters. Given the right challenges and the right preparation in the right environment, they will produce beyond our expectations.

JUDGMENT

We are fond of judging and evaluating. And our children soon pick up our fondness. Generally, our judgments are casual and irrational (that is, we don't arrive at them by rational processes but through received attitudes and "feelings"). And in casual situations perhaps we needn't expect more. However, because so much of our life is run according to our judgments, evaluations, impressions, and so on, it is wise to explore the judgment-making process and to help the student develop sound techniques for making his own judgments. The questions which follow can of course be rephrased to fit anything about which one might make a judgment:

1. Make a list of your pet likes and dislikes. Can you give a convincing reason for your judgment in each case? When you say that you "like" someone or something, what do you mean to convey? Describe your feelings of "liking" something or someone. Do the same for disliking. Are there degrees of liking and disliking? Explain. Does the language seem to have a vocabulary adequate for expressing all the subtleties of liking and disliking that you seem to feel? Does your language

seem in any sense to direct the feelings that you have? Explain.

2. If you read a story and decide that you dislike it, what is it that you dislike about it? Is it just a vague feeling or something else? Explain.

3. Have you ever decided that you disliked something (a new food, for example) *before* you tried it? What made you "dislike" it? Is it actually possible to dislike something before you've experienced it? Explain.

4. What kinds of things are you supposed to believe are "good" for you? And "bad" for you? Why are the "good" things supposed to be "good"? And the "bad" things "bad"? If someone tells you that it is "good" for you to brush your teeth with sand, should you then brush your teeth with sand? Discuss. Or if a person tells you that it's "bad" to put sugar on grapefruit, should you stop putting sugar on grapefruit? Where do people find out what is "good" and "bad"? People used to believe that malaria was caused by damp night air and that only a fool would walk outside in the damp night air or even leave his window open at night. Why did people believe such nonsense? How can we recognize nonsense when we see it? (Incidentally, what *does* cause malaria?) Do you or any of your friends or family have any *superstitions*? Try to develop a way of testing a superstition. What is *luck*? What are some examples of "good luck" and "bad luck"? If everything is the result of a *cause*, what is the cause of "luck"?

5. If your teacher tells you that a certain book is "good" or "bad," what do you suppose is the basis for his judgment?

6. Can you tell the difference between a good musician and a bad musician (that is, between one who plays an instrument well and one who plays poorly)? How can you tell? If you can't tell, how can you learn to tell? Can you tell the difference between a good teacher and a bad teacher? Is judging the quality of a teacher the same as judging the quality of musicianship? What are your standards for judging a teacher? Write a description of your ideal teacher. Write a description of a bad teacher.

7. What is an expert or authority? Are you an expert at anything? How do you become an expert? Are there differences

between the way a person skates who has never skated before and the way a person skates who has been skating for a long time? What are the differences?

8. If a famous person—let's say a popular football player—tells you in a TV commercial that you should use a certain kind of toothpaste, should you? Why? Is the football player an expert on toothpaste? Why does the toothpaste company have a famous football player try to sell you on the product?

9. If you are about to buy something that you need, what would be a sensible way to decide on which brand to buy?

10. If a new child moves to your street or comes into your class, what do you base your judgments about him on? What do *you* prefer to be judged on? What constitutes in your mind a "good" person? A "bad" person? Where do your ideas about these things come from? Do you ever change these ideas? What might cause you to change them?

ETHICAL DECISION MAKING

To prepare a child for life—a much touted purpose of education—is to help the child develop the means of making rational decisions (a rarely achieved accomplishment of education). Our educational system is predicated on the belief that teacher knows best (at the student/teacher level anyway; above that level, the administrator knows best) and that the child's rôle is to accept his judgment on all but the most insignificant matters (even on those at times). One obvious result of this type of education is the degree of insecurity our students exhibit when forced to make a decision. Always the furtive glance to see which way the other guy is going to jump. Always the questions like, "Is it all right if . . . ?" "What am I supposed to do?" "Do you want . . . ?" Our young people, indeed, the society at large, are only too willing to allow others to make their decisions for them. (There will always be a small number of reasonably independent spirits; the high visibility of these few "decision makers" should not blind us to the paralysis of the general.) The ability to make decisions about courses of action to take that will be ethically sound is perhaps the prime requisite of responsible citizenship. We in the schools have an obligation to prepare our children to be responsible citizens. Learning half-truths about American history, putting "God" into the Pledge of Allegiance, and mumbling prayers are poor (and dangerous) substitutes for citizenship. The KKK is first-rate at these "patriotic" activities, but of the ethics of citizenship they know less than my pet iguanas.

The following problems should be explored with the student in great detail. They will provide the basis for writing assignments, panel discussions, and debates. And every student should be drawn out (indeed, one problem is specifically designed to raise this issue of participation).

1. After you and your best friend leave a store, your friend tells you he has stolen something. What will you say to him? What will you do? Explain the basis of your decisions.

2. One of your classmates has offered you some L.S.D. (or some marijuana). What is your response? What action will you take? Explain the basis of your actions and decisions.

3. A student in your class has asked to borrow something from you. You dislike this classmate. What is your response? Explain the basis of your decision.

4. You have found a valuable watch somewhere on the school grounds. What do you do? Explain the basis of your decision. You have found a valuable watch on a park bench in the city. What do you do? Explain the basis of your decision.

5. What do the terms "right" and "wrong" mean to you in regard to the way people interact? Is "wrong" *always* wrong? Explain. Give some examples of "right" and "wrong" behavior. Should wrong behavior ever be forgiven? What's involved in *forgiving?*

6. Two people are drowning. If you act immediately, you can save one of them. No one else is around (nor are there any telephones). The people who are drowning are strangers. Whom will you save? Why? What questions must you ask yourself in order to make the decision? (Clue: the problem isn't really complete yet—you need to know a few more things before you can make your decision. What things?)

7. Your brother tells you that he was responsible for starting the fire that results in a neighbor's house burning down. He says it was an accident. Meanwhile, the police have found a hobo

whom they are convinced started the fire. What do you do? Explain your decision.

8. Two men are running for mayor in your town. One of them is well-dressed and has three children and a pretty (but not beautiful) wife. The other candidate wears a beard and has been divorced. This is a non-partisan election, so political affiliation doesn't mean anything. Who would you vote for and why? What other information do you need in order to make a wise decision? Explain your decision.

9. You have a rare opportunity to travel to someplace that you've always wanted to see, but it will take all of the money you have put away for a special present for your mother. She has several children and an automatic laundry machine would be of great help to her. Since your father barely earns enough to support the family, she has to do all the laundry by hand. On the other hand, your trip may give you a chance to get a very good job (but then again it may not). Do you take the trip or buy the washing machine? Explain your decision.

10. You have found out something about one of your neighbors (who happens to be a close friend of your parents) that *Life* magazine will pay you a lot of money for. Your neighbor will never know who told the magazine, but the information will be extremely embarrassing to the neighbor and his family and will probably cause them to move away. What is your decision? Are there any additional facts that you need to know to make the decision? What are they? Explain your decision.

11. You have succeeded in placing the blame for something bad you have done on one of your classmates, who, of course, will be punished. That night, your conscience begins to bother you. What is your "conscience"? Where does it come from? How does it work? In any case, in order to settle your conscience down, you will have to confess the truth. But confessing the truth will result not only in punishment for what you originally did but acute embarrassment as a result of revealing what you did to your classmate. What is your decision? Try to write a point-by-point analysis of what you had to think about in reaching the decision.

12. What are some real decisions that you have had to make? Were any of them difficult to make? Why? What suggestions

would you make to someone who is faced with making a tough decision (one that *must* be made, not evaded)?

Like most of the questions in this book, these do not resolve themselves into "correct" and "incorrect" answers. Indeed, only the most sterile or most mechanical of questions can properly yield "correct" and "incorrect" answers. A date is a date, a sum is a sum, to be sure, but education built merely on the concept of "correct" and "incorrect" answers cannot be education worth giving or getting.

IN CLOSING

Though children in the middle years seem in many ways to "fall apart," they are nevertheless responsive to challenge and desperately anxious to find out what the world is all about. They often appear to be miles away but are in fact very much involved with Selfhood, with the mysteries inside themselves. Consider, for example, questions from seventh-graders:

What is mental illness? What causes it?
How does mental illness differ from being just plain stupid?
Why do people say things about you that are not true?
Are mind-expanding exercises harmful to you?
Why do some people rob, murder, and commit suicide?
Why are Jews and Negroes made fun of?
Why do some kids in grade seven act so immature?
How can you make a boy like you?
Is 11 too young to "make out"?
Why do kids become hippies?
Should I get upset when my parents fight?
Why do kids rebel against their parents?
What is pregnancy? How do you know you have it?
What are drugs? How many people use them?
How can a person stop using them?
What makes slums? How do we get rid of them?
(From *Teach Us What We Want to Know*, Ch. 4, "Grade Seven.")

They are painfully sensitive, not-quite trusting, eager to know things. If they have been conventionally educated, they already know well how to play the education game, to give the teacher the overt signs ("behaviors") that the teacher wants (in lieu of course of genuine learning). They are, all in all, a curious (in both senses of the word), troublesome lot, who can prove the most exciting students a teacher can have—if the teacher will just allow it.

All of the programs and techniques begun in the early years must be continued and enlarged upon in the middle years. What I have offered in this chapter is by way of a few possible elaborations on the earlier materials. Much more can be done. Substantial classroom time, for example, should be given over to chess, Go, and the many games of logic that were touched on in the previous chapter (and which I describe in some detail in the Appendix). Likewise, students should be encouraged to develop their own variations on these games and to develop, as a further step, their own games in kind. This, too, is a time for closer examinations of the community, of the visual, plastic, and performing arts, the countryside. But not mere one-shot "look-sees." Rather, in-depth examinations following the question-and-problem format. A hurried dash through a museum to the chattering accompaniment of a harried museum guide is not a very assimilable experience. Much time spent with a few things is better, and possibly the hanging of a student art show in the manner of a gallery show, with captions and catalogue, art reviews, perhaps even an opening "tea." Again, the student *becomes* artist, museum director, art critic; sociologist; naturalist; theatergoer, playwright, drama critic; publisher, reporter, and so on. Producer, not passive observer. Actor and reactor, not merely receptor. Now school begins to be the right place to be.

And by now I would hope that even the most skeptical of readers would appreciate the many advantages of teaching without textbooks. With every imaginable kind of book readily and inexpensively available, the textbook merely narrows the educational experience of the child and stultifies the teacher. After all, why look abroad when the officially sponsored book contains all the officially required "information."

6 THE LATER YEARS

Many educators seem unaware of the interest and concern which high school students feel, but cleverly manage to conceal, about the quality of their education.

[B. Frank Brown, *The Nongraded High School*]

Creative intellect is mysterious, devious, and irritating. An intellectually creative child may fail, for example, in social studies because he cannot understand the stupidities he is taught to believe as "fact." He may even end up agreeing with his teachers that he is "stupid" in social studies. Learning social studies is, to no small extent, whether in elementary school or the university, learning to be stupid. Most of us accomplish this task before we enter high school.

[Jules Henry, *Culture Against Man*]

The American world-view is worse than inadequate; it is irrelevant and uninterested, and adolescents are spiritually abandoned. They are insulated by not being taken seriously. The social machine does not require or desire its youth to find identity or vocation; it is interested only in aptitude. It does not want new initiative, but conformity.

[Paul Goodman, *Compulsory Mis-education*]

Most of us are as nervous by the age of five as we will ever be, and adolescence adds to the strain; but one thing a high-school student learns is that he can expect no provision for his need to give in to his feelings, or swing out in his own style, or creep off and pull himself together.

[Edgar Z. Friedenberg, *The Dignity of Youth & Other Atavisms*]

Confined to the classroom, the students crouch, victims of the circumstances that bind them there. In these cages within the larger cage, the major part of the taming process occurs.

[Deborah James, *The Taming*]

If the student has to work with language constantly in the functional way the professional does, he will come to know it in the professional's intimate way. Through reading, writing, and discussing whole, authentic discourses—and using no textbooks—students can learn better everything that we consider of value in language and literature than they can by the current substantive and particle approach.

[James Moffett, *Teaching the Universe of Discourse*]

THE BREAK between the last year of high school and the first year of college is historically fortuitous and has little substantative meaning. In general, the difference between high-school senior and college freshman is not much more than a locative one. Hence, "later years" here subsumes grade 13. (Following grade 13 with perhaps four undergraduate years would from an educational point of view add considerably more than an extra academic year. The additional pre-college year would provide for the student who plans not to go on to college the background required for skilled employment, or at least a solid foundation for that background—neither of which he gets now.)

The ideal school is no *school* (*i.e.*, locus of buildings explicitly designed for instruction) at all—the Parkway Program of the Philadelphia public school district comes very close to this ideal—but in lieu of what may be for many school districts an impracticable ideal, the campus school, embracing nursery through grade 13, is a viable and feasible alternative. The campus school is perforce a multi-purpose learning and cultural center, which in its fully realized form would include libraries, museums, workshops of every kind, film and television production facilities, theaters, and so on, wherein students of all ages and abilities intermingle, working at a variety of interests under the guidance of teachers who themselves have an opportunity to grow and develop both as teachers and scholars (in the best sense of the term). The community campus school would in turn be "plugged in" in a variety of ways to other centers such as sister schools and senior colleges and universities—computer networks, teacher and student exchanges, cultural exchanges, and so on. A utopian vision? Not by any means. We have all the resources to create such a school-community right now. It merely takes the willingness to commit our resources and to free our minds from the classroom boxes we've been trapped in for so long.

What I am leading to is the structure of the educational experience (ideally) of the later years, namely, "education by appointment," a program of independent study such as that initiated by Melbourne High School (see *The Nongraded High School* and *Education by Appointment*). In brief, the student, with minimal guidance, defines his own educational goals and projects and pursues them independent of textbook, teacher, and classroom. (Skeptics, *do* read the books cited.) Since, however, there is an understandable reluctance on the part of "tradition"-oriented parents and administrators to let the student go in search of his own education, so to speak, I will offer here a selection of projects, problems, and questions (touching mainly on language and closely allied matters) that can be successfully worked at in a more-or-less traditional environment, though I would urge at least the abandonment of the rigid forty-minute period. Time boxes are as pedagogically irrelevant as space boxes. The scientist works as his projects direct, not as a clock directs. And if he needs to push out a wall for a new piece of apparatus, he does it. The archaeologist and the astronomer travel through time and space. In the Orson Bean school, children repair to the basement gym (for *un*supervised play) whenever the need to be physical overtakes them. The school is extraordinarily successful in producing healthy-minded, healthy-spirited students. The Parkway Program students are the only students in the Philadelphia public school system who don't run wild in the school buses: the spiritual or psychological freedom of their educational experience leaves them free of the need to explode when the school day is over. When I look into the glass-walled corridors of a "modern" school and watch the measured step of the students marching from class to class at the sound of a bell, I can't help seeing (with a certain *frisson*) those cell blocks we movie addicts of the thirties so well remember! And in some schools, sour-faced teachers (sour-faced, let us grant, because forced to this stupid duty) pace the halls to enforce obedience to the rule of "decorum."

By the time a child pushes into adolescence he desperately needs scope, room to grow. The youngster who is physically sprouting out of his clothes almost daily is likewise emotionally and intellectually sprouting out of the increasingly stifling boxes of his accustomed life. I am convinced that many of the problems of the American adolescent would be significantly eased if his school experience (if not his home experience) would allow him greater growing room than we have hitherto been willing to allow him. Again, we must run the school as though our students were paying admission (which, after all, through their parents they are) and were free to walk out any time they felt that what was going on "inside" was less valuable to them than what they might get elsewhere. Though we hate to admit such home truths, it *is* more often than not less valuable. The student in Typical High School who plays hookey to work on a hot rod is very likely getting more for his time than had he spent that time in school. Think of it: what indeed *does* a student get in a day of school? Forty minutes of this and forty minutes of that— what? A day's total involvement with a piece of machinery has got to be more meaningful than all those "educational" odds and ends.

In the campus school, of course, the student, being free to work on his car (perhaps right in the school shop), will have no cause to be furtive and defiant, will be in a healthy mix of people of many ages, will find a diversity of things to do and discover. There will come a time when he will wish to divide his time between his car and, perhaps, the TV studio or the photography darkroom, even, in time, the library. The point is that he will move around in a place in which it is comfortable to grow and not in a place in which he feels (is made to feel) constantly in conflict. Just because we have set our schools up as we have does not mean that we have brought into being some kind of Platonic Ideal. We could be very wrong. I think we are. The instinct of the child who wants out of the system is probably truer than our conviction that what we are doing is the way of Truth and Righteousness. Wordsworth, if we take him literally, may have been full of beans when he wrote of the child "trailing clouds of glory . . . From God" and being otherwise closer to heaven than adults are. If we take him metaphorically, he was precisely correct. We adults should listen to the kids now and again.

I hope I have made my point. And if it is absolutely impossible to cut the school day up any differently (and one may rightly wonder about such "impossibilities"), then let the teacher manage his string of forty-minute slices with at least some imagination. This might mean, if the project warrants it, not holding formal class for a week or a month. In any case, we should not confuse classroom routine with education.

LANGUAGE AND LITERATURE

Language and literature are properly inseparable and should be kept that way. One of the serious flaws of the English program is the *de facto* isolation of language arts one from the other. There are, to be sure, certain aspects of language that can be examined without regard to what we ordinarily think of as "literature," but never, for example, should student writing be divorced from the language-literature complex. It is clear that literature (and writing) cannot, on the contrary, be properly examined without regard to language.

Set-piece composition assignments are as pointless at these levels of education as they are in the earlier years. Yet language/literature projects should always produce writing, that is, writing as a "natural" consequence of working through the projects. The overburdened teacher need not feel obligated to read and "grade" everything that the student produces. In fact, at this stage of education, the student should be writing for his own satisfaction and to serve functions that are not related to teacher approval or disapproval. Students want to communicate productively with each other (just as adults do), and this is a good time to refine the ear and the judgment. Again, the workshop is the appropriate pedagogical mode. The teacher can very effectively serve as "communications consultant," "literary adviser," "critic-at-large," or whatever. But the students will be the prime movers.

The textbook in the later years is commonly a ponderous anthology freighted with what the editors think the student should be reading and chock-a-block with "apparatus": introductions, footnotes, suggestions for study, questions (frequently inane), and so on. Merely from a bibliophilic point of view, one would never willingly buy such a book. The movement toward the disposable paperback is a healthy one, but better still is a good collection of a wide range of books available in the classroom and added to constantly. The classroom circulating library to which the student can lend his own books (either ones he has chosen to buy or ones he has written, if such is the case) is the best way to handle the question of what the students "should" be reading. It is certainly not a pedagogical necessity for everyone to have read the same things (at the same time or at all). Students are like other people in that all of them at any moment are not ready for the same things. The student who has "discovered" Hemingway or James Branch Cabell should be left to read his fill of his new discovery without being conflicted by a teacher who is meanwhile insisting that snippets of five other writers be read in the same space of time. Works for common study can be dittoed and discussed in forum. And it will doubtless fall out that several students will want to read the same longer work at the same time. A panel discussion may be a useful kind of public presentation. (Talking is as much "composition" as writing is.) And always there should be writing. Several critical reviews of the same work dittoed and discussed and perhaps compared with professional reviews or scholarly studies can be a productive literary project. The permutations and combinations are endless. The teacher need only "let go" and get out from under the dead weight of creaking syllabus and ponderous textbook.

Literature, like any other art, can only be experienced. It cannot be either "taught" or "learned." What we teach and learn is literary criticism. Literary criticism, in turn, broadens and deepens our literary experience (or so it should). The experience of literature is emotional, "visceral." The criticism of literature is intellectual. This means that, when in discussing literature (discussing is *about* the subject, not the subject itself) we find ourselves saying things like "it's so beautiful," "it stinks," "groovey," etc., etc., *ad tedium, ad nauseam,* we are saying nothing to the point about the subject (more accurately, the *object*) though perhaps a bit about ourselves.

In other words, this is neither literary criticism nor in any useful way even literary appreciation. It is a kind of fatuous self-revelation. Even the most tolerant of psychiatrists might be prompted to ask, "*Why* does the work affect you thus?" This is the sticky question that we almost always get hung up on and which almost always yields a "second generation" of "o's" and "ah's," phrased somewhat differently perhaps and invariably ending with "you know what I mean." On the other hand, no one can reasonably be expected to grasp the accomplishment of, say, a poem on the basis of learning how to scan its metrics and label its rhyme scheme. This is the most sterile kind of formalism. Having laboriously scanned a poem and ticked off its rhymes, the student can only say, "so what?" Having heard his teacher rave about the "greatness" of the poet and the "beauty" of the poem, he can only say, "so what?" In neither case has anything worthwhile about poetry been communicated. Further, reducing a piece of literature to a sentence or two of summary (the simple-minded answer to the simple-minded question, What does it mean?) leads the student to properly ask whether plodding through the whole work was worth it after all. Cram-books, he concludes, are just as good as the originals and a lot quicker to read. Where the "read-quiz-analyze" or "read-analyze-quiz" (the word *analyze* not to be taken too seriously in this context) system is not in force, the student will have a far better chance to find the values of literature himself. Again, well-thought-out questions from the teacher will cast light where it is needed, and point directions where they are needed.

During these later years, the student is ready to take on complex, long-range projects in drama, film, literary creation and criticism; media analysis; model building; game development, and the like. The projects will occupy considerable time and will produce results often approximating professional quality—in terms at least of conceptual power and freshness. (The work of student film-makers is a case in point: Students at Northern Valley Regional High School, Demarest, N.J., not only produce extraordinarily fine films, but publish as well *Montage,* a film quarterly of unusual merit.)

THE interrelationship of language and literature is a special case of the interrelationship of language and mind on the one hand and language and culture on the other. The following questions and projects will open these fascinating regions for exploration:

1. What proportion of a typical day's talking is taken up with *contactive* as opposed to *ideational* speech? (That is, speech for merely "making contact" as over against speech for conveying information, etc.?) Does your proportion seem about "normal"? How can you find out? What does this proportion tell you about human communication?

2. Do you use speech fillers of any kind? (*Uh, like, you know, mmm,* etc.) If so, with what frequency and why? Are there different kinds and frequencies for different occasions? Can you classify them? If you do use fillers, can you stop? What happens when you try to eliminate them from your speech? Do people seem to have other kinds of habits associated with speech that are similar to these fillers? What are they and under what conditions have you observed them being used? Are there any analogies in writing to the filler in speech? See if you can find some.

3. How much can you remember of a recent conversation? Are some conversations more easily or fully remembered than others? Explain. What seems to contribute to the "memorableness" of a conversation? Can you remember a lecture or a story or a joke more easily and more fully than you can remember a conversation? Explain. What is it that you remember? Do you, for example, remember the "ideas" primarily or the actual words? What are "ideas" composed of? Do you remember the order of ideas or just a random collection of "ideas"? Do you remember emotional states and how these states came about in the conversation? Discuss.

4. What is *memory*? (Dictionary definitions won't help much.) Can you construct a "memory model"? Devise an experiment for testing memory. You will have to consider such things as type and quantity of items to be memorized, age, sex (?), time of day, and . . . ? Use a book on statistical method (*e.g.,* Monroney, *Facts from Figures,* Pelican A-226) to help you. What useful things might you learn from the study of memory? On the basis of your findings can you figure out a way of improving your memory? Is memory, in fact, just one "thing"? How is language implicated in memory?

5. In Gaelic, the word *flaidireacth* translates as "fishing with a fly, or with any kind of bait dragged rapidly through the water." *Faiteadh* translates as "a striking of the arms and hands against the chest and sides." And *sleabhaire* as "one with a sharp-pointed face." What do these randomly chosen words and their translations tell you about the relationship between language and the way one perceives the world? Here are a few other language "oddities" (that is, they seem odd to us, not to those who normally speak the languages) that might help your thinking: In the Bassa language of Liberia, the spectrum is broadly divided into only two "color" terms (*hui* and *ziza*, roughly approximating the *xanthic* and *cyanic* color groups), even though the Bassa people are as aware of color as we and have a large number of very specific color terms equivalent to such English color terms as aquamarine, cobalt, ultramarine, and so on. Our "everyday" spectrum is red, orange, yellow, green, blue, violet, and indigo —seven color terms. In English, to go along to another example, our "favorite" sentence pattern conveys the notion that we are active agents who cause things to happen: *I opened the window*. In the Navajo language, things just seem to happen: *Opening occurs with the window*. The Subject-Verb-Object, "Actor-Action-Thing-acted-upon," view of reality makes little sense to a Navajo Indian, who sees himself simple as a part of the "universal action," so to speak.

6. Reproduce as accurately as you can a conversation you have had:
   a. With your parents regarding some kind of conflict with them.
   b. With your parents regarding some family activity.
   c. With one or two of your friends about plans for a party.
   d. With your date about some disagreement you had on the date.
   e. With a teacher about a school problem.
   f. With a salesclerk about something you were buying.
   g. With a stranger on a train, bus, etc.
   h. With a policeman or other official representative of the authority of the society.

   What differences do you note in "communication style"

among these various conversations? Try to categorize the differences. Do adults talk differently from your friends? How? Why? Compare the dialogue in a play with the dialogues people actually engage in and with the way you recall those actual dialogues. What are the differences? Can you turn any of your efforts at reproducing actual conversation into the type of dialogue you found in the play? Can you write a one-act play that is built around one or more of these dialogues?

7. How do people talk when they are angry? Try to recall the last "verbal war" you either overheard or took part in. How does angry speech differ from ordinary conversation? Consider vocabulary, intonation ("tone of voice"), sentence structure, meaning, and logic. Can people speak in anger without showing anger? How? What happened to you inside during your last verbal war? What is the language of "making up" like? Do you "make up" with family, friends, boys/girls, and casual acquaintances the same way? If there are differences, what are they? Can you account for the differences?

8. What is an insult? Describe some insults you have given and some you have got. Are there different kinds of insults or do we insult everybody the same way? What happens to you when you are insulted? When you insult somebody? Are there such things as *clever* insults and *crude* or *stupid* insults? If so, exemplify each kind. Is it true, as the old saying goes, that "Sticks and stones may break my bones, but names will never hurt me"? Discuss. Try writing a paper called something like "The Insult: Its Forms and Applications."

9. What words are associated in your mind with *prejudice?* Why is it that these words can make people angry and unhappy? What words make you angry and unhappy? Why?

10. Various moods, events, and objects are described metaphorically with color terms (*e.g., I've got the blues, He made me see red, She was green with envy,* etc.). List all of these you can think of and try to draw some kind of informative conclusion from your evidence. Does one color in particular seem to predominate for negative and unpleasant things? One for positive, pleasant things? Discuss the implications.

11. Read one or two news magazines (*Time, Newsweek,* etc.) and circle every word that gives you a positive or a negative

feeling. List some of these words. How are they used to influence the context in which they were found? Try rewriting an article by substituting words opposite in feeling to the ones you circled. What happens to the tone of the article? Can you manage to neutralize the article? Compare the treatment of a particular news story in a news magazine with the same story as told on the news pages of a daily paper. What differences, if any, did you discover? What are the differences in communication problems between a weekly news magazine and a daily newspaper? How does each type of publication try to solve its own special communication problems?

12. Are there differences between language as used in, say, a deodorant commercial and in the instruction manual that comes with a new appliance? If so, what are they? What other modes of language use can you distinguish as you read and listen at random? Try writing a short paragraph on any suitable subject in each of these modes. Can you contrive a kind of formula for each mode?

13. If you are trying to explain something to somebody and you find yourself saying, "You know what I mean," a great deal, what seems to be the problem? Do you, for example, always really "know what you mean"? Explain. It has been said that if you can't *say* what you mean, then you really don't *know* what you mean. What is your response to this idea? Is "feeling" the same as "knowing"? What difficulties do you have in even talking about these matters? What seems to be the relationship between language and what goes on "inside your head"?

14. What kinds of communication failures have you been involved in? Can you figure out why the communication failed? What might have overcome the failure? Remember that communication requires both a *sender* and a *receiver*, but that each of us plays *both* rôles.

15. We have a variety of verbal formulas that say one thing and mean just the opposite. For example, when people say something like, "We *must* get together soon," they frequently haven't the slightest intention of "getting together." What other formulas like this are you aware of and why do we use

them? Is there a stock of formulas that don't say what they mean in use among your friends and acquaintances? Are they pretty much the same as those you have noticed adults using, or are they different? Discuss.

16. Do you respond more favorably to the styles of speech used by certain people than to the styles used by others? Can you define the differences in both styles and your responses? Do you ever think about the *way* you speak? Do you consciously use certain words and phrases for their style or sound? What are some examples and why in particular do these appeal to you? What is your response to dialects different from your own? Can you explain or account for your responses? What is your response to various foreign dialects (French, German, Spanish, British, etc.)? Can you explain your responses? Why are some jokes told in dialect funnier than when told "straight"? If you could magically change your way of speaking, whose speech would you like to take as a model? Why?

17. What words do your parents use that you don't use, words that seem quaint or "square"? What words do you use among your friends that you wouldn't use with your parents? Why? Can you account for these contrasting vocabularies? How do you suppose they came about? Is this linguistic "generation gap" important or insignificant? Would you like your parents to understand and use your peer vocabulary? Discuss.

18. Why do we think people who talk to themselves are crazy or "weird"? The fact is that we all talk to ourselves, though we generally don't talk *aloud* to ourselves. What do we talk about to ourselves? Why do we talk to ourselves? How do you talk to yourself? If communication requires, as we said, a sender and a receiver, is our "interior dialogue" a form of communication? "Who" is the sender and "who" is the receiver? Try writing a few pages of interior dialogue. What problems do you have in trying to render this "mindspeech" as writing?

19. In what ways do people unknowingly reveal themselves through their use of language? What can you learn about a person through his speech habits? Can you develop a research model for determining such things as level of education, regional background, and other socio-cultural indices

through language analysis? What do you need to know in order to undertake a project like this?

20. How does a typical verbal joke work? What does the listener need to know in order to laugh when he is supposed to? Are there joke "styles"? Make an anthology of jokes and try to categorize them according to style. How is it that the same joke can be told by two different people and be funny one time and not funny the other? Are some people better joke-tellers than others? Can you account for the difference? What seems to account for the degree to which a joke is funny? Ruling out the mysterious "sense of humor," try to explain why the joke that might break you up might elicit "So, what's funny?" from the person sitting next to you. In what ways do jokes seem to have "national" characteristics, that is, we can speak of "American" humor, "British" humor, and so on. What are some examples of non-verbal humor? Why is it difficult to talk about humor? Do you ever make up jokes or do you depend exclusively on others for your jokes? How do you suppose jokes come to be created? Try making up one even if you've never done it before. Try then to explain the process whereby you arrived at the finished product. Perhaps starting with a cartoon might help you get into a "joke-making" frame of mind.

21. What do people mean when they speak of "reading between the lines"? How does one "read between the lines"? Can this be taught? On what occasions do people speak or write with the intention that their listeners or readers will "read between the lines"? Is reading between the lines a useful thing to be able to do? Why? Does it have its dangers? What might they be?

22. Can you explain why man, presumably the most intelligent of earthly creatures, is given to fighting and killing over words? What are some examples of words that people fight and kill over? What words are capable of making you fight or even kill? Why?

23. Language can be used to persuade. Describe how you have been persuaded to do something and how you have persuaded someone to do something. How do you explain this seeming power of "hot air"? How do advertisers persuade? Politicians?

Salesmen? Parents? Teachers? Clergymen? Are there different kinds of verbal persuasion? If so, describe and classify them. How does persuasion seem to relate to the "real" (non-language) world; that is, to what extent does a persuasive argument contain verifiable content? (This must of course be answered by analyzing specific efforts at persuasion.) How can you evaluate the "logic" of an effort of persuasion? What rôle has logic played in those situations in which you have been persuaded to do something or to think in a certain way?

24. The many popular language games on the market are forms of the old-fashioned crossword puzzle. Can you develop a new kind of word game? Try working around the idea of making sentences instead of just words, and try to make the game as little dependent on chance as you can. Keep a record of the problems you ran into and how you solved them.

25. Why does it help to "talk out" a problem? With whom have you found it most useful to talk out your problems? Why is it that strangers are sometimes easier to talk to than people you know?

26. Is talking a pleasurable activity? Why? Are there occasions when it is a painful activity (*psychologically* painful, that is)? What occasions and why?

27. One of the many miracles of the human mind is its ability to distinguish among a vast number of voices. What features do you suppose the mind relies on to make these distinctions? (*E.g.*, you almost always recognize a voice over the phone even though you may not have heard the voice in years.) If you wanted to imitate a person's voice how would you do it? (Try imitating a well known personality. Perhaps the class can put on a show in which everyone in the show is supposed to be a famous actor or entertainer. Try to catch a few performances by impersonators in TV.)

28. Why are we more comfortable when we know the name of the person to whom we are talking or whom we have just met? Why do we want to name all the objects around us? Are there occasions when we prefer not to identify ourselves or know the identity of others? Discuss. What kinds of names do people give their pets? Try classifying these names. How do our own names affect us? Are you pleased with your

names? Why or why not? If you could change your name (without going through a lot of legal red tape) would you? To what? Why? Should children be left to choose their own given names? Why do people change their names (generally their *last* names)? In ancient times names had specific meanings (*e.g., Charles* meant "manly," *Johnson* meant "John's son"—*John,* incidentally, meant "God is gracious"—*Taylor* meant "tailor," *Campbell,* "crooked mouth," and so on). Though we no longer think of these early significations, we do, none the less, have certain associations with various names. List some names that have special meanings for you and explain how they came to have these meanings. How do these meanings affect your relationships with people bearing those names? Track down the original meanings of names that interests you. (You can find surnames originating in the British Isles in books like *The Penguin Dictionary of Surnames* and C. M. Matthews, *English Surnames.*) Do the same for the names of animals (elephant, giraffe, hippopotamus, etc.). Wouldn't it be a lot more efficient just to give everyone a serial number instead of a name? Remember that, for example, *Octavia* simply meant "eighth," feminine (*Octavius,* "eighth," masculine). Why are people so upset about being numbered, to to speak (Social Security, credit cards, bank number, etc.)? Why did a lot of people raise a ruckus about the changeover of phone numbers from words and numbers to straight numbers (*e.g.,* MUrray Hill 9–0000 became 689–0000)?

29. Considerable time and money are expended on choosing *brand names.* Why are businesses so fussy about the names they give their products? Why, for example, doesn't Procter & Gamble simply call its product "Procter & Gamble Toothpaste" instead of "Gleem"? Do various classes of products have characteristic names? One of the reasons given for the failure of the Ford "Edsel" is that the name was a flop. Does "Edsel" sound like an automobile name to you? Discuss. Write a paper on "American Brand Names." What brand names displease you? Why? Suggest changes and explain the benefits of the changes. Are European brand names pretty much like ours? (Get hold of some foreign publications like

Stern, L'Express, Der Spiegel, Réalités, etc.) Do the foreign product names "sound like" the products? Can you develop a "philosophy" or "psychology" of product-naming and company-naming?

30. Are there any aspects of language that are particularly mysterious, puzzling, or interesting to you? How will you attempt to explore these matters? How can an understanding of the workings of language be helpful to you?

A frame project (which can contain other projects) is a "language notebook," a compendium of thoughts, questions, and observations on language. Some students may, for example, get interested in place names (many of which preserve a good deal of local history) or in the technical jargons of various trades, professions, and sports, all of which tell their own interesting stories. The point is that wherever one looks or listens he finds language and learns something about his humanness.

The questions which follow deal rather more explicitly with literary matters and should provide through their working out a reasonable way of critically grasping literature as well as learning a number of useful things about writing.

1. It has been asserted that the art of poetry consists in putting the right words in the right places. Such an assertion, of course, teaches us nothing about the art of poetry. But if we look beneath the assertion, we will find such questions lurking there as these and perhaps we can learn something about poetry as we try to answer them. (We are assuming that learning about poetry is something worth learning about, but that is another whole set of questions that we can explore in due course.)

   a. Can you define "right words"? Read a poem and substitute a "wrong" word for a "right" word. What happens?
   b. Is it useful to distinguish between *lexical* or *referential* words and *structural* words? (Between, that is, words like *bird, big,* and *soar,* on the one hand, and *the, at,* and *but,* on the other.) Apply the "right" and "wrong" distinction to each type in the poem.
   c. How do we recognize "right" words? Is "right" here the same as a dictionary type of "correctness"? Read a poem

by E. E. Cummings (*e.g., anyone lived in a pretty how town*). Can you find all of his words in your dictionary? If you can't, does that mean that he is "wrong"? Does the poet accomplish anything valuable with his language play? How does Cummings' use of words square with the conventions of usage (*e.g.,* have you ever heard of a "how town"?). What does this tell you about the concepts of *norm* and *deviation?*

d. What does "right order" refer to? How can you tell when the order is "right"? (There are, broadly speaking, two kinds of order: the order of syntactic units and the order of elements within a syntactic unit. Thus there is the order *Subject–Verb–Object* [*Jack broke down the door*]; *Subject–Verb–Adverb* [*Jack ran away*], etc. And there is the order within, say, a complex noun: *a chaste, beautiful, and languid maiden/ a maiden chaste, beautiful, and languid,* etc.) Playing around with the syntax of the poem will give you some insights into the problem. See how many different ways you can convey the general sense of the poem, but note carefully the effects of the changes you make. Try this experiment with some of your own writing or with any writing. Then try to write something of your own in the manner of the poet whose work you are examining. Pay close attention always to the ordering of elements in the lines.

e. What is *conventional* syntax? How do you know? Or how can you find out (without looking it up in a grammar, which probably wouldn't be of much help anyway)? Try to arrive at some principles governing conventional ("normal") syntax.

f. Of what use are both conventional and unconventional syntax to a poet? Examine a lot of different poems from several different literary periods.

g. Try paraphrasing a few poems. What happens to the poems as a result? Is the paraphrase or "plain-sense" restatement "really" what the poem is "about"? Even though poems are in some ways very subtle and complex, they are the oldest literary genre, prose coming along only much later in history. Can you account for this apparently curious fact? What is "primitive" about poetry? Why is poetry generally easier to remember than prose? (The easily remembered passages of prose are poetry-like.) Why do young children respond more strongly to poetry than to prose? Why do most adults seem either indifferent to or antipathetic to poetry? Some people charge that a poem is "just a lot of flowery words that add up to very little." Or, "If the poet's got something to say, he should just say it and not beat around the bush." What is your response to these comments? (Undoubtedly there is much truth in the accusation if applied to *verse* such as found in "inspirational" publications, yet this type of "poetry" is apparently quite popular. Can you account for this?) Make an anthology of poems that you particularly like. But do a fair amount of poetry reading before you make your choices. (If you've read only one poem, that one is both the best and the worst, your most favorite and your least favorite, etc.) Examine the poems for the ways in which the poet says his idea. Try writing a collection of your own poems about things that bother you, excite you, "turn you on." Listen to the words and phrases. Try to get hold of a rhythm that moves you along. And try to look at your experience directly and honestly. But remember that a poet is an artist and an artist is a manipulator. He works to make things fit together into a satisfying whole, like an architect, who has to get the entire building looking like a single unity with all the parts properly related to each other, "the right words in the right order."

2. Just as we adjust our conversation to suit the audience with whom we are conversing, so a writer directs his work toward some ideal audience. Examine a range of writing from newspapers and popular magazines to poems, plays, short stories, and novels and see if you can form an impression of the presumed audience of each piece of writing. How can you "identify" an audience? Try writing an article or a short story in different ways to suit different audiences. What do you have to know in order to do this? What assumptions can you make about each audience? What linguistic and semantic features seem appropriate to each audience? What features

seem fairly universal; that is, capable of being understood by anybody who can read? Suppose you wanted to write something to be read *to* an illiterate person (*illiteracy*, remember, does not equal *stupidity;* it simply means that the person has never learned to read or write). To a blind person? Would you have to make any adjustments in your thinking? Can you create a profile of your class as an audience? Your neighbors? Explain how you would do it.

3. One of the "rules" of writing that English teachers are fond of imposing on their students is the prohibition against beginning sentences with conjunctions (*and, but, yet, or, nor, for,* etc.). Read *Gulliver's Travels* (which is, as you will discover, a very entertaining book) and as you go along keep a tabulation of the number of times the author begins a sentence with a conjunction. Then "correct" a few pages of the work to bring Swift in line with the "rule." Compare the "corrected" sentences with the original and then try to decide who is right, the teacher or the author. Where do you suppose such a rule came from? While you've got *Gulliver's Travels* in hand, see if you can write a few paragraphs in the manner of Swift. Since Swift is a *satirist* who found much human foolishness to attack and ridicule in his time (the early part of the eighteenth century), why don't you try to write satirically about contemporary human foolishness. How do you recognize satire? Make a note of some specifically satirical passages in the book. A modern example of satire is *Mad Magazine*. What and how does it satirize? Swift's *A Modest Proposal* is perhaps the most outrageous satire ever written. It makes *Mad Magazine* look wishy-washy and trivial. And it had a real effect on the problem it was attacking (that is, it helped to bring about certain important changes in the economic relationships between Ireland and England). Read it and then make a list of modern issues that might well be given the same harsh satirical treatment. Can you do an imitation of *A Modest Proposal*? Even though Swift was a very angry man, he nonetheless writes with precision and control. Would he have been more effective had he just "let himself go"? Discuss. Do you do better in an argument when you let yourself go or when you keep control of yourself? Are

you more impressed by a person who screams and gets red in the face or one who makes his points calmly and reasonably? There is undoubtedly great use in one's being able to abandon oneself to emotion and just "ventilate," but on the printed page this kind of thing seems contrived and is therefore unimpressive. Who is going to respond to quantities of exclamation points, underlinings, boldface type, and so on? Who is going to respond to ill-considered ranting and raving? In print, it is the emotion felt *beneath* the surface that impresses and affects. Try writing two character sketches of someone you dislike intensely, the first an emotional tirade, the second a biting, well-controlled satire. Test the sketches out on several people. Which one do they feel is *truly* the more devastating? Try to find some satirical writing in contemporary publications (other than *Mad*). Who is being satirized and how is it being done? *Irony* is a major device of satire. How does irony work? Try writing a short satirical play that could be produced in the classroom. Read one of the plays of the French satirical playwright, Molière (*e.g.*, *The Doctor in Spite of Himself*). What is the difference between something that is satirically humorous and just plain humorous? Read *Catch–22* and make a note of the scenes and passages you thought were really funny. Can you account for your reaction? Try writing a scene in the manner of *Catch–22* in which you reveal some facet of the school routine. Test it on various readers for "laughability." How successful were you in being humorous? Polish it and try it out on someone who hadn't read it before. More or fewer laughs? Discuss the problems of making a piece of writing humorous. Is *A Modest Proposal* humorous? *Gulliver's Travels*? Discuss.

4. What is your favorite kind of reading? Why? Try writing something in the manner of your favorite reading. If, for example, you enjoy detective stories, then write a detective story. Try it out on your friends. Describe the problems of writing a readable, enjoyable, and convincing story. Did you, for example, get any good ideas that you found impossible or at least very difficult to work out? What do you feel are your greatest strengths in writing? Your greatest weaknesses? How can these weaknesses be overcome?

5. Make a list of topics that you think would be interesting to read about and write about. Make a recommended reading list for your class and comment on each item on the list. Don't put items on the list because you think your teacher would like to see them there but because *you* think they should be there for *your* reasons (which you will explain in your comments). Before you read a particular book or story or article, how did you decide to bother reading it? *Required* reading doesn't count. What is your honest evaluation of the reading you have been required to do in school? Explain your judgments.

6. Write a speech on the values of reading to be given to a group of people who either don't like to read or don't know how to read. Try to be both lively and informative. Then describe some of the problems you had in writing the speech and how you solved the problems. Try the speech out on a few people, but instead of asking them whether they "liked" it, ask them whether they would be *persuaded* by it.

7. Try the same project for *writing*. Then write a "self-improvement" article for a national magazine (you pick an appropriate one) entitled, "How to Improve Your Writing." Try the article on several people and note their responses. How did you gauge your presumed audience for the article? What were some of the problems you had in doing the article and how did you solve them? Did you learn anything about improving your writing as you attempted to instruct others on improving their writing? What did you learn?

8. There are numerous books and articles which report on and analyze the various issues confronting society (issues of war and peace, race, violence, drugs, and so on). There are also novels, short stories, poems, and plays that deal with the same issues. How do the two approaches (broadly: fiction vs. non-fiction) differ in style, language, tone, purpose, etc.? If one can read a report on, say, juvenile crime, why should one read a novel dealing with juvenile crime? What is your attitude ("set") toward a report as opposed to a novel or a short story? Try writing a report and then a short story on the same topic. A critic has written that there is "no such thing as a morally bad novel: its moral effect depends

entirely on the moral quality of its reader, and nobody can predict what that will be. And if literature isn't morally bad it isn't morally good either." And further that "literature has no consistent connection with ordinary life, positive or negative." Discuss these comments on the basis of your own experience with literature, morality, and life. [Teacher: see Northrop Frye, *The Educated Imagination,* a book pregnant with ideas for the study and teaching of literature. On the question of "morality" in the arts, the issue of censorship is well worth a class debate or a panel discussion. It is reprehensible in a teacher to attempt to avoid confronting controversial issues of this kind.]

9. Are the kinds of things you might learn from a novel set in some historical period the same as the kinds of things you might learn from a history book? How does the actual writing in a history book differ from that in a novel? See if you can track down some books (non-fiction) on history that are interestingly and even excitingly written. How does the author in each case manage to rescue his subject from boredom?

10. Write a scene (for a play) in which A is trying to explain to B how something works but is having a good bit of difficulty because B isn't very adept at mechanical things. Do one version that is more-or-less straight and one version that is comical. What kinds of problems arise from each approach? Invent some other potentially amusing situations for a play and try to work them out. Be sure to include stage directions so that the reader or director will know what the actors are supposed to be doing. If you find this kind of writing particularly appealing, try a complete play on a topic that interests you.

11. Read a short story by each of two writers whose writing styles are quite different one from the other (*e.g.,* Faulkner and Hemingway). Then choose a characteristic paragraph from each and try to present the subject matter in each paragraph in the style of the other writer (*i.e.,* put the material from the Faulkner paragraph into the style of the Hemingway paragraph and *vice versa*). Then write a few paragraphs in which you (1) describe as well as you can the *style* of each

writer and (2) discuss the problems you had in making the switch.

12. The *appositive* is a grammatical resource of the language that is widely used in a variety of ways to achieve certain stylistic effects. Here are a few examples: *The sunlight <u>bright on granite walls</u> . . . ; <u>angry and upset</u>, they left hurriedly; he stood on the corner, <u>willing to talk to anyone who came along</u>; George, <u>completely at home in this strange place</u>, smiled sarcastically at us.* Make a collection of your own examples taken from a variety of sources. Try to find a way of classifying appositives, and then try to determine if certain types occur predictably in certain contexts. Try rewriting each one to convey the same basic meaning as the original but in a different style. For example: *as they were angry and upset, they left hurriedly; they left hurriedly because they were angry and upset,* etc. Can you describe the manipulations you had to perform to get from the original (the *appositive,* in this case) to the rewritten versions? Is there some order or pattern to this?

13. The *absolute construction* is another interesting feature of English syntax. Here is an example; see if you can find some others and play with them as you did the appositives: *The girl on the hill, <u>hair streaming in the wind</u>, shouted to someone in the cabin.* Rewritten: *Standing on the hill, a girl with hair streaming in the wind shouted to someone in the cabin.*

14. It has been postulated that underlying the great variety of sentences we produce are a few simple sentences—more precisely, sentence *forms* or *patterns*—that can be manipulated in a number of ways in order to *generate* that great variety. Thus, we can say that a sentence like *The awkward young sloth dropped out of the tree,* derives from (1) *The sloth dropped out of the tree* + (2) *the sloth was awkward* + (3) *the sloth was young.* This way of looking at grammar allows us to see similarities among sentences (hence relationships of meaning) that look quite different from one another. Furthermore, it gives us a powerful tool for understanding how a piece of writing "works," how the writer manipulates the

resources of the language. Try experimenting as you have been, this time using constructions containing *with: with only twelve hours left, they felt that the search was hopeless; he sat gloomily in the corner with painful memories scratching at his consciousness; she hit him with a dead fish,* etc. The rest of the prepositions will likewise yield a rich harvest.

15. Certain sentences have the annoying characteristic of pulling in two directions (*ambiguity*):

> The boys were ready to eat.
> He likes sailing boats.
> Harry left the hospital a wreck.
> Etc.

Try to find a few more structurally ambiguous sentences and then try to resolve the ambiguity in each by writing the two different sentences which seem to underlie the ambiguous one. Thus (from *The boys were ready to eat*):

> The boys were ready to eat their supper.
> The boys were ready to be eaten.

Try writing a paragraph in which every sentence is ambiguous. Then write two more paragraphs in which all the ambiguities of the first paragraph are resolved. Make an intensive examination of a magazine article to find every possible ambiguity in the article. Try another article or two from different magazines. Can you evaluate writing qualitatively on the basis of ambiguity count? Work up a project and write a report on your findings to be presented to a group of fledgling magazine writers for their guidance.

16. Track down some other kinds of *transformations*. Here are a few clues:

> Sherm ate a woolly worm/ a woolly worm was eaten by Sherm.
> They planned to restructure the program/ they planned the restructuring of the program/ they planned that the program be restructured.
> They thought of flying to the moon/ they thought they would fly to the moon/ to fly to the moon was their thought.
> I gave him a box of bullfrogs/ I gave a box of bullfrogs

to him/ he was given a box of bullfrogs by me/ a box of bullfrogs was given by me to him.

Playing with the transformational resources of the language, write and rewrite a few paragraphs on any subject that interests you. Try the same with poems, passages from books, articles, etc. And try to figure out what the ad writers did with language in a few ads from magazines and newspapers.

17. Copy the first sentence of a paragraph chosen at random from something that you're reading, put away the book or article, and write your own paragraph in such a way that it sounds as though the first sentence (the one you "borrowed") is your own. Try the same exercise with the last sentence of a paragraph chosen at random. In both cases compare your paragraphs with the originals. What differences were there between yours and the originals? What problems did you have in working out your paragraphs? Hunt up something you've already written and try the same experiment; compare the new version with the older one. How many different paragraphs can you write using the same first sentence? Examine a variety of writing samples and try to formulate some principles about the nature of paragraph-initial sentences. Are there different types serving different purposes? Do different types of writing contrast with each other in this matter of paragraph-initial sentences? What about paragraph-final sentences? What other questions can you think of that may lead to useful discoveries about how paragraphs work and how different writers work paragraphs?

18. Read a *biography* and an *autobiography* of the same person. Write two short biographical sketches of the subject, one based on the biography and one based on the autobiography. Does the subject of each sketch seem to be based on the "same man"? If not, what are the differences? Now write a sketch using both books as your source material. Try to be as fair and "neutral" as you can. Finally, write two sketches, one of which shows the subject in as favorable a light as possible and the other of which shows him in as unfavorable a light as possible. In other words, write two heavily *slanted* sketches (but don't misrepresent facts or use highly emotional language in either case—a good job of slanting

avoids the obvious). What did you do to accomplish neutrality? To accomplish bias? Examine several biographies and attempt to establish a set of principles for the writing of biography. Why do you suppose that some people write their autobiographies? Of what value are biographies and autobiographies? Can a person be "trusted" to tell his own story? What qualifications should a biographer have? Try writing your autobiography. Use the biographical works you've already read to give you an approach and some techniques that will make your autobiography interesting. Pay close attention to the style of the writing. Try to achieve some variety, but don't "overwrite," that is, don't stuff your sentences with long series of adjectives, don't try to make trivialities seem important by talking about them in pompous, high-flown language, and so on.

19. Find some examples of what you consider to be "good" writing, that is, writing with the "right sound" to it and writing well suited to its content. Explain your evaluation. Now find some examples of what you consider to be "bad" writing and explain your evaluation. Can you imitate each kind? What can you learn by doing this?

20. Look over an anthology of English literature. Describe its contents. What purpose does a book like this serve? Read some of the earlier selections in the anthology. Describe them. Is there any use in reading this material? Explain. What can you tell about the culture that produced the work? Does, say, a five-hundred-year-old poem "speak" (emotionally) to you? Listen carefully to the words of some contemporary folk and country rock. Now read a few medieval ballads. Compare the modern and the old. What do you discover? Think not only about subject matter but tone, mood, and language as well. Why is an old ballad like *Barbara Allen* still popular? (One of the frustrations of an anthology, as you've probably discovered, is that it contains too little of what you like and too much of what you don't like. What's the solution? Write a prospectus and a Table of Contents for an anthology of literature that would please you. Give some thought to what you mean by "literature." Attempt to define "literature" in a useful way.)

21. What does the term *myth* mean to you? Track down a few definitions—don't rely merely on dictionaries and encyclopedias. (Try, for example, Joseph Campbell's *The Hero with a Thousand Faces*.) What are some of the myths that dominate the world that you live in? What myths do *you* live by? Read outlines of some of the ancient Greek myths (see Edith Hamilton's *Mythology* and Robert Graves' *The Greek Myths*) and see if you can find any parallels between them and some aspects of your world and experience. Try writing modern versions of a few of them. (The Lerner and Loewe musical *My Fair Lady* was adapted from George Bernard Shaw's *Pygmalion*. Read the Greek myth of Pygmalion and Galatea; then read Shaw's *Pygmalion*. What does the story of Henry Higgins and Eliza Doolittle have to do with the Greek myth? Have you had any personal experience with the Pygmalion myth?) Read Shakespeare's *Macbeth* and try doing a modern version of it. (Several years ago, Hollywood tried it in a movie called *Joe Macbeth*, in which Macbeth—*i.e.*, "Joe Macbeth"—is a Chicago gangster who murders the local gangland chief in order to take over the mob.) Or any other play by Shakespeare, or by any of the Greek playwrights. You should, once you've done these experiments, be able to grasp the meaning of this comment by a contemporary critic: "The culture of the past is not only the memory of mankind, but our own buried life, and study of it leads to a recognition scene, a discovery in which we see, not our past lives, but the total cultural form of our present life. It is not only the poet but his reader who is subject to the obligation to 'make it new.' " (Northrop Frye, *Anatomy of Criticism*, p. 346.) Try writing an essay for *Harper's* or *The Atlantic* or *The New York Review of Books* in which you explore and illustrate Frye's point.

22. "Literature, like mathematics, is a language, and a language in itself represents no truth, though it may provide the means for expressing any number of them." (Frye, p. 354.) How is literature a "language"? What kinds of "truths" does literature (and mathematics, for that matter) express?

23. "The body of work done in society, or civilization, both maintains and undermines the class structure of that society."

(Frye, p. 347.) Can you find any evidence to support Frye's assertion? What does the term "class structure" mean to you? Do we have any sort of "class structure" in the United States? If you conclude that we do, on what basis have you arrived at this conclusion?

24. "Nothing is closer to the supreme commonplace of our commonplace age than its preoccupation with Nothing—that is, with the elected experience and deliberate exploitation of Nothing, which may be un-self-conscious non-experience in one sense, but in another is willful submission of oneself to non-experience as an active form of experience." (R. M. Adams, *Nil*, p. 3.) Before attempting to make anything of this statement, read a few "Absurdist" works (*e.g.*, Samuel Beckett's *Waiting for Godot* and *Krapp's Last Tape*; Ionesco's *Rhinoceros*; Albert Camus' *The Stranger*, etc). Then look around at society at large. Is the society preoccupied with Nothing (note the capital N)? Write an article for *The New York Times Magazine* or your school literary magazine (if your school doesn't have one, make believe that it does—perhaps you can get one started) on our preoccupation with Nothing.

25. Read *Howl* (and listen to the recording of it by the poet who wrote it, Allen Ginsberg) and a few other poems by poets who came out of the so-called "Beat Generation" of the fifties. What are Ginsberg and the others bothered by? How does their poetry differ from, say, the poetry of Robert Frost? What are the distinctive linguistic qualities of their poetry? Read Gary Snyder's *Smokey the Bear Sutra*. (This should be read aloud as a chant.) Describe the poem and its effects. Try writing some Ginsberg- and Snyder-type poetry. What are topics worth writing on? Why these? What problems do you have in writing this kind of poetry? Do you think that the originals were worth doing? Explain. Do you think that the imitations are worth doing? Explain.

26. Try writing a short story in three different modes: (1) from the point of view of the all-seeing, all-knowing author, (2) from the point of view of one of the characters in the story *after* the events which he is narrating have taken place, and

(3) from the standpoint of one of the characters in the story through his *stream-of-consciousness* while the events are taking place. Find an actual novel or story for each of these story-telling modes. Compare your technique with that of the novelist. What problems did each mode raise and how did you solve these problems? What are the advantages and disadvantages of each? Which do you prefer to work with? To read? Explain.

27. Make a syllable count of one hundred words of running text in each of the following publications: *Jack and Jill, The Golden Magazine, Reader's Digest, Popular Mechanics, Road & Track, Time, Seventeen, Argosy, The Saturday Review, The New York Daily News, The Times of London, Harper's, Foreign Affairs, The Wall Street Journal, The Journal of the American Medical Association,* a local newspaper, *The Yale Review* (or equivalent). Take your evidence only from articles (no advertising, tables of contents, etc.). Are there differences among the various publications? Do these differences seem to be in any way significant? Does the syllable-count evidence lead you to seek any other kinds of evidence? What and why? Pick two or three different types of publications from the list and write a short piece in the manner of each on a subject appropriate to each. Can you identify the stylistic components that distinguish one magazine style from another?

28. What kinds of experiences really "turn you on"? Do you ever get the urge to write about them or express them to someone else in any way? Can you describe an experience of yours in terms of poetry, story, painting, sculpture, music, and dance? This is a difficult task requiring a good deal of thought, to say nothing of a feeling for each medium of expression. On the assumption that you really want to undertake the task, describe the program you would follow to accomplish it.

With the type of question established and the general approach understood, the teacher and the students should have no difficulty in multiplying the list many times over. These questions blend all the disciplines of English with the disciplines of problem-solving. And—which is very important—the student has plenty of room for following his own interests and capabilities.

MEDIA

The next set of questions is directed toward exploration in depth of the media world. However, none of the questions here or anywhere in the book should be encapsulated. There are innumerable points of contact between and among the broad areas we have defined. For example, it is perfectly obvious that in working on the question about myths (above) the student will inevitably examine the media, the prime promulgator and engenderer in our age of our myths.

1. Pinpoint the ways in which the mass media (radio, TV, motion pictures, periodicals, and their associated advertising) define your life: your sense of reality, your beliefs, your values, etc. How, that is, do the various media "work" on you? Is it even possible to stand apart and examine this relationship between you and the media world? ("After three thousand years of explosion, by means of fragmentary and mechanical technologies, the Western world is imploding. During the mechanical ages we had extended our bodies in space. Today, after more than a century of electric technology, we have extended our central nervous system itself in a global embrace, abolishing both space and time as far as our planet is concerned," Marshall McLuhan, *Understanding Media*, p. 3. Comment on McLuhan's understanding of what's happening to us as a result of the new "electric" media.) How can one develop some degree of objectivity (that is, somewhat less subjectivity) about this relationship? Can the commercial and non-commercial aspects of the media really be distinguished from each other? Do you believe that the media should be subject to any kind of censorship? Explain. Who does the censoring now? If there should be any, who should do it? What should the relationship between the government (federal, state, local) and the media be? What is it now? In many countries, the media (including the arts

as well—theater, ballet, etc.) are supported entirely by the government (through public taxation, of course). Are there any advantages to this system? Disadvantages? What are the advantages and disadvantages to the American system of commercial sponsorship? Make a study of the commercial time per hour of program time (news, entertainment, etc.) on radio and TV. Use your findings to predict the amount of commercial time you can expect to occupy the next half-dozen programs you watch or hear. Do your original findings check out? What do these findings suggest to you? Are you presently satisfied with the quality of programming you are now being given by the stations? Do a study in which you classify the various types of TV programs available during a typical TV week. Then evaluate representative programs from each category according to a set of standards you have developed. These are *your* standards, remember, not the standards you think that your teacher would like you to have. What might you expect from TV were the stations free of commercial pressure? On the question of standards, would you say that your standards of what is good and bad on TV have changed over the years? How? What now interests you that used to bore you? Why? What now bores you that used to interest you? Why? Take the characters from a TV program that you enjoy and write next week's script for them. [The teacher should ditto a sample page or two from a TV script; see, for example, Coles Trapnell, *Teleplay, An Introduction to Television Writing*, Chandler Publishing Company.] Or take a TV play that you've seen and change the focus or the ending, or change one of the major characters, or add a major character. Discuss the problems you had and how you solved them. [The class should form a script-reading committee—which is how the networks do it—and read all the scripts, which should be submitted without the writer's name. Three scripts can be chosen for a class reading. The committee should offer specific reasons for their choices and their rejections.] To make the TV scene complete, write a set of commercials to go with the play, and make certain they are timed properly for the length of the script. Check this out by observing actual TV shows. Choose products or brands that are not currently being advertised on TV (as a way of insuring a fresh approach). What type of thinking has to go into the creating of a good commercial? Study a number of commercials carefully. Note how much is packed into so short a time (often no more than thirty seconds). And note the use of images, movement, sound effects, music, and words. Compare the pace and "stimulation factor" of the commercials with that of the program material. What do you note? Can you explain this?

2. Try a radio script. Since the visual dimension is non-existent, everything has to be done with words, music, and sound effects. The same, of course, is true with the commercials. Try your script out on an audience. (Though virtually all programs on the radio today are music, news, or talk shows, there was a time when various kinds of dramatic programs—radio plays —were the most popular radio entertainment. And that the public could take their radio entertainment seriously is proved by the widespread hysteria generated by Orson Welles' radio broadcast adaptation of H. G. Wells' *The War of the Worlds* —many listeners thought that the Martians had really landed. Your radio script, then, should be a radio play that will hold the attention of your audience.) Try your script out on an audience. Can the audience adequately fill in the missing visual dimension on the basis of your sound effects and verbal clues? Since it is much easier to "grab" you with visual effects than by other means, how does the radio commercial effectively sell its product? How is the "sales talk" structured?

3. What kinds of appeals do commercials make? Choose an ad for a popular product and make a list of the *facts* about the product present in the ad. What *is* a fact? What is an *opinion*? Where do facts come from? Where do opinions come from? Examine ads for a particular product (*e.g.*, soap, toothpaste, etc.) in all the media: TV, radio, newspapers, magazines. Which medium seems to be the most effective for selling what kind of product? The language of advertising has been called "folk poetry." What "poetic" elements can you find in advertising? How do ads play with language? An ad for a brand of men's slacks includes this comment: "They've got the gutsy look that means business!" What does this statement

mean to you? How does the quotation relate to men's slacks? What is the advertiser trying to tell you? Take two or three different (and different *kinds* of) magazines and do a comparative advertising survey. What kinds of products are advertised in each, how are they advertised, and what is the general advertising "tone" of each magazine? How does the advertising relate to the magazine? What can you conclude (tentatively, at least) about the readership of each magazine? Strengthen your assumptions by an analysis of the text material of each magazine: what kinds of articles, stories, and features, how are they written, etc. Do the same analyses (ad and text) of two or three different newspapers (perhaps a weekly, a small-city daily, and a large-city daily). Put all of your material together into an article on the American periodical, written as a feature story for a Sunday newspaper supplement. If you really want to get a good picture of the American periodical, get hold of some Canadian, English, and other foreign magazines and newspapers and add them to your study. Russia puts out several magazines (available in the United States) in English that will give you some perspective in the preceding project and will help you in the following one—propaganda analysis. Many Americans have the mistaken notion that our publications print only the "truth" and foreign publications (particularly those published by our international adversaries) print virtually nothing but lies and distortions. A careful study of a wide range of American and foreign periodicals should open your eyes. Do such a study and report your findings. Try to track down the "facts" and the "interpretations." Sometimes, the truth is distorted by the simple expedient of omitting certain key facts. Sometimes the mere choice of photographs for an article can aim the reader in the direction the editor wants him to go. Look for anything that smacks of "the good-guys-vs.-the-bad-guys" syndrome. Try to sort out the American publications in the order of most fair and honest to least fair and most dishonest. On the basis of what specific observations did you arrive at your classification? In newspapers, do you find that all the editorial material is kept in the editorial columns or are there signs of some degree of editorializing in the news columns? Does the paper *fairly* divide news coverage between opposing candidates or between those holding opposing views on important public issues, or is one side favored by either predominantly greater coverage or by minimal coverage (as a way of keeping the public from finding out something unfavorable about one of the newspaper's "good guys")? Analyze the wording of the headlines, the type and placement of photographs, the quality of the information reported and the tone in which it is reported. Compare a local paper's summary of a speech (by, for example, the President, or a senator, or a cabinet member) with the verbatim text of the speech (which can usually be found in *The New York Times*). What differences, if any, are there in tone and focus and general intent? Using that speech, demonstrate how it can be edited to change its tone, focus, and general intent. (*Editing* does *not* mean *rewriting*.)

4. How many column inches are taken up by ads in a typical edition of your local newspaper? How does this compare with a big-city paper [*vice versa* where appropriate.] What markets do the advertisers seem to be appealing to? How do you know? Give an example of a "good" (*i.e.*, successful) ad, an ad, that is, that has really got you sufficiently excited about the product it is selling to make you want to buy the product. Try to explain why the ad had this effect on you. In general, what kinds of ads really get to you? Why? What kinds leave you cold (even though you might be interested in the product)? Why? Much advertising aimed at the general public partakes of what a contemporary humorist calls "slob culture." He cites the concrete-Mexican-leading-a-concrete-burro lawn ornament as an example of "slob culture." Does the term "slob culture" turn on any lights for you? Write a feature article on "slob culture" and show how the advertiser tunes in on "slob culture" in an effort to sell his products.

5. Has advertising ever played a part in getting you (or anyone you know) to buy something you didn't really need and that you later regretted having bought? How were you convinced? Why did you regret it later?

6. Make up a magazine ad for something you'd like to sell. Use words, pictures, color. What do you have to know about the product and the market (*i.e.*, the readership) to do an effec-

tive job? Make some specific suggestions for revising an existing ad to make it more powerfully appealing to you (as the audience and potential buyer).

7. What are the significant characteristics of ads for (a) the children's market, (b) the pre-teen market, (c) the teen market, (d) the young adult market, (e) the various segments of the mature adult market, and (f) the "golden age" market? Are there other ways of analyzing the market and/or important subdivisions of the categories given above? Revise or amplify if necessary. What proportion of time and space does each market (whatever system of categorization you use) receive in the media? Can a person belong to several market categories at the same time? (Clue: consider occupation, etc., as well as age.)

8. Is there evidence in the media that, as some observers have suggested, America is "youth-crazed"? Discuss.

9. What kind of world does advertising create for us (consider cosmetics, deodorants, cigarettes, mouthwashes, automobiles, etc.)? That is, what are we led to believe makes up the "good life," "success," pleasure, fun, etc.? Write an article on "Advertising's America" for the school paper.

10. What picture of American womankind emerges from the pages of the various women's magazines? (*McCall's*, *Vogue*, *Family Circle*, *Cosmopolitan*, etc.) How does this picture square with your observations? Discuss. Why do some women think that the magazine image is demeaning to women? Do you agree that it is? Discuss the issues that seem to be involved. What picture of American youth emerges from the pages from any random selection of general interest magazines? How do you relate to the picture you see there? Write an article on "Young America: Fact and Fancy," using material you gather from your reading of American magazines.

11. How often do you go out to the movies? What recent movies have you particularly enjoyed? Why? What ones have you disliked? Why? Do you have any definable principles for judging films, or do you just "feel" them? Explain.

12. If you had the expertise, equipment, and budget, what would you make a movie about and why? Do you think that your school should offer a program in student filmmaking? Write

up a proposal for such a program. Be sure to include a well-reasoned, convincing justification that can be submitted to school officials.

13. Should "real" movies (as opposed to "educational films") be shown in the classroom? Why? What movies would you like to see this way? Why these? Develop a program for using movies in school and try to justify your program as a worth-while expenditure of school money and time.

14. Should movies be censored? Why? By whom? What makes a movie "dirty"? Have you ever been embarrassed by anything you've seen in the movies? Discuss. Is sex the only grounds for censorship (assuming that we want censorship)? If not, what other matters should be reviewed for censorship? Why? Does the current rating system have any real meaning or value? On what basis are films classified G, GR, R, and X? See if you can reconstruct the rationale of classification from your own film viewing.

15. Does a black-and-white film affect you differently from a color film? Explain. Should *all* films be in color? What rôle does color play in a recent color film you've seen? What creative uses could color be put to in the art of the film?

16. What in particular interests you most about a film: story? photography? actors and acting? How do you evaluate these elements? Where do we get our standards of judgment? Are the critics always "right"? Discuss.

17. Read two or three reviews of the same film. Compare the reviews to each other and to your own responses to the film. Did reading the reviews help you to understand what you saw? Explain how it is that two reputable critics can often come up with virtually opposite opinions of a film? Under these circumstances, is one "right" and the other "wrong"? Explain. Try writing your own review of a film before you have read any film reviews. How do your comments and observations compare with those of the reviewers? What qualifications do you think a film critic should have? Are film reviews useful? Explain. Does your reviewing a film help you to understand and evaluate a film? How?

18. Do different films seem to be made for different audiences? How can you tell?

19. Are there any distinctive differences between American films and foreign films (other than the fact that the foreign films may not be dubbed in English and will have, therefore, subtitles)? Consider matters of story, mood, acting, photography, "maturity."

20. What kinds of things do you think you might learn from actually making films? Do you think it would be an educationally valid experience to take off a week or more from regular classes to make a film? Write a proposal for such a project and a justification for it to be presented to the principal and school board.

21. Read a few books on filmmaking [see Bibliography] and then put together shooting scripts as follows:
    a. A 30-second "mood" sequence.
    b. A 30-second exposition of a single emotion.
    c. A one-minute comic sequence.
    d. A one-minute suspense sequence.
    e. A short scene from a play or a novel.
    f. A short film commenting realistically on some social problem.
    g. A short film dealing with the same social problem in a surrealistic way.
    h. A short film using only still photographs.
    i. A short film on a flower or an egg or some other single object.
    j. A short film on any subject in any style you choose.
    Write an article called, "Reflections of a Young Filmmaker" (or something like that) in which you discuss the challenges, problems, and rewards of filmmaking. Include the basic technical information needed by anyone who wants to make a film. Don't, incidentally, be shy of suggesting special effects possible with modest equipment, but be sure you work out the technical details.

22. If your school has a video tape recorder, work out some scripts that can be realized with the VTR. While you're at it, make a list of projects that you'd like to see the VTR used for in your school. As a kind of total media project, put together a media package including the following:
    a. A newspaper design. (Make a "dummy" front page and

describe the overall format and contents. Explain the special values and features of your paper. Familiarize yourself with the makeup and style of existing papers, but don't be afraid to do yours a new way—so long as the new way can be justified in terms of the function of a newspaper.)

b. A magazine design. (Same instructions as for *a*, above.)

c. A set of commercials and advertisements for one product conceived as an all-media advertising campaign. (The same product is to be sold through all the media.)

d. An entertainment feature for TV (in outline form).

e. A "public service" feature for TV (in outline form).

f. The same for radio.

g. A prospectus for a full-length motion picture. (Explain the project in some detail and tell why you think the movie is worth making; attempt to convince potential backers.)

h. A multi-media project (music, film, light show, etc., all going on at the same time) for your school. Explain it and justify it.

i. Anything else that you think is potentially interesting and valuable in this general area.

N.B. Be as original as you can—don't copy (though *adaptation* is legitimate).

Wherever feasible, the student should be *doing* not merely theorizing. If he can bring to life at least a few of his ideas through, say, a classroom production of some sort, he will be far more responsive to this type of educational challenge than if he merely talks to himself, so to speak. Critical panels, the talk-show format, newspaper columns, and so on, are all valid ways of exchanging plans, ideas, viewpoints, and feelings. Further, the class should be publishing not only its own newspaper, but its own media journal, literary journal, tape-recorded shows, films, and anything else that allows the student to involve himself in demonstrably productive activity. Media work is, of course, both linguistic and literary. We should never attempt to fix boundaries, for this is both arbitrary and stultifying. In the media age, the printed word must coexist with the other media languages. And I think we need not concern ourselves overmuch with establishing hierarchies of "importance."

IN CLOSING

The teaching materials in this chapter are the core of a program that is virtually limitless. Though subjects like speech and philosophy have not been taken up under their own name, they are of course implicit in the program. Likewise, little time is wasted on "grammar lessons," though substantive questions of language structure and operation are raised and will lead the student into the study of language as a "thing" to be explored and to be used, not a set of "rules" (in effect, prohibitions) to be swallowed. As I have earlier asserted, problems of "correctness" will gradually vanish as the student grows more and more at ease in the use of his language (which he will perforce do because of the very nature of the questions he is being asked to respond to and the projects he is being asked to work out, questions and projects which demand of him not only much reading but a vast amount of writing—and the more he writes, the better his writing will become both from the point of view of "correctness" and from the point of view of grace, fluency, precision, organization, and the rest of the desiderata of good writing). I have offered no reading lists for I think it better to simply make available a broad selection of books and offer guidance on an individual basis. Many of the questions require as part of their solution the reading of certain works (or kinds of works, *e.g.*, poems, biographies, etc.). Certainly I recommend against the massive anthology and the received (and hopelessly outdated—yes, *irrelevant*) reading lists that still beguile a large number of curriculum planners if very few students.

History, political science, mathematics, and the natural sciences, indeed, all the academic disciplines lend themselves admirably at this level to the type of program I am urging for English. (I have throughout the book avoided touching on foreign languages largely because the teaching of foreign languages has long since been updated in most schools, the language laboratory rather than the textbook being the heart of the program, though I would press the introduction of a full-scale foreign language program from the very first year of school. Difficulties in acquiring new and often quite alien speech habits mount rapidly beyond the second or third grade. We have, incidentally, been short-changing our children on the variety of languages it is possible to offer. The Parkway Program, using the resources of the entire community (one sensible solution to the problem of staffing), offers Spanish, French, German, Italian, Polish, Russian, Portuguese, Latin, Greek, Hebrew, and Swahili. (Actually, with a resident professional linguist and a set of tapes, *any* language can be taught.) To reiterate: our students must *be* historians, mathematicians, and so on. And I can list dozens of books far more likely to turn the student in that direction than the usual school texts. Of course, each publisher denies that his is *usual*, but a comparison of the several texts will quickly settle the issue. Likewise, comparison of any school text with such books (on, say, mathematics) as Kasner and Newman's *Mathematics and the Imagination*, W. W. Sawyer's *Prelude to Mathematics*, or even Asimov's little handbook, *Quick and Easy Math*, will underscore the tedium of the textbook. The more advanced student, under the guidance of teachers well grounded in mathematics and history (and why shouldn't our teachers be well grounded in their fields, or move to be so?) can discover a whole new world of ideas in a book like Rashevsky's *Looking at History through Mathematics*. Here is (all rolled into one) theoretical model-building, mathematics, statistics, scientific speculation, history, the study of cultural patterns, and much more. Why do we insist on spooning out pap when the student wants something to really chew on? There is, for example, no textbook that comes within a light-year of Loren Eiseley's *The Immense Journey* on the subject of evolution. And no textbook within a hundred light-years of its superb writing. With a book like this, science and literature become one. And the science is solid, not thinned to barley water, while the writing will stand with the work of any literary figure in business today (and ahead of many). There are others: Sir James Jeans, *Physics and Philosophy*, Sir Arthur Eddington, *The Expanding Universe* and *The Nature of the Physical World*, F. S. C. Northrup, *The Logic of the Sciences and the Humanities*, René Dubos, *So Human an Animal*, etc., etc. Textbook writers seem to labor under the (perhaps unconscious) assumption that their prospective readers can't understand good writing and can't comprehend the whole truth. Or is it that textbook writers can neither write well nor comprehend the whole truth?

WHERE DOES THE FUTURE LIE?

The ethical purpose of a liberal education is to liberate, which can only mean to make one capable of conceiving society as free, classless, and urbane.

[Northrop Frye, *Anatomy of Criticism*]

The more educated adult Americans are, the more they must unlearn as parents.

[Kenneth E. Eble, *A Perfect Education*]

We learn from the study of culture that the patterning of perceptual worlds is a function not only of culture but of *relationship*, *activity*, and *emotion*.

[Edward T. Hall, *The Hidden Dimension*]

Our present-day IQ tests are as good an example of the cognitive barbed wire that surrounds us as you could hope to find.

[George B. Leonard, *Education and Ecstasy*]

The process and the goal of education are one and the same thing. The goal of education is disciplined understanding; that is the process as well.

[Jerome S. Bruner, *On Knowing*]

It is in the schools and from the mass media, rather than at home or from their friends, that the mass of our citizens in all classes learn that life is inevitably routine, depersonalized, venally graded; that there is no place for spontaneity, open sexuality, free spirit. Trained in the schools, they go on to the same quality of jobs, culture, politics. This *is* education, mis-education, socializing to the national norms and regimenting to the national "needs."

[Paul Goodman, *Compulsory Mis-education*]

I think the big mistake in schools is trying to teach children anything, and by using fear as the basic motivation. Fear of getting failing grades, fear of not staying with your class, etc. Interest can produce learning on a scale compared to fear as a nuclear explosion to a firecracker.

[Stanley Kubrick, *The Making of Kubrick's 2001*]

I dwell in Possibility— / A fairer house than Prose—

More numerous of windows— / Superior—for Doors—

[Emily Dickinson]

BECAUSE we have managed (thus far!) to muddle through, because we have had what we long thought were endless riches to draw from, because we have achieved (as the result, we must remember, of the seminal work of a relatively few) some stunning technological and material accomplishments, we have been blinded to the profound failures of our mass education. Only now are we (under continuing crisis) beginning to face up to the obvious bankruptcy of our *Weltpolitik*, to the impending catastrophes of social injustice and environmental destruction. Our tardiness in recognition must be in great measure attributable to a public that has been educated to intellectual flaccidity. Only now are we realizing how close to the wall we are being pushed by a host of problems that our education has ill-prepared us to understand, let alone solve. Our children do millions upon millions of dollars worth of damage to our schools every year ($1.5 million in broken windows in New York City alone in 1968). A strange manifestation for an "enlightened" society. And we are being torn apart by racial, political, and social hatreds. The new barbarism: KKK, Minutemen, SDS, yahoo militancy of every stripe and color. We are swindled and cozened at every level from the flim-flam artist flim-flamming a local innocent to the corporation president flim-flamming the government with phoney contracts or the public with sleazy products. All products of American education: the dupes and the dupers. But why go on giving examples—the evidence is plain to see: we send our youngsters to school and we give them a make-believe education. There are exceptions, of course. Fortunately for all of us, there are always exceptions. They are the ones who make it no matter what. They are the *Wunderkinder* who educate themselves regardless of time, place, or circumstance. It is not for them that this book is written, but for the rest, the ones who are dying in the schools and who willy-nilly will bring the society down around our ears. They have been and will continue. They are us tomorrow. They are the haters, the apathetic, the vicious, the avaricious, the self-content, the narrowly self-interested, the time-servers (teachers and physicians and lawyers and judges and congressmen and. . . .), the timid administrators, and all the rest of the essentially indifferent public by whose slack will and under whose tutelage the society flounders along. The children are the future—but the future is only more of us, more of the same.

It is a dismal picture, and I can no longer jolly myself into being hopeful of its amelioration. I do know, however, that if there is any chance, it is through education and the unremitting labor of the few who genuinely care. Most people will *say* they care (if anyone asks), but when the crunch comes, the concern goes—at least that's been my experience. And I know that we will not survive if our education is not radically changed and very soon. I am pleased to think that the program I offer here—one which did not spring full-blown from my brow, but which has been pieced together from much experience, observation, reading, and reflection—moves toward the kind of education that will hold the "center" Yeats writes of, for if "that rude beast" *is* brought to birth, we, dear reader, have had it.

I have not outlined daily lesson plans or any other of the plans that our schools seem so bent on producing and following. I have presented a philosophy of education largely in the form of specific projects. Creativity in the classroom means (among other things) self-reliance and freedom from preordained ritual. It means the opportunity for teacher and student to launch themselves into the mysteries of existence in an attempt to find out who and what and where they are and how things work. One fails to think in proportion as others think for one. Hence my stress on the avoidance of the textbook program of education. The New Zealand teacher Elwyn Richardson (see *In the Early World*) took his youngsters out into the world for what seems to me to be one of the valid and productive educational experiences I have had news of. John Bremer's Parkway Program, the "school without walls," is another such move toward a genuinely liberating education. Our education should make us independent; instead, it creates a thousand dependencies. It weakens us, forces us into narrow molds, and leaves us selfish and somewhat less than fully human.

This book could have easily been a thousand pages or more. The reader need but open to any of the questions that are the core of the book and in a short time he will have thought of a dozen new ones. This is the ground of education. And each set of actions or answers will in turn generate its new set of questions. What set of textbooks can replace this type of self-generating education? The human mind is laden with riches and potentials far in excess of anything found in our watery textbooks. And a mind that is operating can find all around it all the "texts" it needs. With the classroom and community as library, laboratory, resource center, and base of operations into everywhere the mind wishes to explore, the school day becomes a day of education not servitude. But we have got to break the traditional boxes of time and space, the compulsive urge to stuff our kids with facts, the notion that neatness, silence, and "good grades" are what make good schools.

I am certain that any teacher with any spark of imagination and any willingness to try "letting go" will find endless ways of adding to, improving, and otherwise usefully modifying what I've presented here. This is as it should be. A book like this should never have needed writing.

My penchant for asking questions has not yet (alas) been satisfied. Let me close this brief chapter with a list of questions aimed now at parents (but to which teachers should be prepared to respond). The educational process is mutually the work of the school and the community—a fine proposition that is agreed upon by all hands and acted on by none (except at budget-approval time, but budgets are *dollars* not *education*). Let us now work together on the basis of *educational* issues (the nitty-gritty of what actually goes on in the classroom and in the lives of our children). I mean for this book to stir up both school *and* community. Let teachers and administrators and school-board members be constructively bugged by knowledgeable parents. Let the school establishment make an honest effort at explaining and justifying its programs in clear English, not in "educationese," obfuscation compounded. And let the schools do some constructive bugging of the community in the interests of greater awareness and concern. The questions, then:

1. What seems to be your child's attitude toward school? What leads you to this conclusion?
2. Does your child talk to you about school? What does he tell you?
3. Are you able to engage your child in an informative conversation about anything he is studying in school? What does he do in school that he seems to enjoy a great deal and to be well informed about? What does he seem to lack interest in and to be poorly informed about?
4. What does he seem to be *accomplishing* in school (*i.e.*, *real* as opposed to *report-card* accomplishment)?
5. Does he like to read and write? What does he read/write other than assigned work?
6. What kinds of questions does he ask?
7. Does school seem to be an important part of his life (*i.e.*, not merely from the standpoint of hours-per-day spent in school)?
8. Do you feel that the report-card categories and grades are meaningful? Can you gauge with some degree of accuracy your child's academic, intellectual, and emotional development on the basis of the report card? What kinds of information would you like to see on a report card? Try designing a system of evaluation that would be really valuable to you as a parent.
9. What are your criteria for evaluating (1) a school and (2) a teacher? What are these criteria based on? How much do you know about either the school that your child attends or his teachers?
10. To whom does the neighborhood school really belong and what purposes does it really serve? Take care not to confuse

appearances, expectations, and public relations with reality!

11. Are good grades and a good report equivalent to a good education? How do *you* define "good education"? What, in practice, distinguishes the well educated person from the poorly educated person? Where do you fit into this scheme?

12. Which of your skills, interests, aptitudes, accomplishments, etc., are directly traceable to your formal education?

13. What school subjects do you remember with pleasure (or remember at all, for that matter) and what specifically do you remember about them? Would you say that your formal education was in any sense a *fulfilling* (humanizing, liberating, etc.) experience? Explain. What do you judge to be the weaknesses in your own education? What would you do over if you could? Explain.

14. Do you enjoy reading. Do you read with speed, ease, and high comprehension? If not, what specifically seems to be the problem? What do you read regularly? What magazines, newspapers, books? If reading is not an important part of your life (other than at the level of reading in connection with your job), is it important that it be so for your child? Why?

15. Do you enjoy writing? Do you write with clarity, precision, and fluency? If you do not, what may this tell you about the quality of your education and all the years spent in English classes?

16. Do you see any evidence that your child is doing appreciably better than you in these matters?

17. What is *learning*? How does it take place?

18. A high-school graduate has twelve years' study of "English" behind him. For a large part of those twelve years he has studied "grammar." How much of this "grammar" do *you* know? What do *you* "do" with this "grammar"? Does this tell you anything about rote learning? What has been *learned*?

19. "New Math," "New Science," and "New English" are "new" largely by virtue of their new pedagogy, which (in theory, at least) is a "discovery" or "problem-solving" approach to learning. Does your child show evidence of developing techniques for learning? Can he define a problem and develop a model for its solution? In short, are you satisfied that he is learning to *think* (in the formal, logical sense)?

20. For a society such as ours to maintain its vitality, indeed, even to survive, we need (among other things) what one might call "creative individualism." Does your child seem to be moving toward this goal? Or does he seem to be moving (intellectually speaking) toward a kind of downward leveling conformity?

21. Can you say with any assurance what your child's *values* are? (Not what you'd like them to be, but what you observe them to be!) What should the school's rôle be in building values, and what should those values be? (Arrive at your conclusions through rational thought not through reflex conditioning.) Consider racial, political, geo-political, social, environmental, ethical, intellectual, and educational values, attitudes, and ideals. Can you outline your own presently operational value system? (Again, what it *really* is as opposed to what you may think it should be.) That is, what do you truly value? Is your value system a by-product of your formal education?

22. At home, what topics are taboo for discussion? Why? Should there be any taboo topics for discussion in school? What and why? What, besides routine family matters, do you discuss with your child? Is there any "art of conversation" in your home? Do you sense the existence of the famous *generation gap*? Just what is this generation gap? How might it be bridged? Can the school (or should the school) play a useful rôle in bridging it? How?

23. Have you read any of your child's textbooks? Are they worthwhile? How do you know? Who chooses the books for your child's school? On what basis? Do you think that it is important for parents to be aware of matters like this? Explain.

24. What educational resources are available in your child's classroom and in the school at large? What do you think *should* be available? Have you any means of evaluating these resources?

25. Does the school have a good library? What *is* a good school library and how should it be run? Have you a good home library? What *is* a good home library? Do you really think that a dictionary and a set of encyclopedias constitute a good home library? Why? Does it seem reasonable to expect children to be interested in reading if their parents don't seem to be?

26. What rôle should parents play in the education of their

children? Or is education entirely the job of the school? Discuss. Other than harassing your child about his grades, what do you contribute to his intellectual and academic growth? To his emotional growth and stability? To his general understanding of the ways of the world?

27. What should the schools be teaching? Why? What do you feel you would like to know more about? Why? What efforts are you making to fill these gaps? Or do you feel that since your formal schooling is over and since you have your career cut out for you (as wage-earner, parent, housewife, or whatever), you needn't bother yourself further about your own education? If you are thus indifferent, how can you expect your child to be otherwise with regard to education?

28. What philosophy of education seems to underlie the tests and examinations your child takes in school? What in your opinion does an examination prove or accomplish? Do you feel that the examinations you took in school were educationally useful to you? Explain.

29. How much of what your child is "learning" seems to be immediately applicable to his own world of meanings and experiences? How can you tell?

30. When you hear, read, or observe something, how do you know what it means? Can your child cope with a question like this? What can you learn by trying to cope with a question like this?

31. What is an *idea*? Where do *ideas* come from? Are some ideas more important than others? How do you know? On what basis do we attach "good" or "bad" to ideas? Can "good" ideas become "bad" ideas? How? Or *vice versa*? How? When we say that we *know* something, what does that mean? What does *knowing* consist of? What is *progress* (E. E. Cummings called it a "comfortable disease"), *growth, success, truth*, etc.? How do we evaluate these notions? Does your child ask questions like these? Can he wrestle with them? Are these worthwhile questions to be asking? Explain. Philosophically speaking, what kinds of questions are they? Should one's education point to such questions? Why or why not?

32. How much exposure has your child had to art (museum visits, etc.), music (live concerts), dance, theater, and other

cultural programs? Do you think that this is an important dimension in a person's education? Are you interested in such things? If not, why not? Since we are not born with a taste for, say, ballet, we must acquire it. Would you like to acquire these tastes (assuming, of course, that you don't have them now)? How would you go about it? What should the school be doing in this area that it is presently not doing? What should you be doing insofar as your child's development is concerned? Is a weekly piano lesson (or whatever) sufficient?

33. Does your child like to create (painting, music, sculpture, etc.)? Does the school provide an environment for creativity? Do you do anything creative? Would you like to? (Why not try!) Do you provide an environment for creativity at home? (*E.g.*, a place to mess, materials to mess with, and unforced encouragement.)

34. Do you believe that conformity to teacher-determined (which often means syllabus- and textbook-determined) norms is necessarily desirable for a child? If the teacher has ordained that the child should paint a house that "looks like a house" and the child instead paints a purple blob with green and yellow arabesques around it, is the child "wrong" (or some other pejorative)? How do you arrive at a sensible balance between the demands for conformity on the part of the "establishment" and the need for unique identity on the part of the individual? Does the answer reside simply in "might makes right"?

35. What kind of relationship should exist between the school and the parents? Is the present equation a satisfactory one? Do you *trust* the school and its personnel? What *substantive* information have you been given about the educational programs of the school? How do the Parents' Nights presentations square with your evaluation of your child's education? Would you like to know more about the school and its operations, programs, and resources? (Don't be bashful—you have a perfect right to a full accounting.)

36. Suppose you wanted to make your child's school the best school possible, what would you need to know to do the job?

37. What are the specific functions of the school principal? How

much real authority does he have? How does one become a principal? Should the principal be totally divorced from the classroom (as he is in most schools) or should he have some teaching responsibilities? All of these questions should likewise be asked of the other school executives (vice-principal, assistant principals, etc.). Do you believe that the administrative hierarchy of your child's school earns its keep, as it were?

38. What rôle should the child play in the educational process? Should he, for example, be primarily a passive receiver of "knowledge" transmitted to him from teacher and book?

39. Do you think that compulsory education is still desirable in our society? Compulsory education is so much of a habit that we are inclined to assume that it is just the "way things are." Perhaps the concept needs some serious rethinking. As an exercise in thinking, draw up a convincing set of arguments *both* pro and contra compulsory education.

40. Is our present system of education appropriate to the type of world we are living in? This question requires much serious thought and discussion.

And, I might add, "Will we survive?" But contemplation of that one gives me, as they used to say, the fantods. The fact is that I am not convinced we will survive, though on this point I shall be happy to be proved wrong. Surely without some serious second and third thoughts about what we are doing to our children and ourselves through our ways of education, our chances for survival as a free, healthy, humane, and productive people are negligible.

Appendix 1

GAMES

Where does education begin? Surely it begins in play and continues in play all our lives. Yet no sooner does education become formalized than it becomes solemnized.

[Kenneth E. Eble, *A Perfect Education*]

Childhood is playhood; and any community system that ignores that truth is educating in a wrong way.

[A. S. Neill, *Summerhill*]

It is not difficult to imagine a school of the future as a "laboratory school" —a school making massive use of educational stimulation games, laboratory activities, and creative projects—a school in which almost everything to be earned is manipulated, physically or mentally. Students will have the chance to investigate their subject matter, to feel comfortable with it, to familiarize themselves with it, and to do so in communication with other students, thereby giving to all students the benefit of additional ideas and insights. The students will be in an almost totally active learning environment, exploring and discovering for themselves.

[Clarke C. Abt, *Serious Games*]

WE commonly think of games either as a kind of frivolity or as a way to "relax." Chess addicts will of course appreciate that chess playing is a pretty tense kind of relaxing, but by and large we don't consider game playing as much more than idle amusement. Yet it is perfectly possible (perhaps desirable) to build an entire educational program around game playing, a program that will result in the child's acquiring more theoretical and practical knowledge than he now acquires in school and acquiring it in a way that will make his school experience continually engaging and challenging to him. For the child, games are anything but "frivolous." The spontaneous game-playing of children (exhaustively documented in Iona and Peter Opie, *Children's Games in Street and Playground*, Oxford University Press) is one of the ways, a very important one, in which the child acculturates himself and learns to identify and manipulate the dynamics of social existence. And, as the Opies tell us, this type of game-playing had better be left alone by the adult world. (Consider the concomitant demise of kid's baseball with the advent of the "Little League" madness, adults playing games through their children and infecting the game with all the adult sicknesses.)

The formally "educational" game is of a somewhat different order than mumbley-peg, but its play component is what gives it its unique value in the educational program. Every classroom should have an ample stock of these games (some representative examples of which are described below). Most of them are cheaply bought, copied, or invented. It should, for example, be well within the capabilities of first-graders to make chess and checker sets of cardboard, construction paper, and so on. One of the most attractive chess sets on the market is a "do-it-yourself" set in which the various pieces are made of interchangeable nuts and bolts.

TRADITIONAL BOARD GAMES

Of the traditional board games, chess and *Go* offer the greatest learning potential. Both games are not only infinitely challenging but their rules and moves are simple and can be taught in a very short time. It surely says something about the quality of our education that our young people occupy themselves with the witless games fobbed off on the public by toy manufacturers and are so little intrigued by, say, chess, the "basic" game of Russia and Persia. The challenge of the American fad games rarely lasts longer than a week. Chess and *Go* players find that a lifetime isn't sufficient to mine the riches of the games. A chess or *Go* game is an exercise in creative logic, sequencing, and projective thinking. It requires the understanding of local and immediately identifiable relationships as well as the ability to anticipate the consequences of these relationships in the future and the ability to plan for the satisfactory resolution of these consequences. I see very little in the usual school curriculum that is as productive of high order logical operations. The invention of *Go* is attributed to the Chinese Emperor Shun (2255–2206 B.C.), who (tradition tells us) invented it to sharpen his son's dull mind. The tendency of our education, on the contrary, seems to be toward dulling rather than sharpening minds! The child is naturally an experimenter, and if we give him things to do which preclude experimentation, we effectively dull his mind. (The Emperor Shun's pedagogical instincts were certainly good.) The great beauty of these classical board games is the scope they allow for experiment while at the same time providing an intellectually satisfying framework in which to range. And, of course, there is the excitement of the clash of forces that makes up the external shape of the games.

Chess

Compared with man's great achievements, what does Chess have to offer? Why be concerned about it? Strangely, Chess is one of the few man-conceived phenomena to which man has been enslaved, for he has not been able to solve the mystery of it. We are dealing with a *finite* concept—a board consisting of *exactly* 64 squares and two opposing forces each consisting of *exactly* 16 pieces, and each of the pieces locomoting within the bounds of the board in accordance with *specific* rules. Yet man, who has tackled the "infinity" of the cosmos with highly respectable results, has not been able to conquer Chess. (I. A. Horowitz and P. L. Rothenberg, *The Complete Book of Chess*, Collier Books.)

Simply put, the aim of chess is *checkmate* (etymologically quite different from what it sounds like: *shāh*, "king"; *māt*, "dead" [Arabic]; hence, *check mate*, "kill the king" or "the king is dead"). This situation arises when the opposing king is under an attack that cannot be turned. Checkmate can be accomplished in as few as three moves and as many as dozens of moves. After the opening move (which is fairly standardized), the endless possibilities of the game open up. For equally matched opponents (whether equally good or equally poor), the game is continually exciting and great fun. Plans are made and wrecked and remade; there are unexpected attacks and thrilling resolutions. As is true of anything worth exploring, the deeper one goes, the more one discovers that there is more to know. In the *Games* section of the Bibliography, I have listed a few of the numerous chess books currently available. An adult can teach himself the rudiments of the game in half an hour. The rest is practice. And if the entire class is starting out on an equal footing, the teacher can learn a great deal in games with his students. To make the most of this and other board games, the class should from time to time examine the logical and mathematical features of the games, play a few games in common (on the blackboard), work out alternate moves and consequences, and so on. Advanced players should be encouraged to attempt developing a model for approximating the total number of chess games possible. (It has been determined that in a game of forty moves, 25×10^{115}—*i.e.*, $25 + 116$ zeros—moves are possible. Through only the *fourth* move, there are 288 billion possibilities!) And to make things even more interesting, students should be asked to try working out alternate kinds of chess games. There is, for example, a "space chess," which is a kind of three-dimensional version of the game. (Likewise, there are three-dimensional tic-tac-toe and three-dimensional checkers.)

Go

Chess and Go are both in a sense military games, but the military tactics that are represented by Chess are of a past age, in which the king himself entered the conflict—his fall generally meaning the loss of the battle—and which victory or defeat was brought about by the courage of a single nobleman rather than through the fighting of the common soldiers. Go, on the other hand, is not merely the picture of a single battle like Chess, but of a whole campaign of a modern kind, in which the strategical movements of the masses in the end decide the victory. Battles occur in various parts of the board, and sometimes several are going on at the same time. Strong positions are besieged and captured, and whole armies are cut off from their line of communications and are taken prisoners unless they can fortify themselves in impregnable positions, and a far-reaching strategy alone assures victory. (Arthur Smith, *The Game of Go, The National Game of Japan,* Charles Tuttle Co.)

(Looking at a map of the Vietnam War, one is inclined to believe that the North Vietnamese and the NLF are *Go* players!)

From Smith's comments one might judge that a game of *Go* in progress is busy, even frenetic. The contrary is so. The game is played on a board scribed with 19 by 19 lines, making 361 intersections upon which stones are simply placed, each player having a sufficient supply to completely fill the board between them (black, 181, white, 180). Black (given to the weaker player) always plays first, hence the extra stone, which serves as a handicap stone for black. The stones are placed or, if "killed," removed. There are, in a sense, no *moves,* only placements and removals. The aim of the game is to enclose territory, neither to "kill" opposing stones (though this is inevitably done in the course of play) nor to checkmate, but rather to take under one's control as many intersections (*mei,* "eyes") as one can. With as many intersections to work with, the possibilities for play are, as in chess, astronomical. And, as in chess, while it takes but a few minutes to learn the very simple rules, "It is said in Japan that a player with ordinary aptitude would have to play ten thousand games in order to attain professional rank of the lowest degree." (There are *nine* professional degrees.) Yet, equally matched players can have a rousing good time with the game despite the fact that their playing may be execrable by professional standards. (In Japan, some people play *Go* for a living, the way some Americans play golf for a living.) The classroom activities for *Go* are the same as for chess. Boards are easily made, and bottle caps painted contrasting colors (black and white, to be traditional) will do very well for the stones. In fact, round, flat stones about ¾-inch in diameter are fine if the local geology affords such. (Not at all impossible: There are places on the Maine coast, for example, that abound in first-rate *Go* stones.) A good way to get into the game would be to give the class a *Go* board and stones and let them devise a game to suit the components. And once *Go* is learned, it might be worthwhile asking the class to devise variations. (Several abbreviated versions of the game are played.)

In both of these games, the *problem* (*e.g.,* discovered check in two moves) is an excellent technique for probing their complexities. At first, the players can work on the great variety of readily available problems. (Almost any book on chess contains examples of chess problems.) But as soon as players have had some experience in problem-solving, they should get to work on *creating* problems. The value to the student of this type of intellectual challenge cannot be overestimated.

GAMES OF LOGIC
AND MATHEMATICS

> Introduction of the first WFF'N PROOF game . . . was, in our estimation, a significant event in the teaching of logic—as significant in its field as the launching of the first satellite in the space race field. If this seems extravagant, let us point out that challenging, competitive games capable of teaching with unadulterated enjoyment still are a rarity. . . . Therefore, we enthusiastically recommend the new WFF'N PROOF games. . . . WFF'N PROOF can be the first exhilarating challenge to children of 6 and, as the games progress, stimulate the intellect of people of any age or capability. (*Data Processing Digest*, quoted by the WFF'N PROOF Publishers in their promotional material.)

The educational worth of the WFF'N PROOF academic games is amply demonstrated in the quarterly *Newsletter* that came into being as a result of wide interest among students and teachers in the games as teaching devices. The Spring, 1969, *Newsletter*, for example, reports preparations for the fourth National Academic Games Olympics (held at the Nova School, Ft. Lauderdale, Florida, April 23–26, 1969). And academic games workshops are being set up around the country, coordinated by the WFF'N PROOF *Newsletter*, and staffed by teachers experienced in the use of the games in the classroom. And in almost any issue one can read items like this letter from a thirteen-year-old boy from Jericho, N.Y., who "would like to know if there are any mathematicians in the New York metropolitan area interested in working on a mathematical analysis of the WFF'N PROOF games." I have no wish to sound as though I were peddling these games (and if any sales are attributable to my enthusiastic endorsement, that is to the benefit of the company and to those who buy the games, not to me!), but I am urging their use, for their value is beyond question. Where the games have been used as a regular part of the school program, there have not only been dramatic improvements in computational skills but mathematics has become a truly living subject. (For detailed information about the classroom use of the games, write to WFF'N PROOF *Newsletter,* 1111 Maple Avenue, Turtle Creek, Pennsylvania 15145.)

The major games in the WFF'N PROOF series are these:

1. WFF'N PROOF. A kit of 21 games of logic, for six-year-olds to Ph.D.'s. The games are progressively more difficult (or *challenging,* if you prefer) and represent in their totality a complete course in symbolic logic. Although there are no numbers, some elements of mathematical logic can be learned through the games. (WFF = "well-formed formula.")
2. EQUATIONS. A five-game kit (grades 1 to 12) using real numbers and affording practice in the basic numerical operations.
3. ON-SETS. A 3-game kit (for six-year-olds and up) that teaches the principles of set theory (the basis of "modern math").
4. CONFIGURATIONS. A variety of mathematical and geometrical puzzles and games designed to afford insights into projective geometry.
5. THE PROPAGANDA GAME. The games in this set are not symbolic but based rather upon actual instances of faulty logic in everyday contexts. These games can be very effectively used in conjunction with a study of the media: news presentation, advertising, editorials, etc.

The WFF'N PROOF games are, of course, not the only academic games available. They do, however, have the advantages of being developed by teachers and scholars (as opposed to toy manufacturers), being widely tested and proved, and being inexpensive. A trip to any well-stocked toy and game store will turn up a number of other useful classroom games of this general type. And books like *Serious Games, The Gentle Art of Mathematics, Adventures in Mathematics,* and *Vision in Elementary Mathematics* (see Bibliography) will provide an embarrassment of riches to the imaginative teacher.

WORD AND LANGUAGE GAMES

The archetype of most boxed word games is the crossword puzzle. In some language arts workbooks, the authors include a few dull crossword puzzles, but the game manufacturers have appreciated the crossword puzzle's potential far more than the textbook writers as the success of SCRABBLE and similar games demonstrates. Various kinds of crossword puzzle tournaments (whether done on paper or with the commercial games—or classroom copies of the games, my recommendation in the interests of saving money and further involving the student in the materials of his education) would do a lot for spelling and vocabulary, though it would be a mistake on the part of the teacher to approach these games simply as an easy way to shove spelling at the kids. A fairly complex type of thinking is required to work puzzles of this kind and it would be illuminating to explore this process with the student. And as he becomes more aware of the operations involved, he should be urged to develop his own word puzzles—based on puns, perhaps, or other word play mechanisms (see Dmitri Borgmann, *Language on Vacation*). The real benefit of "word-gaming" is a heightened *Sprachgefühl* or sensitivity to one's language. Once a child is put onto the track of an idea that teases his imagination, he will usually carry it to extraordinary lengths. On this point, consider the student (cited above) who wants to do a mathematical analysis of the WFF'N PROOF games. Or the youngsters who have discovered strategies that the inventor of the games hadn't even thought of. This is creativity; this is education.

SPILL AND SPELL and SCRABBLE are the basic "configurations" of the boxed crossword games. (PROBE is an interesting and very appealing variation.) Crossword puzzle games can be easily made. Letters can be drawn on large sheets of railroad board and cut on a print trimmer. The class should do some thinking about how many of each letter to include. This is an interesting problem in determining letter frequencies in English.

GAME-MAKING

Though a wide range of games is currently available on the market, many of these are either trivial or overpriced. Once game-playing as a legitimate classroom activity has been introduced and the student is urged to think about the logic and structure of games, he should be set to work on developing specific kinds of games: a game to teach number concepts to very young children, a sentence-producing game, an etymology (word-origin) game, geo-political games, economic games, and so on—the possibilities are limitless. In *Serious Games*, the author discusses such marvelously imaginative and genuinely productive games as SEPEX, a game "designed to aid educational decision-makers in the application of electronic systems to educational services, both instructional and administrative" (pp. 157ff.). At any rate, game-making is a point at which *Homo sapiens, Homo loquens, Homo faber,* and *Homo ludens* meet. And here is learning in action.

Appendix 2

BOOKS

Books, like men, are subject to manners, behaviour; they are well or ill-bred; well dressed or badly dressed. You can tell them for what they are at a glance.

[Holbrook Jackson, *The Anatomy of Bibliomania*]

The anthologies should make the English teacher wonder about what an editor's judgment and a publisher's necessity have put together. An examination of high school literature texts suggests that more attention is being paid to four-color printing (certainly more money expended on it) than to contents.

[Kenneth E. Eble, *A Perfect Education*]

The text-book mill of exercises, boring and inefficient, is preserved by poor material and administrative conditions.
The bulk of classroom text-books are grotesquely Philistine. . . .

[David Holbrook, *English for the Rejected*]

The source of publishers' information about what teachers can do is the sales staff, which will never willingly shoulder the extra load of selling something really original. The result is a despairing, defensive criticism which hangs over the entire textbook field.

[Martin Mayer, *The Schools*]

As a genuine, unregenerate bibliophile, I have a powerful instinct for doing just what the maxim advises us against, namely, judging a book by its cover. My instinct in this regard, may I say, is rarely wrong (if I am allowed as well a bit of hefting and of feeling of paper and of examination of typography). I grew up with books and even when I didn't read them, I liked them. One of my greatest pleasures was (and is today) browsing in bookstores (preferably ones without fluorescent lights—a crotchet of no consequence), tormenting myself (deliciously) over which volumes I shall buy and which I shall with regret leave for another day when my checkbook is again able to accommodate my fancies. And I confess to buying, even when funds were needed elsewhere, innumerable books for no greater reason than they felt right and promised by this token a lifelong friendship. Romantic and imprudent, no doubt, but bibliophiles are, after all, just that way—it is the mark of the breed.

Books seem to distinguish themselves from non-books (textbooks and the like) by some quality of design, of feel, of that *je ne sais quoi* that every true bibliophile will recognize. More seriously (and objectively), the honest books are the primary works of creativity and scholarship, the novels and other literary works (*ohne apparat*), the whole range of scholarly and scientific writing produced by scholars and scientists for their peers and for an educated public. These, too, are the great reference works: *The New English Dictionary on Historical Principles* (all thirteen volumes), *Webster's Third New International Dictionary of the English Language,* the *Deutsche Brockhaus Sprachwörterbuch,* the *Nouveau Larousse;* the *Enciclopedia Italiana,* the *Deutsche Brockhaus,* the *Espasa;* Frazer's *The Golden Bough* (complete), Graves' *The Greek Myths,* and so on. And the children's books by writers who *respect* children (A. A. Milne, Kenneth Graham, Antoine de Saint Exupéry, E. B. White, and the rest) and realize that children are entitled to grace and charm and not commercial fakery (in the form, for example, of "controlled vocabularies" that almost invariably yield graceless and witless stories). At all events, the books that are books are almost without exception not textbooks.

Throughout this book (which I blush to admit is something of a textbook), I have spelled out my objections to textbooks—a stratagem appropriate enough for one who is urging a program of education that is not dependent on textbooks; and it is perhaps redundant to reiterate those objections. Nevertheless, I will do so briefly as a summary statement. (The major villain in the textbook trade, as I see it, is the textbook *series,* and it is toward this particularly pernicious form of the textbook that my strictures mainly apply.)

1. Textbooks tie down both teacher and student through *de facto* control of the curriculum by the series.

2. They are written down to the lowest common denominator, both teacher and student.

3. They enmesh the teacher in a tangle of "guides," "aids," "manuals," etc., that effectively preclude the teacher's doing anything original on his own. Caleb Gattegno, quoted in *The Center Forum,* March 1, 1969:

   > Our picture of children is distorted . . . because we don't grant them what they are. We develop schema into which we fit their actions. There's no such thing as a frustrated one-year-old who can't talk. He's content to see the world from where he is with his own senses. It's the adults who get frustrated. SRA [a textbook publisher] develops reading material based on the average student, and puts it in a little box. Its concept of reading is reached *a priori.* It doesn't take the individual child into consideration. It's concerned with "you" getting through the box. (P. 6.)

4. They are the antithesis of creativity (which all the books and sets of materials promise but don't deliver) by virtue of the simple fact that they pre-digest and predict everything that they are supposed to be "creative" about.

5. With the rarest of exceptions, they are poorly written, tastelessly designed, and filled with (a) outright misinformation, (b) gross oversimplifications, (c) subtle distortions, (d) nonsense, and (e) non-information. (That is, in an American history textbook, for example, they simply overlook anything which puts America in an unfavorable light, or so gloss over the facts as to blatantly misrepresent the truth.) They are, furthermore, tendentious, pretentious, portentous, and patronizing.

6. All of the preceding makes them monumentally boring.

7. And it helps them admirably to serve the cause of making school a tiresome place to be and books tiresome things to bother with.

In my list of encyclopedias, I pointedly overlooked the big American productions for the simple reason that I think of them as another species of non-book. I am appalled at the money schools waste on those flashy sets. Somehow, school librarians (or whoever manages the job in lieu of a librarian) at every school level from elementary on up have got the idea that encyclopedia sets are desirable acquisitions. I know of many an elementary school that is virtually barren of books but which feels satisfied that several hundred (hard-to-come-by) dollars are well spent on a new encyclopedia. The question that immediately comes to mind is, What are the kids supposed to do with an encyclopedia? Of course, in order to give the encyclopedia a workout, the teachers require the kids to look things up in it. Well, if that's the point of having an encyclopedia, who can argue with it? So the kids look things up and copy them out? Then what? Everybody is happy because the encyclopedia is being used and the kids are "doing research." Since of course there is only one article on each subject covered by the encyclopedia, they are going to get a pretty limited view of things. And suppose, for example, they want to find out something about movie-making (an interest they've come on by themselves, let's say, not as a result of being told to look it up). What does any encyclopedia tell one about movie-making in a few columns of print, however fine that print may be? For $1.50 the school can get a 250-page book on movie-making (with sixty-five photographs and all manner of drawings, charts, diagrams, etc.) done in clear, readable language (Edward Pincus, *Guide to Film-making*, Signet W3992). American encyclopedias are very slick and very weighty (physically so), but they are of the most limited use, for unless one wants a fast fact or two (see the handy one-volume Columbia desk encyclopedia for that), the typical encyclopedia article is both oversimplified and overly general. I am unimpressed by encyclopedia references in student papers at the college level, and why they should be of any greater value at other levels I don't know. Good research is good research; otherwise it's busy work. Copying or paraphrasing encyclopedia articles is plagiarism, though an awful lot of teachers apparently think that it's in a noble cause. Let the school spend money on books. Fill the gaps in the library with books of substance that will give the young inquiring mind something to really dig into. The "diggings" one culls from an encyclopedia are thin stuff indeed. A work like the *Enciclopedia*

Italiana is another matter entirely. This mammoth undertaking (an official publication of the Italian government) is probably the best single source of information on matters of art (Italian art in particular, as one might suppose). It is of course in Italian and is not the sort of reference work a public school can ordinarily invest in. But there are innumerable inexpensive books on art that offer riches vastly in excess of the few pages of watered-down art history offered by the big commercial encyclopedias. They are strictly American business enterprises and are, understandably, in business to please their stockholders. Their sales pitch is keyed to the fallacious but appealing notion that owning an encyclopedia is of great significance to a child's education. It isn't. I venture to say that most of the impressively bound volumes gather dust in the handy bookcase that comes as a part of the package. Not only is the general multi-volume encyclopedia worth little as an educational tool, but it preempts both book space and book budgets. Instead of one's building a proper library, which can be so inexpensively done today, with worthwhile books bought at the moment of need (ideally for the student through a school-run paperback bookstore, a service being introduced by more and more schools), three hundred to six hundred dollars' worth of encyclopedia squats reproachfully in the bookcase. Not that an encyclopedia might not make entertaining casual reading (if one enjoys stuffing his head with odds and ends). Unfortunately, the volumes are far too stiff and heavy to make pleasant companions of this sort. In the eighteenth century, when the first great general encyclopedia of knowledge was published (a product of the French Enlightenment), it met a real need. Now, it is redundant.

America's neurosis regarding "correctness" has created (and, interestingly, been created by) a flourishing branch of the publishing world that addresses itself aggressively to this large and willing market. We are afloat on a sea of dictionaries (more of which are sold in supermarkets, dime stores, and drugstores than in bookstores) and books that promise to correct all of our spelling, writing, and speaking "errors" and to improve our "word power in 30 days." With the few exceptions I will discuss shortly, the dictionaries are a flat-out waste of money. (The name *Webster*, incidentally, is in the public domain, which means that anybody who wants to publish a dictionary—or what he hopes will pass for one—can call his book *Webster's Dictionary*. Webster is so indelibly associated in the American mind with dictionaries that we fall for the fraud without giving it a second thought. The fact is that even the respectable dictionaries of the G. & C. Merriam Co., the more-or-less legitimate heirs to the original Webster's dictionary, contain nothing whatever of Noah Webster in them. Nor would we want a modern dictionary to do so. Eighteenth- and nineteenth-century lexicographical crotchets have no place in the twentieth century.) And the books that are aimed at our linguistic insecurities are likewise fraudulent. More non-books. It takes a lifetime to achieve that "powerful vocabulary," for we develop our linguistic skills only through genuine use—speaking, reading, writing. Memorizing vocabulary lists with synonymic "definitions" is about as futile a way to idle away one's time as I can think of. In the matter of our correctness neurosis:

> No one flourishes in an atmosphere of repression. It is possible, of course, for a person with special aptitudes and a special drive to bull his way past the prohibitions and achieve an individual style. But with the negative attitude that attends all our writing, those whose main interest lies elsewhere are inhibited by fear of "error" and the nagging doubt it stirs up from setting pen to paper, until the sight of a blank white page gives them the shakes. It is no wonder that their expression is halting and ineffective. They cannot fulfill the demands of a prissy propriety and trace the form of an idea at the same time. They thus arrive at adulthood victims of the steely eye of Mr. Sherwin Cody, whose bearded face stares at them from countless ads for his correspondence school, demanding, "Do YOU make these mistakes in English?" The locutions he lists are not mistakes, and Mr. Cody knows they are not; but his readers do not know it, and they do not know that they don't matter anyway. (Donald J. Lloyd, "Our National Mania for Correctness," *The American Scholar,* Vol. 21, No. 3, Summer, 1952.)

These books, then, are in the same category of books that "teach" you how to make a million in the stockmarket, how to resolve all of your worries and anxieties, how to think "positively," how to win friends and influence people, how to lose weight without dieting, how to find new love in marriage and new joy in sex, how to. . . . And so forth. There is no end, it would seem, of finding ways of parting a fool from his gold.

Two so-called unabridged dictionaries are currently in print in the United States (not counting supermarket junk), the Merriam-Webster *New International Dictionary, Third Edition* and *The Random House Dictionary of the English Language.* I say "so-called" because the size of the English vocabulary is unknown. Hence, these dictionaries are merely less abridged than the "desk" or "college" dictionaries. Of the two, the Merriam-Webster is by far the superior. G. & C. Merriam have a long tradition of dictionary-making (and that is all they do).

Of the desk dictionaries, by far the best is the new *American Heritage Dictionary of the English Language* (Houghton Mifflin), which is not only typographically the most readable and the best illustrated but includes the comments on key items of a "usage panel," a group of about a hundred major figures on the contemporary literary and media scene. This feature answers the needs of those who are in fact uncertain, for example, whether to use *disinterested* for *uninterested, like* for *as,* etc. Lack of unanimity on most items is in itself illuminating and underscores the fluidity of the language. The usage comments obviate the need (for the nervous native speaker) of additional "rule books" and usage guides. *Funk & Wagnalls, The American College Dictionary, Webster's New Collegiate Dictionary* and *Webster's New World Dictionary* (no relation to the G. & C. Merriam products) are the only other desk dictionaries currently in print that are worth owning. Those impressively large supermarket dictionaries that are bought piecemeal are wholly without merit. They are dated, poorly edited, lack many useful features of the legitimate dictionaries, and are altogether shoddy goods. Do some comparing. Check the prefatory and appended material, check copyright dates, editorial staffs, revision dates, typography, paper quality, pronunciation symbols, definitions, etymologies, cross referencing, and (that subjective matter) "feel." A definition, for example, that merely sends you running in circles through the dictionary only to end where you started with a word left undefined, is not very useful in the very area where you will probably use the dictionary most for—namely, finding out the meanings of technical and exotic words. A proper dictionary can be among the most fascinating of books, a poor one among the dullest and most useless.

Perhaps a few questions (of course!) will suffice to guide the reader in search of real books:

1. Who is the author? What are his credentials? (As there are

non-books, there are non-writers, non-experts, non-scholars, etc.)

2. When was the book first published? Is it a reprint? A reprint can be very valuable, but it can also be something of a fraud. The reader can be lead to believe (by virtue, say, of a modern cover design) that he is getting the latest in scholarship on a certain subject whereas in fact he may be getting something that was first published in 1902. Some careful browsing in the book will provide the answer.

3. If the book is a collection of essays on a particular subject, are the essays substantive or merely general statements that offer little in the way of evidence, examples, or supporting material? Or are they merely snippets taken from larger works by well-known figures? The market is flooded with worthless collections and anthologies of all kinds.

4. Does the book have an index? An index isn't necessary for every kind of book, but it certainly is useful for any kind of book that may be used for reference, and an index can tell the reader a good deal about the book. And just as there are non-books there are non-indices. A non-index is one that is so sketchy and general as to cause one to wonder why the writer bothered at all. An impressive example of a genuine index is that in William L. Shirer's *Rise and Fall of the Third Reich.*

5. What is the shape of the book's content? Check the Table of Contents for this. Many books helpfully include summaries of each chapter in the Table of Contents. On the other hand, chapter titles are sometimes cutesy and uninformative at best and misleading at worst. In the latter cases, the book must be considered suspect.

6. Who is the publisher? This perhaps used to be a more useful question than it is today in this age of corporate conglomerates. It's getting so you can't trust anyone. Be that as it may, some publishers specialize in non-books.

7. What does the book look and feel like? How is it bound (or put together, if a paperback)? What kind of paper? Is the print readable? Are margins and spacings ample for marginalia and interlineation? (I love books, but I also love to write in them.) Is the book designed with some aesthetic sensibility?

8. Does the book seem to be well written? Try a few paragraphs

at random. I have, for example, a considerable number of unreadable books on subjects of great interest to me. To push through a chapter or even a few pages takes a great effort of will. And it is not because the subject matter is intrinsically difficult (as a page of advanced economic theory might very well be) but because the writer just has no feeling for language and no sense of audience.

9. Does the subject seem to be adequately covered for your purposes? Is it either sufficiently nontechnical or sufficiently technical? Does it represent the original work of the author or is it the work of others popularized, homogenized, sanitized, explained, interpreted, or whatever? Generally speaking, nonbooks are watery stews put together wholly from the work of others. This gives the books a certain lack of focus, character, style, and vitality. It can also mean that they are not especially reliable. Consider, for example, a typical social studies textbook. Just as an experiment, read Cash's *The Mind of the South* alongside any American history textbook you choose. Were I teaching American history in junior high or high school, I would do very nicely with Cash, Brogan, de Tocqueville, Parrington, Commager, and any number of other commentators on the American experience. All these writers are accessible, readable, and informed. The school textbooks may be accessible, but that is all they are.

10. What are the merits and defects of each of the several editions of the same work that may be available? This multiplicity is common among the classic (out of copyright) writers. Let us suppose that the reader is looking for a new copy of *Hamlet*. There are a dozen or more to choose from in paperback alone. I would try for the best combination of sturdiness, readability (typographically speaking), price, and scholarly apparatus. Under whose direction is the edition being edited? How heavily or lightly is it annotated? (The general reader probably wants less apparatus than the student or teacher.) Is the introduction cursory or well packed with helpful commentary? Will the edition, all in all, serve my needs?

11. What is the relationship between advertising puffery on the cover and what's inside? I have found it generally true that the more a book claims for itself, the less it delivers.

12. And finally: Does the book seem to warrant its price? Many books are more wisely bought at second hand, on remainder, or in paperback. Your expected use of the book will have to be considered. I just bought a book in paperback for $1.95 that I wanted but could not bring myself to buy at $12.50 in hard covers. As the book will not be *heavily* used, the paperback edition is adequate.

Specialized reference works present certain technical problems. I would urge the buyer of foreign language dictionaries, technical manuals, atlases, and the like to ask the advice of someone with expertise in the field. If that is not feasible, he should look for evidence of scope, detail, authorship, usefulness of layout, and so on. This brings us back to the elementary school and its encyclopedia. Prior consultation by the principal with someone other than an encyclopedia salesman and the well-meaning but uninformed PTA parents who commonly scratch up the money for these projects might convince him to spend the money more wisely. I am much impressed by the institutional selling the encyclopedia industry has accomplished over the years. I was told, for example, that the first thing parents look for in the library of a prestigious private school nearby is the encyclopedia shelf. Finding one or more sets of the various well-known brands, they are quite satisfied with the quality of the library.

Whatever is worth learning or knowing about is worth the time and effort it takes to explore it with reasonable thoroughness. There is, as was well said a long time ago, no royal road to education. Knowledge cannot be taken like pills. Who offers me the cheap and easy way, I suspect. The book that offers the world in fifteen minutes of easy reading a day is no book for my library. The book or set of books that offers all that classroom magic and solves all those classroom problems and does all the teacher's work (or so it would seem) is no book for the classroom. Only the teacher can do the teacher's work and only the teacher can create the classroom "magic." Books are for thinking; non-books are cheap substitutes for thinking.

BIBLIOGRAPHY

No book can be so good as to be profitable when negligently read.

[Seneca]

THE books cited here include both those which have contributed some-thing to *The Creative Classroom* and those which can serve the diverse needs of the creative teacher. In total, they constitute (in the proper hands) the foundation stone of a first-rate educational program. Likewise, they provide the interested parent with the knowledge he must have to effectively monitor public funds (and private, for that matter) for educa-tion and to oversee the programs being developed in the schools. For while I believe in the freedom of the teacher to run his classroom accord-ing to his best judgment of what needs to be done at any given moment as well as over the long term, I also believe that the public has the re-sponsibility to advise and consent, a responsibility the public at large has generally failed to either wholeheartedly accept or to vigorously (and knowledgeably) discharge. The administrator has arrogated to himself the responsibilities of the teacher on the one hand and the responsibilities of the public on the other. (The school board, the agency which presumably represents the public, has mainly concerned itself with business matters: bricks and bucks, as it were.) The administrative hierarchies of most schools are absurdly overgrown and have fallen victim (as they must) to institutional entropy. The brilliantly successful operation of the Parkway Program is compelling proof that schools need very little in the way of "administration." In any event, it is not an issue that should be considered closed. The public can and must exert great pressure here.

A thoroughgoing bibliography of works pertinent to the substance of this book would fill a sizable volume of its own. As lengthy as this Bibliography is, then, it is highly selective (and almost entirely from my personal library). It surely overlooks many works that might well have been included. "This whole book is but a draught—nay, but the draft of a draught. Oh, Time, Strength, Cash, and Patience!" (Of course, Melville was writing about other matters.) To any who would task me for having missed this or that "basic" or "absolutely necessary" work, I can only answer that my work will not stand or fall on this or that inclusion or omission.

For the reader's convenience, I have divided the Bibliography into several sections. Though since categories of these kinds are not mutually exclusive, the decision to put a particular book into one rather than another category may seem an arbitrary one. This occasional uncertainty in classification should afford the reader no special difficulty. Broadly, all the books have to do with education (education, at least, as I conceive of it). Nevertheless, the division is handy. In an effort to give some guidance to the reader, I have in most instances annotated the entries—often with a quotation from the cited work.

The divisions:
1. *Education.* Diverse works on educational theory and practice.
2. *English Teaching.*
3. *Linguistics.* Work on language, the science of language, and related fields (psychology, anthropology, etc.).
4. *The English Language.* Works on the history and structure of English.
5. *The Arts.* Critical and analytical studies of literature and the other arts.
6. *Mathematics and Science.*
7. *Media.* Mass communication (film, TV, advertising, etc.).
8. *Games.* Works on games in education and on specific games (Chess, Go, etc.).
9. *Community.* Works on the city and the society.

EDUCATION

Ashton-Warner, Sylvia. *Teacher*. New York: Bantam Books, Inc., 1967.
°191 pp.

"The school should be conceived, in the author's phrase, as 'a créche
of living where people can still be changed,' and where creative activities are the agents of this change. If we want humanity to have a future
—a future of any kind—*this is all that matters*. That is why I say that
this book, however unprofessional or unacademic it may seem, is a
book of fundamental significance. Without exaggeration it may be said
that the author has discovered a way of saving humanity from self-
destruction. We should not ignore her method because it is so unas-
suming, so unpretentious. Great changes in the destiny of mankind can
be effected only in the minds of little children," Sir Herbert Read, Preface.

All teachers and parents should know this book well.

Aylesworth, Thomas G. and Gerald M. Reagan. *Teaching for Thinking*.
Garden City: Doubleday & Company, Inc., 1969. °270 pp., index.

"A skill most often overlooked by teachers of the academic subjects is
that of critical thinking: that is, the mental skill of solving problems
in the manner of the practitioner. Critical thinking is the lifework of
the academicians, and learners are rarely given the opportunity to behave in this manner," p. 4.

An introduction to logic. Applications in the form of student-teacher
dialogues.

Barnes, Douglas, James Britton, and Harold Rosen. *Language, the
Learner and the School*. Baltimore: Penguin Books, Inc., 1969. °128
pp.

To "study the language of the classroom is to study both the learning
process and some of the internal and external constraints upon it," p.
11.

Three essays by British educators on problems of communication in
the classroom.

Birmingham, John, ed. *Our Time Is Now. Notes from the High School
Underground*. New York: Frederick A. Praeger, Inc., 1970. 262 pp.

"Perhaps the best way of destroying the stereotype is to let the high
school underground speak for itself in all its variety of voices. Maybe
only 5 per cent of high school students are actively involved in the
underground movement, but that 5 per cent is enough to lead, to
cause some change in the high schools, and to cater to the needs of

---

(*Paperbound* volumes are *starred* thus: °191 pp.)

high school students in ways that teachers and administrators never could," p. 6.

What's wrong with our high schools from the mouths of perhaps the least understood segment of our society: high school students. No one seriously interested in young people can afford not to read this book.

Black, Hillel. *The American Schoolbook*. New York: William Morrow & Co. Inc., 1967. 193 pp., index.

"In appearance at least the American textbook has few peers. Profusely illustrated, laid out in the same fashion as the mass consumer magazines, most schoolbooks are far more inviting than the textbooks used thirty years ago. In contrast there has been little change in the actual content of nearly all history books, most readers, grammars, and civics books. Devoid of controversy, stylistically dull, they remain vacuous and boring. The wonder indeed is not that Johnny can read . . . but that Johnny, after a twelve-year diet of schoolbooks, wants to read at all," pp. 5–6.

Popularly written, but generally sound in its observations and conclusions.

Brenton, Myron. *What's Happened to Teacher?* New York: Coward-McCann, Inc., 1970. 280 pp., index.

The teacher today: successes, failures, and vulnerabilities. Popularly written.

Brown, B. Frank. *The Nongraded High School*. Englewood Cliffs: Prentice-Hall, Inc., 1966. 223 pp., index.

A description of the Melbourne, Florida, experiment in nongraded education by the then principal of the high school.

"Although the student is responsible for getting his own education and moving ahead at his own pace, the nongraded high school is not student-centered but rather learning-centered—learning-subject- and learning-to-think-centered. The teacher does not 'give' students education; he helps the students get it. In classes the emphasis is on raising questions and on skillfully helping students find answers for themselves. When a student does independent work, the teacher must know when to leave the student alone, when to help by raising good questions, and when to get out of the student's way," p. 9.

Every teacher must read this book.

————. *Education by Appointment*. W. Nyack, New York: Parker Publishing Co., 1969. 175 pp., index.

"What is most needed in the educational establishment is a variety of styles for bringing about educational change. This book deals with several strategies for improving learning and considers some very major changes in the establishment. The matter of 'education by appoint-

ment,' or independent study, may be one of the most effective ways to draw from the student his desires, his objectives—and his participation," pp. 10–11.
Background and methods of the "quest curriculum" by the former principal of the Melbourne High School, a pioneer (and a highly successful one) in both nongraded and independent education.

Bruner, Jerome S. *The Process of Education.* New York: Vintage Books, 1963. °97 pp., index.
A seminal work in educational theory and philosophy. The central concept is that of *structure.* "Grasping the structure of a subject is understanding it in a way that permits many other things to be related to it meaningfully. To learn structure, in short, is to learn how things are related," p. 7.

————. *Toward a Theory of Instruction.* New York: W. W. Norton & Company, Inc., 1968. °176 pp., index.
Essays on educational theory. How children learn and how they can be helped to learn.

————. *On Knowing.* New York: Atheneum Publishers, 1969. °165 pp.
Psychological and philosophical explorations of the processes of creation and learning. Touches on a diversity of topics including art, literature, and mathematics. Extremely valuable for the teacher.

Byler, Ruth, Gertrude Lewis, and Ruth Totman. *Teach Us What We Want to Know.* New York: Mental Health Materials Center, Inc., 1969. °179 pp.
An outstanding example of imaginative and far-sighted curriculum planning.
"While its original purpose was to assist health teachers, it is very apparent that individuals and groups who may have specialized health interests such as drug abuse education, smoking and health, family life and sex education, prevention of numerous diseases, and particularly mental and emotional health, to mention only a few, will find this an invaluable sourcebook," ix.

Callahan, Raymond E. *Education and the Cult of Efficiency.* Chicago: University of Chicago Press, 1962. °273 pp., index.
"Americans who are concerned about their schools and who understand that the future of our free society depends upon the quality of education our children receive must realize that as a result of the developments in educational administration since 1911 we are, in the 1960's, caught in a vicious circle. The continuous pressure for economy has produced a situation in which many men with inappropriate and inadequate training are leaders in our public schools," p. 260.

An illustration of "Parkinson's Law" and "The Peter Principle" at work in the educational establishment.

Chall, Jeanne. *Learning to Read: The Great Debate.* New York: Mc-Graw-Hill Book Company, 1967. 372 pp., index.

The only comprehensive study of current methods in the teaching of reading. Useful evaluations of virtually all the reading programs (*i.e.,* philosophies) in force. Evaluations, likewise, of a number of reading textbook series. However, leaves important questions of educational priorities pretty much alone.

Cianciolo, Patricia J. and Jean M. Le Pere. *The Literary Time Line in American History,* ℞ *For Social Studies.* Garden City: Doubleday & Company, Inc., 1969. °313 pp.

"The fundamental purpose of [the book], for students in grades five through nine, is to identify significant political, economic, and social influences which form the ideologies upon which the United States of America is built. Therefore, in the various time periods which are designated along the time line, significant events and personalities are identified. Trade books suitable for children in grades five through nine are indicated as they relate to each of these significant personalities and events. Materials include both fiction and nonfiction. The range of readability and interest is necessarily widespread in order to attempt to meet the varying needs of a group of children within a single classroom at any of the grade levels specified," p. 9.

Excellent annotated bibliographies make this a valuable resource.

Crary, Ryland W. *Humanizing the School: Curriculum Development and Theory.* New York: Alfred A. Knopf, Inc., 1969. 481 pp., indices.

The book "makes precise definitions; then it holds to them, applies them, and uses them. It tells what and why; it also tells how. Its specifics are not the specifics of educational folklore or of easy words assigned by one committee or another. Its specifics are the realities and hard sense of the school in a troubled world," p. 9.

Pedestrian writing (a characteristic of many books on education) adds to the book's already considerable weight and length. But it is an informative guide to curriculum theory.

DeGrazia, Alfred and David Sohn. *Revolution in Teaching: New Theory, Technology, and Curricula.* New York: Bantam Books, Inc., 1964. °310 pp. Much of the material in this diverse collection of essays is already dated, but there are valuable nuggets to be found. Anthologies like this are useful in generating discussion and argument.

Dennison, George. *The Lives of Children: The Story of the First Street School.* New York: Random House, Inc., 1969. 309 pp.

A major contribution to the *art* of education.

"We had no administrators." "We did not give report cards." "We didn't give tests, at least not of the competitive kind." "Our housing was modest." "We treated the children with consideration and justice," pp. 7–8.

The program, people, and operations of an experimental (and highly successful) "ghetto" school in New York City.

Eble, Kenneth E. *A Perfect Education.* New York: Collier Books, 1968. *215 pp.

"Learning begins in delight and flourishes in wonder. Surely the greatest gift a parent can give a child, once heredity has done what it can, is to let that child experience the delight of learning. Response is everything. Parents worry too much, and probably the more educated they are, the more they worry. No parents could be more concerned with the education of their children than American parents. And yet that very concern often discourages the delight in which all learning should begin," p. 3.

A wise book by a sensitive teacher.

Eckstein, Rudolph and Rocco L. Motto, *et al. From Learning for Love to Love of Learning, Essays on Psychoanalysis and Education.* New York: Brunner/Mazel Publishers, 1969. 282 pp., index.

"In order to maintain the perspectives of a free and open society, we must not allow the current desire for mass solutions, the raw quest for power, the wish to find answers for the millions to overwhelm us. For along with such concerns, it behooves us to maintain an individualistic approach in the field of education. This book is dedicated to psychoanalysis and education. It is designed to strengthen and enlarge the living bridge between education and psychoanalysis. It is directed to psychoanalysts, educators and to professional workers in related fields. It is an expression of much work that has been carried on here at the Reiss-Davis Child Study Center," Editors' Introduction, xvii–xviii.

"Only he who can remain a student forever will be a good teacher forever," p. 65.

A most valuable collection. Should be read by anyone who has the slightest concern with education.

Engelmann, Siegfried. *Preventing Failure in the Primary Grades.* New York: Simon & Schuster, Inc., 1969, 395 pp.

"This book details a catch-up program for the child who is seriously behind in basic arithmetic and reading skills. It does not contain detailed descriptions of culturally disadvantaged and slow-learning children. It is not designed for those who look at these children from the often remote viewpoint of the school administrator, psychological diagnostician, or social reformer. Rather this book is designed for the teacher who watches these children fail year after year and has never learned to live with such failure. This book promises that teacher nothing but hard work—an effort far in excess of that implied by the size of her paycheck," pp. 1–2.

A sourcebook of practical classroom activities—though it should not be swallowed whole.

Fader, Daniel N. and Elton B. McNeil. *Hooked on Books: Program and Proof.* New York: Berkley Publishing Corp., 1968. °244 pp.

"Because the reasons seem as compelling as those for asking teachers *in every classroom* to teach English, the second part of this program is based on the principle of SATURATION, meaning the replacement, whenever possible and in whatever classroom, of customary texts and workbooks with newspapers, magazines and paperbound books," p. 17. Includes useful study guides and an excellent bibliography of inexpensive paperbound books on a wide range of topics.

"In the words packaged between the covers of paperbound books and magazines I think we have finally found a common and exciting ground for conversation and contact between the dominant and dominated socio-economic groups in our society," p. 236.

Featherstone, Joseph. *The Primary School Revolution in Britain.* Washington: *The New Republic.* (Reprint of three articles by Featherstone that appeared in *The New Republic* August 10, September 2, and September 9, 1967.)

Fisher, Dorothy Canfield. *The Montessori Manual for Teachers and Parents.* Cambridge: Robert Bentley, Inc., 1964. (First published, 1913.) 126 pp., index.

A companion volume to *Montessori for Parents* (*q.v.*).

"The central idea of the Montessori system, on which every smallest bit of apparatus, every *detail of technic rests solidly, is a full recognition of the fact that no human being is educated by anyone else. He must do it himself or it is never done,*" pp. 19–20. (Emphasis in the original.)

————. *Montessori for Parents.* Cambridge: Robert Bentley, Inc., 1965. (A reprint of *A Montessori Mother*, 1912.) 240 pp., index.

A sensitively written introduction to the Montessori system by a perceptive observer.

(The Montessori schools—at least in this country—have grown rather cultish over the years and rather compulsively attached to the special [and expensive] Montessori apparatus, most of which should be produced by the children as they discover the need or value of devices for measurement and so on.)

Friedenberg, Edgar Z. *The Dignity of Youth & Other Atavisms.* Boston: Beacon Press, 1966. °270 pp.

Essays on education by a teacher who is at the same time a shrewd critic of American education. Civilized and literate.

Gattegno, Caleb. *Towards a Visual Culture, Educating Through Television.* New York: Outerbridge & Dienstfrey, 1969. 117 pp.

How television can be used as a major tool in education in ways quite different from the usual "educational" programming. A revolutionary book that may prove to be the most important single work on education in our time.

Goodman, Paul. *Compulsory Mis-education* and *The Community of Scholars.* New York: Vintage Books, 1964. °339 pp.

"In these remarks on the schools, I do not try to be generous or fair, but I have seen what I am talking about and I hope I am rational," p. 7.

Stimulating and acerbic observations on American education not designed to please the Establishment. Attacks all aspects of American education without favor. Goodman is a prophet well worth listening to. (See also, *Growing Up Absurd,* New York: Vintage Books, 1962. °296 pp.)

Gross, Ronald and Judith Murphy, eds. *The Revolution and the Schools.* New York: Harcourt, Brace & World, Inc., 1964. °250 pp.

Essays on new developments in educational theory and practice.

Harvard Educational Review & Teachers College Record. *Problems and Issues in Contemporary Education.* Glenview: Scott, Foresman & Co., 1968. °290 pp.

A diversity of essays on education. "The mood of the anthology, like the mood governing education today, is adventurous, open-minded, activist. The implicit challenge of the book is in the *how*," Preface.

Hentoff, Nat. *Our Children Are Dying.* New York: The Viking Press, Inc., 1969. °141 pp.

"Are we to tell children now in slum schools—and their parents—to wait until 'across the board' changes are made? The thrust of this book is that we need not tell them that. And we cannot, for they know when they're being conned," Author's Note, xiv.

An important (and passionate) book about the problems of urban education and how one principal, Elliott Shapiro, tried to solve them.

Hoffmann, Banesh. *The Tyranny of Testing.* New York: Collier Books, 1962. °223 pp., index.

"All methods of evaluating people have their defects—and grave defects they are. But let us not therefore allow one particular method to play the usurper. Let us not seek to replace informed judgment, with all its frailty, by some inexpensive statistical substitute. Let us keep open many diverse and non-competing channels toward recognition. For high ability is where we find it. It is individual and must be recognized for what it is, not rejected out of hand simply because it does not happen to conform to criteria established by statistical technicians. In seeking high ability, let us shun overdependence on tests that are blind to dedication and creativity, and biased against depth and subtlety. For that way lies testolatry," pp. 216–17.

A persuasive corrective to "standardized" tests. ETS comes in for some severe (and well deserved) buffets.

Holt, John. *How Children Fail.* New York: Dell Publishing Co. Inc., 1964. °181 pp.

"Mr. Holt has given us a book which should be immensely helpful. It is not like the performance of a musical virtuoso to which we can listen appreciatively without any expectation that we can play as well. Mr. Holt's virtuosity as a teacher is laid before us in terms of insights we all can use; we are stimulated to use them as rapidly as we glean them from each page of his text," Introduction by Allan Fromme.

———. *How Children Learn.* New York: Pitman Publishing Corp., 1969. °193 pp.

"This book is more concerned to describe effective learning than to explain it, or give a theory about it," viii.

Like all of Holt's books, a valuable contribution to the art of teaching.

———. *The Underachieving School.* New York: Pitman Publishing Corp., 1969. 209 pp.

"If the educational reformers do not see more clearly than they do, it is not because they have not good eyes, but for two other reasons. The first is that they tend to start talking before they have done enough looking, and their theories obstruct and blur their vision and the vision of others. The second is that their contact with schools is so special and artificial that they don't really know what school is like," pp. 13–14.

Hutchinson, Michael and Christopher Young. *Educating the Intelligent.* Baltimore: Penguin Books, Inc., 1962. °240 pp., index.

"The reason for writing the book is that we believe that in many ways the secondary education at present offered to our more intelligent children is out of date," p. 11.

Rather an understatement. The problem from the British point of view.

James, Deborah. *The Taming, A Teacher Speaks.* New York: McGraw-Hill Book Company, 1969. °156 pp.

"This book is designed to help you prepare for the conditions you will meet when you enter the school as a teacher," Preface.

The school as a cage, its students inmates to be tamed. A fascinating and in many ways depressing book.

Jones, Richard M. *Fantasy and Feeling in Education*. New York: New York University Press, 1968. 276 pp., index.

"In schoolrooms, conditions are created which invite expression of controlled emotions for the purpose of imbuing curricular issues with personal significance. The power of emotion to generate interest and involvement in subject matters which would otherwise find children uninterested and uninvolved lies in their deep personal familiarity—such familiarity being a consequence of emotion having been integral to every phase of personal development from infancy on. The value of emotional involvement in the learning process thus lies in its potential for aiding assimilation of new or remote experiences in idiomatically illuminating ways," p. 174.

The focus is primarily on the social studies. Specific classroom examples are the most valuable (practically speaking) materials in the book.

Kagan, Jerome, ed. *Creativity and Learning*. Boston: Beacon Press, 1967. °289 pp., index.

"The papers in this volume touch most of the vital social, educational, political and psychological issues bearing on creativity," Introduction, x.

Kay, Harry, Bernard Dodd, and Max Sime. *Teaching Machines and Programmed Instruction*. Baltimore: Penguin Books, Inc., 1968. °173 pp., index.

A balanced account of this branch of educational technology. The authors conclude that we have yet to determine the long-range effects of "programmed education."

Kimball, Solon and James E. McClellan, Jr. *Education and the New America*. New York: Random House, Inc., 1966. °403 pp., index.

The task "is no less than that of bringing into contemporary focus the traditional message of the professional educationist, namely that the schools must change to meet the demands of a changing society," Preface.

An impressive study of the relationships between school and society.

Kohl, Herbert. *36 Children*. New York: New American Library, Inc., 1968. °224 pp.

A compelling account of how a young teacher made education worthwhile for a class of ghetto kids.

Kozol, Jonathan. *Death at an Early Age*. New York: Bantam Books, Inc., 1968. °242 pp.
"I hope some of those congressmen who are now looking into the causes of the riots will find time to read this honest and terrifying book . . . ," Introduction by Robert Coles.
A young teacher's experiences in the Boston Public schools. Enlightening and depressing (for the sad truths it reveals).

Leonard, George B. *Education and Ecstasy*. New York: Delacorte Press, 1969. 239 pp.
"The idea of education as the most effective human change agent is by no means new. But I have tried to broaden and simplify education's definition, to expand its domain, to link it with the new technology and to alter the relationship between educator and learner. As a chief ingredient in all this, as well as an alternative to the old reinforcers, I have named 'ecstasy'—joy, *ananda,* the ultimate delight," p. 230.
An antidote to the sterility and joylessness that pervade the typical American school. Strongly recommended for all teachers.

Lieberman, Myron. *The Future of Public Education*. Chicago: University of Chicago Press, 1965. °294 pp., index.
A stimulating and vigorously stated examination of the educational establishment, setting forth its weaknesses, failures, and confusions, and making recommendations for its improvement. "The reality is that public education is not in the mainstream of American life," p. 284. "At the present time, public education presents a paradox: the work of teachers is dominated by political considerations but the teachers themselves are political nonentities," p. 285.

Mayer, Martin. *The Schools*. New York: Harper Brothers, 1961. 446 pp., index.
The impressive result of "thirty months of observing, interviewing, reading and (briefly) teaching." A broad survey of the principles and practices of education in America (revealed through a large number of specific schools). Detailed and highly informative.

Miller, Richard I. *The Nongraded School, Analysis and Study*. New York: Harper & Row, Publishers, 1967.
"This book is about *one* dimension of 'loosening the plaster'—the nongraded school. The effort is not to sell the nongraded school but to analyze, to offer useful strategies for implementation, and to carefully evaluate this innovation," Preface, ix.
Should be read in conjunction with B. Frank Brown, *The Nongraded High School* (*q.v.*) and B. Frank Brown, *Education by Appointment* (*q.v.*).

Minuchin, Patricia, *et al. The Psychological Impact of School Experience, A Comparative Study of Nine-Year-Old Children in Contrasting Schools.* New York: Basic Books, Inc., Publishers, 1969. 521 pp., index. "This is a complex, honest, and provocative book, one long awaited by those who have been attracted by earlier partial reports of the 'Bank Street Study.' As an evaluation of 'modern' versus 'traditional' educational strategies, it is far from conclusive—both for methodological reasons and because, even where clear differential effects appear, evaluation depends crucially upon competing value perspectives that can be brought to bear on them. But it greatly enriches our understanding of schools and of school children. It provides a usefully detailed natural history of four differing school-and-classroom cultures. It exemplifies a serious and skilled attempt to assess the impact of schools on children . . . ," Foreword by M. Brewster Smith, v.
Impressive in both detail and meaningful presentation of detail. Provides an exemplary model for educational research.

Moffett, James. *Teaching the Universe of Discourse.* Boston: Houghton Mifflin Company, 1968. °215 pp.
"Mr. Moffett would teach the Universe of Discourse not by analyzing language but by having students use it in every realistic way," Introduction by Roger Brown.
Essential reading for every teacher.

————. *A Student-Centered Language Arts Curriculum, Grades K–13: A Handbook for Teachers.* Boston: Houghton Mifflin Company, 1968. 503 pp.
"This book is for teachers on the job, student teachers, and all others concerned with teaching the language arts. I have tried here to describe and illustrate particular language activities that students and teachers would engage in from kindergarten into college," Introduction.
A flexible, imaginative approach to the language arts, requiring flexibility and imagination on the part of the teacher. Contra textbooks and the "prepackaged curriculum." A must for every teacher. *The Creative Classroom* owes a spiritual debt to Moffett.

Neill, A. S. *Summerhill, A Radical Approach to Child Rearing.* New York: Hart Publishing Co. Inc., 1960. °392 pp. index.
"I hold that the aim of life is to find happiness, which means to find interest. Education should be a preparation for life," p. 24.
"Parents are slow in realizing how unimportant the learning side of school is. Children, like adults, learn what they want to learn. All prize-giving and marks and exams sidetrack proper personality development. Only pedants claim that learning from books is education," p. 25.
"In twenty-five years of reading and reviewing books on education, I

have yet to find one as stimulating, exciting and challenging as the story of SUMMERHILL. I commend this book to all educators and laymen who are interested in children," Dr. Benjamin Fine (quoted on book cover).

Despite its crochets and its occasional overstating of the case, this is a basic book in the annals of the teaching art.

Nesbitt, Marion. *A Public School for Tomorrow*. New York: Dell Publishing Co. Inc., 1967. °168 pp., index.

A teacher looks at her own "school of tomorrow," Matthew Fontaine Maury School, Richmond, Virginia, in many ways a model school.

"The school of tomorrow will need teachers of scholarship, imagination, and creativity, for they must choose content from the whole wide world and they must be able to impart this richness so that it becomes the children's own," p. 152.

Oettinger, Anthony G. *Run, Computer, Run: The Mythology of Educational Innovation*. Cambridge: Harvard University Press, 1969. 303 pp.

The "average American school inspires neither passionate praise nor passionate denunciation, mainly because it is so familiar. It is disquietingly like the schools we went to thirty years ago. Peace, quiet, and order are prominent among its objectives. The librarian is happiest when all the books are in their proper places on the shelves. The science teacher keeps to the lesson plan no matter what the children may be interested in. The new textbooks are six weeks overdue and both the record player and projector are broken.

"Will computer terminals in every classroom change all this? The advocates say yes, with conviction. The book says no, pugnaciously. It does so by puncturing some of the myths that have grown up around education and educational technology and by casting doubt on some too-facile notions about how technology can serve social purposes," Foreword by Emmanuel G. Mesthene, viii.

The educational gadget addicts had better read this before signing any contracts!

O'Neill, William F., ed. *Selected Educational Heresies*. Glenview: Scott, Foresman & Co., 1969. °372 pp.

"The selections in this book are not safe, dull, and respectable. They are intended to excite, arouse, provoke, and even irritate," Preface by editor.

If only all these exciting and provoking statements would excite and provoke!

Osborn, Alex F. *Applied Imagination*. New York: Charles Scribner's Sons, 1963. °417 pp., index.

A practical approach to creative problem solving. Lots of useful, detailed information.

Parnes, Sidney J. and Harold F. Harding, eds. *A Source Book for Creative Thinking*. New York: Charles Scribner's Sons, 1962. °393 pp., index.
Essays on all aspects of creativity. Detailed appendix on research in creativity.

Plumb, J. H., ed. *Crisis in the Humanities*. Baltimore: Penguin Books, Inc., 1964. °172 pp.
"Old, complex, tradition-haunted societies find change as difficult to make as aged rheumatoid arthritics to move; old men, however, die and are replaced, but in old societies young men grow up, frustrated, crippled, distorted by them," p. 10.
Essays by divers hands on current problems in the humanistic disciplines.

Postman, Neil and Charles Weingartner. *Teaching as a Subversive Activity*. New York: Delacorte Press, 1969. 219 pp.
"The new education, in sum, is new because it consists of having students use the concepts most appropriate to the world in which we all must live. All of these concepts constitute the dynamics of the questing-questioning, meaning-making process that can be called "learning how to learn." This comprises a posture of stability from which to deal fruitfully with change. The purpose is to help all students develop built-in, shockproof crap detectors as basic equipment in their survival kits," p. 218.
A lusty attack on education vacuity and irrelevance. Offers a number of valuable suggestions for an "education for survival."

Richardson, Elwyn S. *In the Early World*. New York: Pantheon Books, Inc., 1964. 217 pp., plates.
"Every piece [of children's poetry, painting, etc.] illustrated grew out of an individual history, out of an encounter with the materials of an art, and out of confident self-acceptance. In the school as a whole, too, teaching expressed Elwyn Richardson's nature by giving children the opportunity to reach their full height as artists, as craftsmen, as scientists, and as students, through the establishment of a community where self-respect demanded this generosity in giving and receiving. In this sense every classroom can uniquely express its own mode of co-operative individualism. As teaching becomes more conscious an art the journeyman will move closer to the satisfactions of this kind of teaching, and new generations of children will learn to recognize and understand the value of work into which love has flowed," Introduction by John Melser, ix.

What good education can and should be. A must for all teachers and all parents.

Riemer, George. *How They Murdered the Second "R"*. New York: W. W. Norton & Company, Inc., 1969. 322 pp.

"In this book I present evidence which shows how writing was killed in the grades. It died as all beings die, its body separated from its soul—its body the symbols, its soul, human communication. It was separated from reading, then led to a deserted part of education and there done in.

"A variety of devices was used to complete the crime. I have tagged and exhibited them: (1) controlled-word lists, (2) multiple choice and fill-in sentences, and (3) a most insidious tool called 'child-to-teacher dictation'," p. 17.

Education through the Initial Teaching Alphabet (a combination writing-reading approach). Informed, informative, and persuasive, though the author's intemperance in flaying the "reading establishment" will overheat some collars.

Schramm, Wilbur, Jack Lyle and Edwin B. Parker. *Television in the Lives of Our Children*. Stanford: Stanford University Press, 1965. *324 pp., index.

A detailed and fairly technical research study, the findings of which should be known to parents and teachers alike. The only generally available academically sound work on the subject.

Scobey, Mary-Margaret and Grace Graham, eds. *To Nurture Humaneness*. Washington: Association for Supervision and Curriculum Development, National Education Assn., 1970. 257 pp.

Essays from the publications of the ASCD on the elusive concepts of humanness and humaneness in education. The writing is generally lumpy and "institutional," but the intentions are good.

Silberman, Charles E. *Crisis in the Classroom. The Remaking of American Education*. New York: Random House, Inc., 1970. 533 pp., index.

The culmination of a three-and-a-half year study commissioned by the Carnegie Corporation, this book is far and away the most thoughtful and detailed examination of public education in America of all the many such books currently in print. It is not, however, a book for the Caspar Milquetoasts of our educational Establishment, for its intent is to make waves aplenty. The author, for example, writes:

"If mindlessness is the central problem, the solution must lie in infusing the various educating institutions with purpose, more important, with thought about purpose, and about ways in which techniques, content, and organization fulfill or alter purpose. And given the tendency of institutions to confuse day-to-day routine with purpose, to transform the means into the end itself, the infusion cannot be a one-shot affair. The process of self-examination, of "self-renewal," to use John Gardner's useful term, must be continuous. We must find ways of stimulating educators—public school teachers, principals, and superintendents; college professors, deans, and presidents; radio, television, and film directors and producers; newspaper, magazine, and TV journalists and executives—to think about what they are doing, and why they are doing it. And we must persuade the general public to do the same," p. 11.

The responsibility for vital change in American education does not finally lie with remote forces and institutions but with each of us as concerned citizens.

Trubowitz, Sidney. *A Handbook for Teaching in the Ghetto School.* Chicago: Quadrangle Books, 1968. °175 pp., index.

"This book illustrates how teachers can develop meaningful curriculum content by knowing children's experiences, their interests, their feelings, their needs, their strengths, and their weaknesses. It attempts to help teachers understand a school and a community in the ghetto by exposing them to the perceptions of the children, the parents, and other people in the neighborhood," p. 7.

By a school principal and based on a great deal of practical experience. Can be read profitably by *all* teachers and administrators. The suggestions for school and classroom activities are applicable, *mutatis mutandis,* in *any* school.

Wallach, Michael A. and Cliff W. Wing, Jr. *The Talented Student: A Validation of the Creativity-Intelligence Distinction.* New York: Holt, Rinehart and Winston, Inc., 1969. °142 pp., index.

"What we have found can be put quite directly. Within the intelligence range defined by our sample—and it is a sample that falls overall within the upper part of the intelligence continuum—intelligence level is indeed strongly related to grades. But only to grades. Intelligence is not at all related to level or quality of attainment in any of the diverse forms of extra-curricular involvement that we studied—and these covered the entire range from literary and artistic pursuits through dramatic and musical performance, social service activities, and scientific work on one's own to leadership in student organizations," Preface, vi–vii.

The implications of this study are of profound importance to the development of new educational programs. A must for all parents, teachers, and administrators.

Wilson, John, Norman Williams, and Barry Sugarman. *Introduction to Moral Education.* Baltimore: Penguin Books, Inc., 1967. °463 pp.

A laudable attempt to come to grips with an extraordinarily complex and intractable subject. The questions raised in the book should be raised and discussed by every parent, teacher, and student. The book can yield a vast amount of exciting classroom material.

ENGLISH TEACHING

Brengleman, Fred. *The English Language, An Introduction for Teachers.* Englewood Cliffs: Prentice-Hall, Inc., 1970. 157 pp., index.
"This book is an introductory survey of current findings about the English language. It focuses on the aspects of current linguistics research which in the author's judgment have the clearest application to the teaching of English. The topics it examines have been under discussion for some time and form a solid part of the developing body of knowledge about the English language, particularly as related to the traditional responsibilities of the language arts teacher," Preface, vii.
Sketchy, but well provided with stimulating questions and projects.

Brown, Marshall L., Elmer G. White, and Edward B. Jenkinson. *Two Approaches to Teaching Syntax.* Bloomington: Indiana University Press, 1967. °239 pp.
Resource material for grammar study, grades 7–9, with a chapter on teaching basic sentence patterns to slow learners, grades 7–11. Linguistically sound but wearisomely programmatic.

Christensen, Francis. *Notes Toward a New Rhetoric.* New York: Harper & Row, Publishers, 1967. °110 pp.
Six essays attempting to establish a generative approach to rhetoric. May be of some value in developing a sense in the student of sentence style and paragraph structure.

Fries, Charles C. *Linguistics and Reading.* New York: Holt, Rinehart and Winston, Inc., 1963. 265 pp., index.
Valuable insights into the reading process by one of the pioneers in modern linguistics. Much of the material can be adapted to the approach to reading I suggest in Chapter 4.

Gleason, H. A., Jr. *Linguistics and English Grammar.* New York: Holt, Rinehart and Winston, Inc., 1965. 519 pp., index.
"This is in many respects a guide book to English grammars. It is a little like a Baedecker—rather unenlightening reading at home in your own living room, but useful as you travel through the regions described. It should not be read alone unless you are already so familiar with the territory that you can visualize as you read. Rather, it should

be read with two or three grammars at hand, so that features pointed out may be identified and examined closely," Preface, v.

Lucid, informative (even without "two or three grammars at hand"). *Part Three, Points of Contact and Implications* is especially useful to the teacher attempting to bring language study and literature study and writing together.

Hogan, Robert F., ed. *The English Language in the School Program.* Champaign: National Council of Teachers of English, 1966. °280 pp. Essays on language theory, usage, and curriculum. A good resource book.

Holbrook, David. *English for the Rejected.* London: Cambridge University Press, 1965. °291 pp., index.

"The present book is written with the conviction that with the 'backward' child the 'unseen' elements of sympathetic respect for the creature, and the imaginative-creative element in teaching are the most important and efficient means to develop the child's capacities. In fact, I suppose, I have tried to insist once again that teaching is an art, and to suggest how this art may be made more efficient with the most unacademic, unexaminable children—those whom our society rejects because they yield no 'results'," p. 3.

Packed with first-rate ideas for teaching *all* children (not merely the "backward" ones).

———. *The Exploring Word.* London: Cambridge University Press, 1967. °283 pp., index.

"This book has a simple purpose, which is to set out to define the disciplines of teaching English, in order to suggest ways in which the education of teachers can be improved," p. 3.

"But this is not a book which belongs to 'education' as a subject, nor to 'method' as split off from 'English' in the unreal way in which such things tend to become divided in departments and colleges of education," p.3.

Packed with valuable insights into "English" and into the ways of English teaching.

———. *English for Maturity.* London: Cambridge University Press, 1965. °255 pp., index.

"This book is offered to those who profess to teach English, or who have to teach English in the secondary modern school, to help them consider their work as part of all English teaching—whether in the university, in the grammar school, primary school, or secondary modern school—and as of equal value," p. 7.

A thorough examination of the nature and values of the discipline of English along with practical suggestions for teaching.

Hunt, Kellogg W. *Grammatical Structures Written at Three Grade Levels.* Champaign: National Council of Teachers of English, 1965. °159 pp. A research report based on observations of "average" students in grades 4, 8, and 12 of Florida State University School. The findings are neither startling nor even unexpected, but they are objective and clearly tabulated. In grossly simple terms: older children write more complicated grammatical structures than do younger children. The study specifies the contrasts of structural types.

Jenkinson, Edward B. *What Is Language? And Other Teaching Units for Grades Seven through Twelve.* Bloomington: Indiana University Press, 1967. °246 pp. A resource book for the study of several important aspects of language (the nature of language, words and meanings, lexicography, dialect, etc.).

Joos, Martin. *The Five Clocks.* New York: Harcourt, Brace & World, Inc., 1967. °108 pp. "The book is designed to overcome what the author calls the English-usage guilt-feelings of the normal American," Introduction by Albert H. Marckwardt, xii. The "five clocks" are the five basic modes of English discourse (as Joos defines them): frozen, formal, consultative, casual, and intimate. A must for English teachers.

Leavitt, Hart Day. *The Writer's Eye.* New York: Bantam Books, Inc., 1969. °224 pp., illustrations. Imaginative writing assignments based on paintings and photographs.

Lodwig, Richard R. and Eugene F. Barrett. *The Dictionary and the Language.* New York: Hayden Book Companies, 1967. °181 pp., index. An interesting resource book on words, meanings, lexicography, and dictionary-making. Good exercises.

Muller, Herbert J. *The Uses of English (Guidelines for the Teaching of English from the Anglo-American Conference at Dartmouth.* New York: Holt, Rinehart and Winston, Inc., 1967. °198 pp. An informative synopsis of the Conference. Touches on all aspects of English teaching. Readable and free of educational jargon.

O'Donnell, Roy C., William J. Griffin, and Raymond C. Norris. *Syntax of Kindergarten and Elementary School Children: A Transformational Analysis.* Champaign: National Council of Teachers of English, 1967. °115 pp. A research report on 180 children, grades K, 1, 2, 3, 5, and 7. Attempts to answer some basic questions regarding the child's acquisition and use of language. Among the interesting conclusions is the assertion that "deletion transformations may be better indicators of development than are subordinate clauses." A good introduction to applied linguistic research in an area of importance to the English teacher.

Opie, Iona and Peter Opie. *The Lore and Language of School-Children.* London: Oxford University Press, 1967. 417 pp., index.
The fascinating and, to the adult, little-known world of children's language, jokes, insults, stories, slang, taboos, etc. An excellent resource for the imaginative teacher in search of fresh ideas.

Postman, Neil and Charles Weingartner. *Linguistics, A Revolution in Teaching.* New York: Dell Publishing Co., Inc., 1967. °209 pp.
"What, then, is linguistics?"
"Linguistics is a way of behaving. It is an activity, a process of doing something. More specifically, it is a way of behaving while one attempts to discover information and to acquire knowledge about language. The information and knowledge that result from such inquiry-behavior become part of what is meant by linguistics," p. 4.
A vigorous *apologia* for the "new English." Offers a number of sensible teaching suggestions.

Sledd, James and Wilma R. Ebbit. *Dictionaries and THAT Dictionary.* Glenview: Scott, Foresman & Co., 1962. °273 pp.
A case book on lexicography and dictionary-making focused primarily on the controversy surrounding the publication of *Webster's New Third International.* Resource for class discussion. Good exercises.

Sohn, David A. *Pictures for Writing.* New York: Bantam Books, Inc., 1969. °192 pp., illustrated.
"Here is a proven way to effective writing. Based on the principle that good writing depends on accurate and keen observation, this book teaches the student to see life through the perceptive eye of the photographer and the writer. Using as examples the writing of William Faulkner, Somerset Maugham, James Joyce, Colette, Eudora Welty, Isak Dinesen and others, the student is exposed to the best of modern writing and photography," flyleaf blurb.
Lots of good ideas for writing assignments. The book will not make the student a good writer, but will help to sensitize him to the problems of description and explanation.

Tiedt, Iris M. and Sidney W. Tiedt. *Contemporary English in the Elementary School.* Englewood Cliffs: Prentice-Hall, Inc., 1967. 376 pp., index.
"This is a methods book; it is a book of strategies and ideas. Our own experience has shown us that successful teaching is directly related to

knowledge of content combined with effective teaching strategies," To The Reader, v.

Sensible, linguistically-based materials for English (*i.e.*, language arts) teaching. A genuine effort at making the language arts synoptic.

Williams, Joseph M. *The New English; Structure/Form/Style*. New York: The Free Press, 1970. 421 pp., index.

"If you teach either grammar or rhetoric as a WAY to learn about human language, as a way to recognize, explore, and attempt to solve problems, you have no need to hesitate teaching something that is not eternally right.

"In other words, the value of teaching something about the structure of English (that is, the structure of grammar that describes English) is not in the CONTENT of the grammar but in asking questions and testing answers," Preface, x.

An excellent resource book.

LINGUISTICS AND RELATED FIELDS

Allen, Harold B. *Linguistics and English Linguistics*. New York: Appleton-Century-Crofts, 1966. °108 pp., index.

A bibliography of linguistics. Lists without annotation a broad selection of books, articles, bibliographies, and dictionaries. A vast amount of material has of course been published since the publication of this bibliography.

Black, Max. *The Labyrinth of Language*. New York: Frederick A. Praeger, Inc., 1968. 178 pp., index.

"The purpose of this work will be at once more modest and more ambitious: to extract, from what is already known and what can plausibly be guessed about language, some productive *concepts* and controversial *issues*. In short, to develop a tentative linguistic perspective, a way of looking at men, their activities, and their relations to each other and to the universe as they perceive it, *sub specie linguae*," p. 19.

A stimulating look at language by a philosopher. Eminently readable.

Bollinger, Dwight. *Aspects of Language*. New York: Harcourt, Brace & World, Inc., 1968. °326 pp., index.

An excellent (though at times highly idiosyncratic) introduction to language. Stimulating questions close each chapter.

Burling, Robbins. *Man's Many Voices: Language in Its Cultural Context*. New York: Holt, Rinehart and Winston, Inc., 1970, 222 pp., index.

"Unlike many anthropologists who have written on language and culture, I am not concerned with the way in which the rest of culture is

dependent upon or similar to language, but I am concerned instead with the way language is affected by the rest of our culture. On the other hand, unlike most linguists, I am not primarily concerned with the internal structure of language, but only with the way that structure is affected by and dependent upon things other than language," Preface, v.
Readable and relatively non-technical.

Chadwick, John. *The Decipherment of Linear B.* New York: Random House, Inc., 1958. °159 pp., index.
A fascinating excursus into linguistic problem-solving. This account of Michael Ventris' translation of the Minoan Linear B script reads like a detective story. Great potential for classroom work on language.

Chao, Yuen Ren. *Language and Symbolic Systems.* London: Cambridge University Press, 1968. °240 pp., index. A readable introduction to the study of the phenomenon of language, with an emphasis on the relationships between language and other dimensions of culture.

Chatman, Seymour and Samuel R. Levin. *Essays on the Language of Literature.* Boston: Houghton Mifflin Company, 1967. 450 pp.
A diverse collection of papers brought together to "reconcile linguistic and literary studies." One of the best collections of its kind.

Chomsky, Noam. *Syntactic Structures.* 'S-Gravenhage: Mouton & Co., 1957. °116 pp.
The seminal work of Chomskyan linguistics. It is mainly from this brief monograph that transformational-generative grammar has sprung. Not overly technical.

————. *Aspects of a Theory of Syntax.* Cambridge: The M.I.T. Press, 1965. °251 pp., index.
Demanding.
Modifications and amplifications of ideas presented in *Syntactic Structures.*
"This monograph is an exploratory study of various problems that have arisen in the course of work on transformational grammar, which is presupposed throughout as a general framework for the discussion," Preface, vi.

————. *Language and Mind.* New York: Harcourt, Brace & World, Inc., 1968. °88 pp.
Expansions of three lectures. "The first is an attempt to evaluate past contributions to the study of mind that have been based on research and speculation regarding the nature of language. The second is devoted to contemporary developments in linguistics that have a bearing on the study of mind. The third is a highly speculative discussion of

directions that the study of language and mind might take in coming years," Preface, v.

A philosophical view of linguistic study.

Cleator, P. E. *Lost Languages.* New York: New American Library, Inc., 1962. °192 pp., index.

A very readable account of the discovery and decipherment of ancient languages.

de Saussure, Ferdinand. *Course in General Linguistics.* New York: Mc-Graw-Hill Book Company, 1966. °240 pp., index.

A seminal book in modern linguistic theory.

Erikson, Erik H. *Identity, Youth and Crisis.* New York: W. W. Norton and Company, Inc., 1968. 336 pp., index.

An important contribution to the psychology of identity. Worth any number of undergraduate textbooks in "educational psychology."

Fishman, Joshua A. *Readings in the Sociology of Language.* The Hague: Mouton & Co., 1968. °808 pp., index.

A treasury of essays and papers on many aspects of language as a social force. All are informative, virtually none is too technical for the interested general reader.

Gelb, I. J. *A Study of Writing.* Chicago: University of Chicago Press, 1963. °319 pp., index.

A standard work on the subject of writing systems. Well illustrated and well written.

Greenberg, Joseph H., ed. *Universals of Language.* Cambridge: The M.I.T. Press, 1966. °337 pp., index.

Essays on the interesting and controversial issue of linguistic universals. Many of the essays are quite readable and do not require a great deal of technical knowledge.

Hall, Edward T. *The Silent Language.* Greenwich: Fawcett Publications, Inc., 1959. °192 pp., index.

"Culture is communication and communication is culture," p. 169.

A most perceptive and illuminating examination of the ways in which we communicate without language.

————.*The Hidden Dimension.* Garden City: Doubleday & Company, Inc., 1969. °217 pp., index.

"The central theme of this book is social and personal space and man's perception of it," p. 1.

A significant contribution to the study of the systems of intra- and inter-cultural communication.

Hall, Robert A., Jr. *Introductory Linguistics.* Philadelphia: Chilton Books, 1964. 508 pp., index.

"A possible subtitle for this book might be 'Linguistics Made Accessible.' Not 'linguistics made easy': this latter goal would be both impossible and undesirable," Preface, vii.
A wide-ranging, structuralist-oriented overview of linguistics.

Hörman, Hans. *Psycholinguistics: An Introduction to Research and Theory*. New York: Heidelberg-Berlin, Springer-Verlag, 1970. 377 pp., indices.
An excellent introduction to the important and rapidly growing field of linguistic psychology. Reviews and elucidates all significant works in the field.

Hunter, I. M. L. *Memory*. Baltimore: Penguin Books, Inc., 1964. °329 pp., index.
The nature, functions, and limitations of memory. Touches on questions of learning, memory disorders, brain damage, etc. A good introduction to a complex subject.

Jakobovits, Leon A. and Murray S. Miron, eds. *Readings in the Psychology of Language*. Englewood Cliffs: Prentice-Hall, Inc., 1967. 636 pp.
A broad sampling of important studies in psycholinguistics. Not particularly easy reading, but many of the papers are well worth the effort (especially in Part Three, "The Problem of Meaning").

Koestler, Arthur. *The Act of Creation*. New York: Dell Publishing Co., Inc., 1967. °751 pp., index.
"The first part of this book proposes a theory of the act of creation—of the conscious and unconscious processes underlying scientific discovery, artistic originality, and comic inspiration. It endeavours to show that all creative activities have a basic pattern in common, and to outline that pattern."
"The aim of Book Two is to show that certain basic principles operate throughout the whole organic hierarchy—from fertilized egg to the fertile brain of the creative individual; and that phenomena analogous to creative originality can be found on all levels," p. 21.
An ideal book for triggering worthwhile discussion. Any page affords a dozen research projects.

Landar, Herbert. *Language and Culture*. New York: Oxford University Press, 1966. °274 pp., index.
A valuable contribution to cultural linguistics built around the "sociology of knowledge." "A sentence, no less than each of its parts, is a creature of social convention and part of a larger and grander sociocultural perspective," p. 5.
A rich resource for a wide variety of classroom discussions (as well as linguistic field work).

Lenneberg, Eric H., ed. *New Directions in the Study of Language.* Cambridge: The M.I.T. Press, 1966. °194 pp., index.
A heterogeneous collection of essays representing current views of the nature and origin of language. Included are studies by a biologist, an anthropologist, and a psychologist.

Leed, Jacob, ed. *The Computer and Literary Style.* Kent: Kent State University Press, 1966. °179 pp.
A collection of fairly technical papers in which stylistic analysis is approached through computational linguistics. Can be fruitfully used in the classroom to stimulate thinking on matters of style.

Lester, Mark, ed. *Readings in Applied Transformational Grammar.* New York: Holt, Rinehart and Winston, Inc., 1970. °314 pp.
Of the collection, those essays on style and composition are of particular value to the teacher.

Lilly, John Cunningham. *The Mind of the Dolphin.* New York: Avon Books, 1969. °286 pp.
"This book emphasizes man's communication and its close relationship to mental health. The science of interspecies communication can illustrate and some day help our human communication. 'Learning of a nature gifted with special powers' we can become healthier," p. 11. A book of great importance to anyone interested not only in communication but in scientific creativity. (By the author of *Man and Dolphin,* New York, Pyramid Publications, 1962.)

Lindgren, Henry Clay, ed. *Readings in Educational Psychology.* New York: John Wiley & Sons, 1968. °474 pp., index.
Forty-five papers on all phases of psychology in relation to learning.

Love, Glen A. and Michael Payne, eds. *Contemporary Essays on Style.* Glenview: Scott, Foresman & Co., 1969. °307 pp.
Recent essays on style. Linguistically oriented.

Lyons, John. *Introduction to Theoretical Linguistics.* London: Cambridge University Press, 1968. °519 pp., index.
"My purpose in writing this book has been to provide a relatively self-contained introduction to the most important trends in contemporary linguistic theory. Although the book is intended primarily for students of linguistics, I hope that it will also prove useful to students of psychology, anthropology, sociology, biology, computer science, and a number of other disciplines which are concerned, in various ways, with the analysis of human language, as well as to students of literature and the 'humanities' . . . ," Preface, p. 1.
Among the best introductions to linguistic science currently available.

Menyuk, Paula. *Sentences Children Use*. Cambridge: The M.I.T. Press, 1969. 165 pp., index.
A highly technical linguistic examination of the grammar of children (ages 2–7). Hard evidence as opposed to impressions. Can be studied by those who have some background in transformational grammar.

Odgen, C. K. and I. A. Richards. *The Meaning of Meaning*. New York: Harcourt, Brace & World, Inc., 1963. °363 pp., index.
A classic work on language and thought (first published in 1923). Slow going, but stimulating and informative.

Oldfield, R. C. and J. C. Marshall, eds. *Language*. Baltimore: Penguin Books, Inc., 1968. °392 pp., index.
Fairly technical papers on psycholinguistic topics.

Parlett, D. S. *A Short Dictionary of Language*. London: The English Universities Press, Ltd., 1967. 154 pp.
A brief guide to the world's languages. Should be in the class library (along with the entire set of "Teach Yourself Books" published by the same house).

Pedersen, Holger. *The Discovery of Language*. Bloomington: Indiana University Press, 1962. °360 pp., index.
An account (first published in English in 1931) of the growth and development of linguistics in the nineteenth century. Specimen texts of exotic languages greatly enrich the book. A good resource.

Robins, R. H. *General Linguistics, An Introductory Survey*. Bloomington: Indiana University Press, 1966. 390 pp., index.
Among the better introductions to linguistics. Well within the grasp of the layman.

Sebeok, Thomas A., ed. *Style in Language*. Cambridge: The M.I.T. Press, 1966. °470 pp., index.
Papers and discussion from the Conference on Style (1952), offering insights into the broad question of style in language from the viewpoints of anthropology, folklore, linguistics, literary criticism, philosophy, and psychology. A rich resource book.

Staats, Arthur W. *Learning, Language, and Cognition*. New York: Holt, Rinehart and Winston, Inc., 1968. 614 pp., index.
A worthwhile effort at developing the basis for a new theory of learnning and new methods in research toward that end. Language is the focal area of the study.

Ullmann, Stephen. *Semantics, An Introduction to the Science of Meaning*. Oxford: Basil Blackwell, 1962. 278 pp., index.
Informed, well-exemplified, and readable.

Vygotsky, L. S. *Thought and Language*. Cambridge: The M.I.T. Press, 1967. °168 pp., index.

"Vygotsky represents still another step forward in the growing effort to understand cognitive processes. His is a mediational point of view. Concepts and the language that infuses and instruments them give power and strategy to cognitive activity. The capacity to impose superordinate structures in the interest of seeing things more simply and deeply is seen as one of the powerful tools of human intelligence," Introduction by Jerome Bruner, ix.

A classic study of the growth and development of intellect. Should be read in conjunction with Jean Piaget, *The Language and Thought of the Child*, New York: Meridian Books, 1957.

Waterman, John T. *Perspectives in Linguistics*. Chicago: University of Chicago Press, 1963. °105 pp., index.

A thumbnail sketch of the history of linguistic science.

Whorf, Benjamin Lee. *Language, Thought, and Reality*. Cambridge: The M.I.T. Press, 1966. °278 pp.

A selection of Whorf's important papers on the relationships between language and our perceptions of reality. (A useful companion volume is Edward Sapir, *Language*, Harvest Books, Harcourt, Brace, 1949.)

THE ENGLISH LANGUAGE

Cattell, N. R. *The New English Grammar: A Descriptive Introduction*. Cambridge: The M.I.T. Press, 1969. 162 pp., index. (Also in paperback.)

"This book is an attempt to provide students, teachers, and other interested people with an account of English grammar which will be in step with the knowledge provided by modern linguistics, and yet will be comprehensible to readers with no specialized linguistic training," Preface, xix.

A clear explication of structuralism and transformationalism.

Clark, John W. *Early English*. New York: W. W. Norton & Company, Inc., 1964. °176 pp., index.

A lively and well-written glimpse of the early forms of our language. The outlines, at least, of this material should be part of the teacher's professional kit.

Cook, Walter A. *Introduction to Tagmemic Analysis*. New York: Holt, Rinehart and Winston, Inc., 1969. °210 pp., index.

Presupposes some background in linguistics.

Cottle, Basil. *The Penguin Dictionary of Surnames*. Baltimore: Penguin Books, Inc., 1967. °334 pp.
The family names of the British Isles and their meanings. Should be in the classroom library (along with C. M. Matthews, *English Surnames, q.v.*) as a resource for what always proves to be a very engaging project.

Hathaway, Baxter. *A Transformational Syntax, The Grammar of Modern American English*. New York: The Ronald Press Company, 1967. 315 pp., index.
A non-diagrammatic approach to transformational grammar. Densely written but packed with valuable insights into the language. Excellent projects follow each chapter. Highly recommended for those teachers (and students) who can't abide diagrams.

Herndon, Jeanne H. *A Survey of Modern Grammars*. New York: Holt, Rinehart and Winston, Inc., 1970. °208 pp., index.
"This handbook is intended for all those who would like to know something of the findings of linguistic scholarship—especially with regard to the workings of the grammar of the English language—without necessarily wanting to become accomplished linguists themselves," Preface, v.

Jacobs, Roderick A. and Peter S. Rosenbaum. *English Transformational Grammar*. Waltham: Blaisdell Publishing Co., 1968. 294 pp., index.
An examination and explication of the main outlines of transformational theory. Heavy use of diagrams. Exercises.

Joos, Martin. *The English Verb, Form and Meanings*. Madison: University of Wisconsin Press, 1964. 251 pp., index.
A fascinating attempt to describe the English verb system using evidence gathered at a murder trial. An excellent introduction to method in linguistic research. Provides an eminently usable model for classroom explorations into linguistic phenomena.

Krapp, George Philip and Albert H. Marckwardt. *Modern English, Its Growth and Present Use*. New York: Charles Scribner's Sons, 1969. 316 pp., index.
A thoughtful revision of an eminently clear and sensible introduction to the history of English.

Langendoen, D. Terence. *The Study of Syntax*. New York: Holt, Rinehart and Winston, Inc., 1969. °174 pp., index.
An introduction to generative-transformational grammar.

Markman, Alan M. and Erwin R. Steinberg, eds. *English Then and Now*. New York: Random House, Inc., 1970. 462 pp.

A well-chosen selection of essays on the history of the English language. Challenging and imaginative exercises.

Matthews, C. M. *English Surnames.* New York: Charles Scribner's Sons, 1967. °367 pp., index.
The whys and hows of English family names. For the classroom library.

Myers, L. M. *The Roots of Modern English.* Boston: Little, Brown and Co., 1966. 323 pp., index.
A history of the language that is sound, readable, and not overburdened with minutiae.

Palmer, F. R. *A Linguistic Study of the English Verb.* London: Longmans, Green & Co., 1966. 199 pp.
An attempt quite different from that of Joos (*The English Verb, q.v.*) to describe the English verb system. A useful reference work.

Pyles, Thomas. *Words and Ways of American English.* New York: Random House, Inc., 1952. 310 pp., index. (Also in paperback.)
A witty account of the "origins, growth, and present state of the English language in America." Requires no technical background. Should be in classroom library (as should H. L. Mencken, *The American Langauge: The Fourth Edition and the Two Supplements,* New York, Alfred A. Knopf, Inc., 1963).

Reibel, David A. and Sanford A. Schane, eds. *Modern Studies in English.* Englewood Cliffs: Prentice-Hall, Inc., 1969. 481 pp.
Papers on the transformational syntax of English. Those by Chomsky of particular interest and value.

Warfel, Harry R. *Language: A Science of Human Behavior.* Cleveland: Howard Allen, 1962. 188 pp., index.
A curious and curiously misnamed book that offers some valuable insights into language. The sections on language in relation to literature are very worthwhile.

THE ARTS

Bernstein, Leonard. *The Joy of Music.* New York: New American Library, Inc., 1967. °299 pp.
Showmanship, excitement, and great understanding are whipped together in this delightful ramble through the world of music. Bernstein is unquestionably one of the great teachers.

Empson, William. *Seven Types of Ambiguity.* New York: New Directions Pub. Corp., n.d. °256 pp.

"An ambiguity, in ordinary speech, means something very pronounced, and as a rule witty or deceitful. I propose to use the word in an extended sense, and shall think relevant to my subject any verbal nuance, however slight, which gives room for alternative reactions to the same piece of literature," p. 1.

Seven types of ambiguity as touchstones to the understanding of literature.

Frye, Northrop. *Anatomy of Criticism*. New York: Atheneum Publishers, 1966. °383 pp., index.

"This book consists of 'essays' in the word's original sense of a trial or incomplete attempt, on the possibility of a synoptic view of the scope, theory, principles, and techniques of literary criticism," p. 3.

Formulations by the leading critical theorist of our time. No one seriously interested in the study of literature can fail to read, re-read, and know Frye.

————. *Fables of Identity: Studies in Poetic Mythology*. New York: Harcourt, Brace & World, Inc., 1963. °265 pp.

Critical theory and its applications through essays on Homer, Shakespeare, Byron, Emily Dickinson, Joyce, etc.

————. *The Educated Imagination*. Bloomington: Indiana University Press, 1969. °156 pp.

"Read this book. It tells us what we believe and never quite convey to our students: literature is the most valuable of studies because it educates the imagination, where we live every day of our lives, in all our private and public decisions. . . . And of course it enables us to read our books with joy," *College English* (quoted on cover).

Six essays that no teacher can be without.

Hall, James B. and Barry Ulanov, eds. *Modern Culture and the Arts*. New York: McGraw-Hill Book Company, 1967. °560 pp., index.

"Coming to terms with modern culture can be an uneasy confrontation, both for the novice and for the initiate," Preface, ix.

Essays on all aspects of the arts in the twentieth century. An excellent resource book.

McMullen, Roy. *Art, Affluence, and Alienation*. New York: New American Library, Inc., 1969. °320 pp., index.

Stimulating insights into the arts in the twentieth century. This and the preceding book will serve very well to make the "contemporary experience" rather more accessible than it seems to be to so many of its children.

Sontag, Susan. *Against Interpretation*. New York: Dell Publishing Co., Inc., 1966. °304 pp.

Essays, articles, reviews on the arts by a penetrating and disturbing observer. Controversy guaranteed! "What is important now is to recover our senses. We must learn to *see* more, to *hear* more, to *feel* more," p. 14.

Zuckerkandl, Victor. *The Sense of Music*. Princeton: Princeton University Press, 1967. °246 pp., 32 pp. of scores.

"It is in . . . the search for a listener's knowledge of music that this book will engage the reader. It takes its stand definitely among the audience, not on the stage. Its starting point is the point where tones meet a listener's mind," p. 9.

One of the best introductions to the appreciation of *music* (*music*, that is, not *music history*).

MATHEMATICS AND SCIENCE

Asimov, Isaac. *Quick and Easy Math*. Boston: Houghton Mifflin Company, 1964. 180 pp.

An entertaining introduction to shortcuts in computation.

Berkeley, Edmund C. *A Guide to Mathematics for the Intelligent Non-Mathematician*. New York: Simon & Schuster, Inc., 1966. °352 pp., index.

Mathematics in layman's language. Good source book for interesting projects and problems.

Barnard, Douglas St. Paul. *Adventures in Mathematics*. New York: Funk & Wagnalls, 1968. 130 pp., index.

Mathematics as an art. A source of mathematical puzzles. Presupposes a certain mathematical sophistication.

Clarke, Arthur C. *Profiles of the Future*. New York: Bantam Books, Inc., 1967. °235 pp.

"It is impossible to predict the future, and all attempts to do so in any detail appear ludicrous within a very few years. This book has a more realistic yet at the same time more ambitious aim. It does not try to describe *the* future, but to define the boundaries within which the possible futures must lie," xi.

Scientific speculation at its best. Can provide much stimulation for classroom explorations.

Cohen, Donald. *Inquiry in Mathematics Via the Geo-Board*. New York: Walker & Company, 1967. °61 pp.

An excellent resource for using the *geo-board* (typically a 5 x 5 square array of nails, each set 2 inches from the other, and over which rubber bands are stretched to form line segments and polygons), a "physical model of a set of points."

"Children enjoy learning when they are actively involved, when they are not always being lectured to or being told how to do something. Working with the geo-board enables them to *do* things and discuss their work with their classmates; they learn from each other this way," p. 8.

Danto, Arthur and Sidney Morgenbesser, eds. *Philosophy of Science*. New York: Meridian Books, 1960. °477 pp.

Twenty-nine essays on philosophical issues in science. A valuable resource book for the classroom library.

Dantzig, Tobias. *Number*. New York: The Free Press, 1967. °340 pp., index.

A reissue of a classic work on number theory.

"The author holds that our school curricula, by stripping mathematics of its cultural content and leaving a bare skeleton of technicalities, have repelled many a fine mind. It is the aim of this book to restore this cultural content and present the evolution of number as the profoundly human story which it is," Preface.

Eddington, Sir Arthur. *The Nature of the Physical World*. Ann Arbor: University of Michigan Press, 1958. °361 pp., index.

A philosopher-scientist's look at the modern scientific thought. Beautifully written.

Eiseley, Loren. *The Immense Journey*. New York: Random House, Inc., 1957. °210 pp.

Brilliant essays on evolution. Superb writing. A must for the classroom library, along with *The Invisible Pyramid*, New York: Charles Scribner's Sons, 1970. 192 pp.

Goldberg, Lazar. *Children and Science*. New York: Charles Scribner's Sons, 1970. 146 pp., index, annotated bibliography.

"Difficulties in the schools will not be decreased by refinements in testing procedures. They will be exacerbated. Educators will not cultivate a scientifically literate population by perfecting 'scientometers' which, when inserted into children's mouths, register the degree of scientific mastery. The need is for recognition of the real, lasting, humane goals for which science is taught. Parents and educators must find the will to struggle against whatever obstacles may stand in their way to provide opportunities for *all* children to reach for these goals as well as they can. They must give greater attention to children, to what is happening to them, and when they have noted, exercise their judgment about what changes will urge the children to reach a little higher," p. 130.

A wise and well-written guide to introducing the child to the scientific spirit of inquiry.

Jeans, Sir James. *Physics & Philosophy*. Ann Arbor: University of Michigan Press, 1958. °222 pp., index.
The aim of the book "is to discuss—and to some extent explore—that borderland territory between physics and philosophy which used to seem so dull, but suddenly became so interesting and important through recent developments of theoretical physics," Preface.

Kasnar, Edward and James R. Newman. *Mathematics and the Imagination*. New York: Simon & Schuster, Inc., 1963. °380 pp., index.
" 'Haute vulgarisation' is the term applied by the French to that happy result which neither offends by its condescension nor leaves obscure in a mass of technical verbiage. It has been our aim to extend the process of 'haute vulgarisation' to those outposts of mathematics which are mentioned, if at all, only in a whisper; which are referred to, if at all, only by a name; to show by its very diversity something of the character of mathematics, of its bold, untrammeled spirit, of how, as both an art and a science, it has continued to lead the creative faculties beyond even imagination and intuition," Introduction. (First published in 1940.)
Lively, entertaining, and informative.

Kline, Morris. *Mathematics, A Cultural Approach*. Reading: Addison-Wesley Publishing Co., 1963. 701 pp., index.
A college textbook that "attempts to show what mathematics is, how mathematics has developed from man's efforts to understand and master nature, what the mathematical approach to real problems can accomplish, and the extent to which mathematics has molded our civilization and our culture," Preface, v.
Mathematics in a matrix of history and philosophy. A rich resource book.

Marsh, L. G. *Children Explore Mathematics*, Second Ed. London: A. & C. Black, 1968. 160 pp., index.
An excellent practical guide for teacher and parent to the introduction of mathematical experience to children. Emphasis is on manipulative approaches to grasping number concepts. "Mathematic symbols refer to activities," p. 19.

Moroney, M. J. *Facts from Figures*. Baltimore: Penguin Books, Inc., 1967. °472 pp., index.
A clear, readable, and well-illustrated introduction to statistics.

Pedoe, Dan. *The Gentle Art of Mathematics*. Baltimore: Penguin Books, Inc., 1969. °160 pp., index.

A pleasant introduction to modern mathematics. Includes a number of mathematical games and puzzles.

Rashevsky, Nicolas. *Looking at History through Mathematics*. Cambridge: The M.I.T. Press, 1968. 199 pp., index.

"Our purpose is to illustrate in a number of different, sometimes almost disconnected, examples how mathematical reasoning *could in principle* be used in attempted explanations of *some* historical phenomena," Preface, vii.

Difficult but very stimulating. For advanced students.

Sawyer, W. W. *Prelude to Mathematics*. Baltimore: Penguin Books, Inc., 1966. °214 pp.

"This is a book about how to grow mathematicians," p. 7.

"*Mental venturesomeness* is characteristic of all mathematicians. A mathematician does not want to be told something; he wants to find it out for himself," p. 19.

An exploration of "mathematics for mathematics' sake," so to speak, or "mathematics for pleasure."

————. *Vision in Elementary Mathematics*. Baltimore: Penguin Books, Inc., 1964. °346 pp.

Teaching mathematics via *vision*. An excellent introduction to sets and other devices for *picturing* mathematical concepts.

Way Things Work, The. New York: Simon & Schuster, Inc., 1967. 590 pp., index.

"This volume is not a reference book in the ordinary sense. It has been designed, instead, to give the layman an understanding of *how things work*, from the simplest mechanical functions of modern life to the most basic scientific principles, and complex industrial processes that affect our well being," Foreword, p. 5.

A must for the classroom library. Worth any number of science textbooks now in use in the schools.

MEDIA

Agel, Jerome, ed. *The Making of Kubrick's 2001*. New York: New American Library, Inc., 1970. °368 pp., 96 pp. of photos.

A McLuhanesque "happening" in print about what may prove to be the most significant film of the period. Packed with information on every phase of the film's production and reception.

Bluestone, George. *Novels into Film*. Berkeley: University of California Press, 1966. °237 pp., index.

A very informative examination of the ways in which fiction has been translated into the film.

Bobker, Lee R. *Elements of Film*. New York. Harcourt, Brace & World, Inc., 1969. °303 pp., index.

"The structure of the book reflects the filmmaking process itself. The early chapters follow the order in which a film is made: script, image (camera, lighting, composition) sound, and editing. I have devoted special attention to the roles of script-writers, cameramen, film editors, actors, and directors, and their relationships to one another. A separate chapter on the work of the major contemporary directors—the complete filmmakers—who shape every element of the film, from acting techniques and optical effects to the final editing, and whose 'style' pervades the entire production. A final chapter defines the function of film criticism and analyzes the work of important film critics," Preface, v.

Perhaps the best available introduction to the film. Well illustrated with still shots from films discussed.

Geduld, Harry M., ed. *Film Makers on Film Making*. Bloomington: Indiana University Press, 1969. °302 pp.

Comments on the art by leading filmmakers.

Kracauer, Siegfried. *From Caligari to Hitler*. Princeton: Princeton University Press, 1966. °361 pp., index.

A brilliant examination of the German psyche as revealed in the films made in Germany from the post-World War I period to the Hitler era. Creative scholarship at its best. (See also, S. Kracauer, *Theory of Film*, New York: Oxford University Press, 1965.)

Lawson, John Howard. *Film: The Creative Process*. New York: Hill and Wang, Inc., 1967 (2nd Ed.). °380 pp., index.

A broadly ranging book that brings film history and technique to bear on film art and aesthetics. Well illustrated.

Lindgren, Ernest. *The Art of the Film*. New York: The Macmillan Co., 1968. °258 pp., index.

A standard work on the craft of filmmaking. Readable and well illustrated.

Manoogian, Haig P. *The Film-Maker's Art*. New York: Basic Books, Inc., Publishers, 1966. 340 pp. index.

"This book is written to whet the artistic imagination, to stir up the aesthetic sensibilities," p. 2.

The nuts and bolts of filmmaking by a professional teacher of filmmaking. Clear and thorough.

Mascelli, Joseph V., ed. *American Cinematographer Manual*. Hollywood:

American Society of Cinematographers, 1967 (2nd ed.). 626 pp., index.

The "bible" of the professional cinematographer.

A basic reference work on all aspects of motion picture photography.

McCann, Richard Dyer, ed. *Film and Society*. New York: Charles Scribner's Sons, 1964. °182 pp.

A research anthology including selections on film propaganda and film censorship.

McLuhan, Herbert Marshall. *Understanding Media: The Extensions of Man*. New York: McGraw-Hill Book Company, 1965. °364 pp.

One of the seminal documents of the age. A rich source of stimulating (and often highly irritating) ideas—"probes," McLuhan calls them. No media work can go far without coming to grips with McLuhan.

O'Hara, Robert C. *Media for the Millions*. New York: Random House, Inc., 1961. 421 pp., index.

A perceptive analysis of the processes of mass communication. Part Three, "The Media View of Life," is especially interesting (and rather frightening in its implications).

Pincus, Edward. *Guide to Filmmaking*. New York: The New American Library, Inc., 1969. °256 pp., index.

"This book is addressed both to filmmakers and to people who want to be filmmakers. By 'filmmakers' we mean people who use motion picture film to achieve some conceptual whole. This can range from a well-done home movie to a full-length feature film," Preface, xi.

Reisz, Karel, *et al. The Technique of Film Editing*. London: Focal Press, 1966. 285 pp., index.

The craft of film editing explored in detail through a wide variety of films. Fairly technical but extremely valuable in understanding editing principles. Editing, wrote the Russian director, V. I. Pudovkin, "is the creative force of filmic reality. . . ."

Renan, Sheldon. *An Introduction to the American Underground Film*. New York: E. P. Dutton & Co., Inc., 1967. °318 pp., index.

A detailed, and well-illustrated examination of the personal (*i.e.*, "avant-garde," is idiosyncratic, low-budget, etc.) film. Much that is filmically fresh and exciting in today's commercial films derives from the special visions of the underground filmmakers.

Ross, T. J., ed. *Film and the Liberal Arts*. New York: Holt, Rinehart and Winston, Inc., 1970. °419 pp., index.

"The essays in this book use film as a common core, but not in isolation. Rather, each set of essays revolves around film and one or more of the liberal arts . . . ," Preface, viii.

The essays are grouped around film and (1) rhetoric, (2) literature, (3) visual arts, (4) music, (5) society, and (6) aesthetics. Exercises.

Sheridan, Marion C., *et al. The Motion Picture and the Teaching of English*. New York: Appleton-Century-Crofts, 1965. °168 pp., index.

"There are many reasons why we have considered the role of the moving picture in the teaching of English. First, the film has an unparalleled power to transmit information and inferences. Second, it may illuminate and augment the study of literature. Third, it has form, structure, theme, irony, metaphor and symbol—aspects of any work of art, and hence subject to examination and isolation. And finally, it is concerned with ethics, values, and truth—which may be embodied or distorted in films as in any other medium," Foreword, viii.

Comprehensive (though superficial) examination of the film art.

Smallman, Kirk. *Creative Film-Making*. London: Collier-Macmillian, Ltd., 1969. °245 pp.

A good introduction to low-budget filmmaking. Clearly written and well illustrated.

Talbot, Daniel, ed. *Film: An Anthology*. Berkeley: University of California Press, 1966. °404 pp., index.

A first-rate collection of essays on all aspects of the film art.

Trapnell, Coles. *Teleplay, An Introduction to Television Writing*. San Francisco: Chandler Publishing Co., 1966. °245 pp., index.

The theory and practice of television script-writing. An actual script (from the TV series, *Slattery's People*) is included.

Willis, Edgar E. *Writing Television and Radio Programs*. New York: Holt, Rinehart and Winston, Inc., 1967. 372 pp., index.

"The objective [of the book] is two-pronged: first, to provide practical instruction for those seeking a career in broadcasting; and second, to help guide students in writing courses for general education purposes toward the achievement of fruitful creative experiences. The principal program types in American radio and television writing are discussed and a chapter on the writing of commercials is included," Preface, v. Includes a wide variety of actual script material.

Wollen, Peter. *Signs and Meaning in the Cinema*. Bloomington: Indiana University Press, 1969. °168 pp.

A sometimes perversely obscure exposition of the *auteur* theory of cinema and an attempt to find a *semiology* of cinema (making an interesting association between this "science of cinema signs" and linguistics).

GAMES

Abt, Clark C. *Serious Games*. New York: The Viking Press, Inc., 1970. 176 pp.

"The classic Greek ideal embodied both thought and action, both individuation and participation, *in the same activities.* Today, intense participation in social decision-making is limited to a few individuals appointed, elected, or permitted to represent the larger society. Yet individuals can once again become involved, and thought and action can again be integrated, in games created to stimulate these social processes. The zest for life felt at those exhilarating moments of history when men participated in effecting great changes on the models of great ideas can be recaptured by simulation of roles in the form of serious games," p. 4.

An extremely valuable book in the "new education." *Serious,* incidentally, does *not* mean *dour!*

Borgmann, Dmitri A. *Language on Vacation*. New York: Charles Scribner's Sons, 1965. °318 pp., index.

"The first objective of this book . . . is to help reverse the trend of more than half a century, and to elevate recreational linguistics to the same high level of esteem now enjoyed by recreational mathematics. You will find a generous assortment of word diversions here, to stimulate an appetite jaded by the ubiquitous crossword puzzle," p. 2.

A rich source book of word games of every kind. A must for the classroom library.

Chernev, Irving and Kenneth Harkness. *An Invitation to Chess*. New York: Simon & Schuster, Inc., 1945. °221 pp.

A clearly written introduction to the game. Includes a large number of illustrative problems.

Gardner, Martin. *Mathematical Puzzles & Diversions*. New York: Simon & Schuster, Inc., 1958. °178 pp.

Mathematical games and puzzles.

Hart, Harold H. *Grab a Pencil*. New York: Hart Publishing Co., 1958. °190 pp.

A miscellany of word games, acrostics, etc.

Horowitz, I. A. and P. L. Rothenberg. *The Complete Book of Chess*. London: Collier-Macmillan Ltd., 1969. °372 pp.

Chess rules, lore, problems, famous chess games, chess recreations, etc. A good resource book.

Howard, Kenneth S. *How to Solve Chess Problems*. New York: Dover Publications, Inc., 1961. °171 pp., index.

An orderly and rational approach to solving chess problems. First section of book is for novices. Problems from actual games are used.

Huizinga, Jan. *Homo Ludens, A Study of the Play Element in Culture.* Boston: Beacon Press, 1967. °220 pp., index.
A major work in the philosophy of history. It is listed in this section because it provides the philosophical-historical rationale for game-playing. Should be required reading for all teachers.

Hurwitz, Abraham B. and Arthur Goddard. *Games to Improve Your Child's English.* New York: Simon & Schuster, Inc., 1969. 352 pp., index.
Despite the title, a rich compendium of language games (alphabet, word, grammar) for classroom (and home, of course) use.

Kishikawa, Shigemi. *Steppingstones to Go.* Rutland: Charles E. Tuttle Co., Inc., 1965. 159 pp.
A well-illustrated introduction to the Japanese game of *Go.*

Lasker, Edward. *Go and Go-Moku.* New York: Dover Publications, Inc., 1960. °215 pp., index.
Expanded version (first published in 1934) of a good introduction to the game of *Go* by a chess master.

Loyd, Sam. *The Eighth Book of Tan.* New York: Dover Publications, Inc., 1968. °52 pp.
"According to encyclopedia lore, the game of Tangrams is of very ancient origin, and has been played in China for upward of 4,000 years, somewhat in the nature of a national pastime. It consists of seven flat pieces of wood, cut upon the geometrical angles of 45 and 90 degrees, with straight edges which fit together so as to produce a variety of changes which baffles the science of mathematics to compute," p. 1.
The modern toy-store puzzles like *Mr. Pythagoras* and *Madagascar Madness* derive from the Chinese Tangrams. The book contains a large number of tantalizing shapes to contrive from the original seven pieces. Solutions provided.

Luckiesh, M. *Visual Illusions.* New York: Dover Publications, Inc., 1965. °252 pp., index.
A good sourcebook for visual puzzles as well as for the study of "optical illusions."

Reinfeld, Fred, ed. *Chess Tactics for Beginners.* Hollywood: Wilshire Book Co., 1968. °128 pp.
A good collection of beginner's chess problems.

Simon, William. *Mathematical Magic.* New York: Charles Scribner's Sons, 1964. °187 pp., index.
Fun and games with mathematics.

Smith, Arthur. *The Game of Go*. Rutland: Charles E. Tuttle Co., Inc., 1959. 224 pp.
The best available introduction to the Japanese game of *Go*. First published in 1905.

COMMUNITY

Bacon, Edmund. *Design of Cities*. New York: The Viking Press, Inc., 1967. 296 pp., index.
A beautifully illustrated book on the history and principles of city design. The author has for many years played an active rôle in the redevelopment of Center City, Philadelphia.

Chermayeff, Serge and Christopher Alexander. *Community and Privacy*. Garden City: Doubleday & Company. Inc., 1965. °255 pp.
"It would be easy to call this book a sort of exercise in human biotechnical engineering. It certainly is that, and masterfully so. It seems to me it is more than that. It is an exercise in creative or constructive humanism," Foreword by Kenneth Rexroth, pp. 16–17.
An important resource book in this day of environmental disaster. Well illustrated.

Mumford, Lewis. *The Urban Prospect*. New York: Harcourt, Brace & World, Inc., 1968. °255 pp.
The city's present problems and future possibilities.

Peets, Elbert. *On the Art of Designing Cities*. Cambridge: The M.I.T. Press, 1968. °234 pp. index.
Witty and intelligent essays on the problems of municipal design. Several essays are devoted to the city of Washington, D.C.—its original design and its changes (good and bad) over the years.

Saarinen, Eliel. *The City: Its Growth, Its Decay, Its Future*. Cambridge: The M.I.T. Press, 1966. °385 pp.
A great architect looks at the problems of city design. "Civilization produces mass actions. Cultural movements originate from individual mental growth. The greater the number of those having opportunity to become culturally influenced in the city's atmosphere, the stronger and more lasting the social order in the city will be," p. 5.

Weimer, David R., ed. *City and Country in America*. New York: Appleton-Century-Crofts, 1962. °399 pp.
A research anthology of writings on the urban, suburban, and rural worlds. Touches on philosophical issues and sociological and aesthetic problems. Illustrated.

A FEW HOURS exploring the periodicals room of a good library will be time well spent, for it is in current periodicals in all fields (art, architecture, business, design, education, music, current events, film, science, theater, etc., etc.) that the world of "right now" can be apprehended. Likewise, occasional browses in bookstores will turn up much that is useful to the classroom. At all events, teachers must learn to free themselves from their long dependence on book salesmen and advertising campaigns.

"Only he who can remain a student forever will be a good teacher forever."